The
HETERO[illegible]Y
Handbo[illegible]

The HETERODOXY Handbook:

How to Survive the PC Campus

Edited by
David Horowitz and Peter Collier

Regnery Publishing
Washington, D.C.

Library of Congress Cataloging-in-Publication Data

The Heterodoxy handbook : how to survive the PC campus / edited by David Horowitz and Peter Collier.
p. cm.
Includes index.
ISBN 0-89526-731-4 (acid-free paper)
1. Popular culture--United States. 2. Political correctness--United States. 3. Education, Higher--United States. 4. Education. Higher--Political aspects--United States. I. Horowitz, David, 1939- . II. Collier, Peter. III. Heterodoxy (Studio City, Los Angeles, Calif.)
E169.04.H47 1994
306'.0973--dc20 94-27551
CIP

Published in the United States by
Regnery Publishing, Inc.
An Eagle Publishing Company
422 First St., SE, Suite 300
Washington, DC 20003

Distributed to the trade by
National Book Network
4720-A Boston Way
Lanham, MD 20706

Printed on acid-free paper.

Manufactured in the United States of America.

10 9 8 7 6 5 4 3 2 1

Books are available in quantity for promotional or premium use. Write to Director of Special Sales, Regnery Publishing, Inc., 422 First Street, SE, Suite 300, Washington, DC 20003, for information on discounts and terms or call (202) 546-5005.

Table Of Contents

Preface

A moment of truth occurred at the annual meeting of the American Studies Association in Costa Mesa last year. It took place during a special panel convened at the request of Laurence Jarvik of the Heritage Foundation, who had asked the sponsoring organization the previous year why—at a conference of 2,000 academics in the field of American Studies—there was not a single conservative panelist or panel. Alice Kessler-Harris, president of the ASA responded by offering a spot at the 1992 meeting to a conservative panel, if funding could be found. The Heritage Foundation provided the funding.

The panel was chaired by Wilcomb Washburn of the Smithsonian and was called "Change of Course for American Studies?" In fact, there was no change of course and only one of the panelists, Charles Kessler, a political scientist at Claremont, was actually both a conservative and a currently credentialed academic with a university post. The other panelists were a *Heterodoxy* editor, who holds no academic position, and the historian John Diggins, who holds an academic position but is not (except by the extreme standards prevailing in today's politically correct academy) a conservative. The moment of truth occurred after the panel moderator asked Diggins to respond to a question from the audience about a charge the panelists had made.

The charge was that despite lip-service to the idea of diversity, the university had become for all intents and purposes a monolithic institution, intolerant of any intellectual attitude of doctrine that was not approved by the academic Left. In his reply, Diggins said: "When my generation was in control of university faculties in the Sixties, we were the liberals. We opened the doors to the hiring of radicals in the name of diversity. We thought you would do the same. But you didn't. You closed the doors behind you."

There it was, simply put. In one academic generation, America's universities had been transformed from institutions devoted to intellectual dialogue and the pursuit of learning, into a vast patronage machine for the political Left. So complete was this transformation, that today it can be baldly acknowledged by radicals themselves, without a hint of guilt over their cynical betrayal of an intellectual trust. At a recent conference of activists in Virginia, the philosopher Richard Rorty was actually brimming with praise for this development: "The power base of the Left in America is now in the universities since the trade unions have largely been killed off," he crowed. "The universities have done a lot of good work by setting up, for example, African-American Studies programs, Women's Studies programs, Gay and Lesbian Studies programs. They have created power bases for these movements." So the Eliots and Lowells of the contemporary university now take their place beside the Hoffas and Reuthers as the institutional godfathers of the radical faith.

If any explanation were needed for the launching of *Heterodoxy*, whose first issue appeared in April 1992, Richard Rorty has provided it. Given the fact the Cold War has come home, *Heterodoxy* has the status and is meant to have the feel of a *samizdat* publication inside the gulag of the PC university. It is self-consciously designed to be something the commissars of political correctness can't take: irreverence toward their smelly little orthodoxies; a breath of freedom in the chill air of their passe dogmas.

Heterodoxy, then, is a *journal de combat*. The following pages collect its worthiest salvos, which means they document a story that is unpleasant to contemplate but necessary to tell. *The Heterodoxy Handbook* is the second in a series of many such efforts we intend to undertake in what promises to be a long twilight struggle with the totalitarian demons that many had erroneously concluded were exorcised and gone.

PETER COLLIER
DAVID HOROWITZ

It's The Culture, Stupid!

It's The Culture, Stupid!

by Peter Collier

People are aghast at the appointment of Donna Shalala to a Cabinet post in the Clinton Administration, and rightly so. But the true epiphany in the pre-inaugural process preceded Shalala's ascension and might have been covered up by the compliant media if not for a story that first surfaced in the *Jewish Forward.* It was the President-elect's naming of Johnnetta Cole to head the transition team's talent search in the areas of education, arts, labor and humanities.

Cole is presently President of Spellman College. Yet the institutions of higher education have become so subordinated to political agendas that this just opens the question. In Cole's case it is not so much what she is as what she has been. And thereby hangs a tale. In the early 70s Cole was a member of the Venceremos Brigade, a New Left organization that went to Cuba to cut sugar cane for the dictatorship and wound up serving the DGI, Castro's intelligence service. By the late 70s, Cole was president of the U.S-Grenada Friendship Society, a clone of the US-Soviet Friendship Societies that Stalin invented, in this instance fronting for Marxist dictator Maurice Bishop. In 1980, she was again in Havana with an elite handful of others in orbit around the U.S. Communist Party discussing ways to help the Cubans export revolution to Central America. A year later Cole was actively involved in the Soviet front and CP subsidiary, the U.S. Peace Council, which had been reactivated to set up a fifth column in America for the Marxists in Nicaragua and El Salvador.

We could go on. But the point is clear. This is a profile of one of those left wing apparatchiks who spent the Big Chill rededicating themselves to the leftover Left's solidarity mode. The only thing missing from Cole's dreary curriculum vitae, in fact, is any indication of remorse for fifteen years spent doggedly working in the vineyards of pro-Communist anti-Americanism. If it is a tragedy that such a record did not stop Cole from working her way onto an affirmative action fast-track in higher education, it is a farce that Clinton should have chosen her to play a key role in staffing his administration. What was such a person doing on his short list for Secretary of Education? Why, when some of the more disgraceful episodes in Cole's background were made public, did the Clintonites merely shrug, as if collaboration with the most oppressive tyrannies of this century meant nothing at all? Did transition chairman Vernon Jordan define the new Administration's idea of political morality when he said regarding Cole that all these things happened a long time ago and anyway who cares?

It would be nice to think that Cole's selection was the result of a computer malfunction, or that some sort of random dialing process inadvertently called up her name. But Cole is a protege of Donna Shalala, whom she served at U Mass in the People's Republic of Amherst. It was no glitch. Nor was it merely, to turn Milan Kundera's famous quote on its head, the triumph of forgetting over memory. It is hard to believe that Clinton is so disoriented by the dubious commitments of his political adolescence that he really sees no difference between trying it once and not inhaling and sucking up to Castro for twenty years; between failing to fight for your country's cause and supporting your country's enemies. Sadly, Vernon Jordan is right: Johnnetta Cole's past commitments don't matter to the Clinton crowd; what matters is that she's on the right track now, one of them who has finally found a popular front that works, in multiculturalism and radical feminism.

The media treated the Cole episode as a tiny closet drama. Yet it stands as the first stirring of the rough beast of political correctness now slouching toward Washington, a mentality that is forgiving of America-bashing because it has been nurtured on a vision of the rampant white, heterosexual male—a synecdoche for America the bad—running roughshod over the country and the world.

In his unctuous endorsement of the Democratic ticket in *Rolling Stone*, Jann Wenner said that he supported Clinton and Gore because they had "come of age in the Sixties and [had] sensibilities and value systems" which were formed then. Right. That's exactly the problem. Probably out there this very minute buying a party hat and noise maker for his box seat at the inaugural, Wenner probably thinks he is helping usher in an era of good vibes, a don't-stop-thinking-about-tomorrow view of the world. But the change about to overtake the country is less generational than ideological. And if there is an irony here it is that Clinton, more than any other politician, seemed to have understood the tragedy of the Sixties — the unloosing of a 25-year night of the long knives that allowed the Left to subvert institutions of the center like the university and his own Democratic Party. Clinton came to power, after all, by portraying himself as someone anxious to rescue the party from its ideological tar pits, rebuild the damaged center and purge it of the alienating extremism of the Left. Yet by the first few weeks of his Presidency-elect, he was already feeding the animals.

Midway through the appointment process, when half of the cabinet was chosen, Clinton came under fire. He had said, after all, that he wanted a cabinet that looked like America. Where were the women? Perhaps Donna Shalala's gender didn't qualify. (Subsequently outed by Queer Nation, Shalala denied she was gay, but who knows these days except the vanguard, in their secret consistories, what is what?) In any case, the feminists felt that *they* had a right to know. Clinton responded with his jive-angry act, saying that he refused to be bound by quotas. It was a clumsy imitation of an independent politician, exactly what he had done during the campaign when he attacked Sister Souljah. Yet at the time of the Souljah outburst he was mortgaging his future to Maxine Waters, an L.A. Congresswoman from Jesse Jackson's camp, and to the other interest groups of the rainbow who would later demand a payoff. (An early warning of the form this might take is Clinton's promise to lift the ban on HIV-infected Haitians now quarantined at Guantanamo, presumably to award them the indispensable tools of citizenship under the new dispensation: a green card, a condom, and a hospital bed.) Shortly after his demarche with the harridans of NOW, Clinton appointed a bevy of females, including some even less qualified than Shalala for their jobs. Thus, at the very moment he was complaining about quotas he was capitulating to the quota-mongers' demands.

True, Clinton's National Security apparatus is middle of the road, and loaded with Carter re-treads. But because Ronald Reagan and George Bush knitted together the damaged threads of Truman's containment policy and brought the USSR to its knees, foreign affairs, while perhaps no more manageable, is potentially less decisive than before. It is the social agenda that is now at the center of American concerns and this agenda is in danger of being handed to what we will probably soon be calling the Hillary Left.

The point person is Donna Shalala, only 4'11, but so committed to the cause that even *Newsweek* had to concede her credentials as "the high priestess of political correctness." The people at Madison she bedeviled while working as chancellor of the University of Wisconsin breathed a sigh of relief at her departure. She had been a disaster there, backing hate speech rules that the courts threw out as hateful to the First Amendment, implementing draconian Ethnic Studies requirements, along with hiring and admissions rules that had the feel of one of the Great Helmsman's Five Year Plans.

Shalala avoided the explicit foreign entanglements which attracted the likes of Johnnetta Cole. Her career has rather been a triumph of boring from within. Yet in her views one sees a holograph of the Sixties. Two years ago, for instance, when the U.S. government was still withholding recognition from Vietnam in an attempt to get a straightforward final response to the POW-MIA issue, Shalala was sponsoring "scientific exchanges" with an eye toward pressuring for unconditional resumption of relations with the sadists of Hanoi. She was willing to condemn the vile Louis Farrakhan, but only by coupling her expression of doubts with a far stronger denunciation of fraternities on the Madison campus who had done a tasteless skit involving Fiji Islanders. This idea of moral equivalence was one which the leftover Left made familiar in the 80s: criticize the Soviet Union but only by coupling it with the equally culpable U.S.A.

Shalala is only one appointment, it has been said. (Yes, but to an agency whose budget is larger than the national budgets of every country except Germany and Japan). There are no doubt other appointments to come in domestic affairs which will buttress the Left's seizure of the culture. (It is rumored that Joseph Duffey, who has made appeasement of the radicals into performance art at the University of Massachusetts, is on the short list to take over USIA and thus to dictate how America is portrayed abroad; and that Catharine Stimpson, whose lugubrious advocacy of PC as head of the Modern Language Association is legend, may be given control of the National Institute of Humanities.) With her connections with Hillary, Marian Wright Edelman and the Children's Defense Fund (an organization which may be a 90s version of the Trilateral Commission), Shalala is more than a Secretary; she is a symbol. In her, the long march through the institutions is complete. No one believed it possible back in the early 1970s when the first burned out New Leftists re-enrolled in the universities they had spent the previous years trying to destroy, but this was always a march on Washington.

During the last few weeks before the election, some warned that we were headed for a PC administration. But they were told that Clinton himself would stand against such nonsense. That was why he had created the Democratic Leadership Council, after all. The DLC was an organization based on political common sense and recreating the vital center. Yet at least from the time of the Democratic convention it has been clear that the President-elect was a paper hound dog. The convention itself had the feel of a 12-step clinic. "Recovery" was in the air — a psychological as well as an economic imperative. Everyone there seemed to be "in recovery" — from AIDS, from abuse, from harassment, from prejudice. They were overcoming co-dependency, a Yuppie version of guilt; and low self esteem, the Yuppie version of sin. Everyone had a tale of how they had overcome. The robotic Al Gore had the story of his son — a nightclub imitation of a moral quickening. Clinton's self-defining vignette was doctored with a slightly different spin. When he was presented as the boy who had stood up against an abusive stepfather, it was an attempt to impress them with the heroism he never achieved in war on the battleground of the dysfunctional family. The subliminal message was that this primal trauma had left a mark. No wonder that he had perhaps strayed from the course during a life lived in these psychological shadows. But the important thing was that he had seen the light and was in recovery, and the misdeeds he never admitted committing in his marriage were behind him.

Despite the clumsy attempt at premature closure it was easy to see the subtext: Clinton had signed not just a truce with his wife, but an unconditional surrender. Every marriage conceals a deal. But not since FDR has the deal had such national repercussions. It is easy to imagine the terms of it: yes, I'll stay with you despite the bimbo, but there's a price; I want a hand in it if you make it through the primaries. Her feminism had given the First Partner the insight Clinton might have learned if he had gone to Vietnam: if you have them by the balls, their hearts and minds will follow.

Hillary is not the thick-ankled virago her enemies make her out to be, no more than she is the philosopher queen portrayed in gushing mash notes from Eleanor Clift in *Newsweek* and Susan Faludi in the *New York Times.* Garry Wills certainly flatters her by reviewing a body of work that is anorexically thin. Like her friends Shalala and Cole, she grew up in the woman's movement, imbibing the cliches which are its mother's milk and which helped create political correctness. She is an activist, like Shalala and Cole, with an agenda for transforming the domestic arrangements that structure our society.

It is Hillary, much more than her husband, who is the policy wonk. Back in the Sixties, radicals were upfront about what they wanted: smash monogamy and nuke the nuclear family. Now, the feminists push the same ideas not as slogans but as "national priorities." Marriage is akin to the institution of slavery, Hillary once told us. The family is not the site of enduring ties, she believes, but a bloody ground of unremitting negotiation where that which is nuanced, voluntary and not immediately reciprocal is dangerous; where every duty must be defined and every right prescribed. (Only such a mentality could use a depressing phrase like "cherished, albeit fantasized, family values").

For Hillary and her comrades, the family is not a building block of autonomy, but an obstacle in the path of social progress and a psychological ghetto of dysfunction. What these people want to do may seem liberal: protect children from arbitrary power. But what they really want to do, as Christopher Lasch has observed, is to protect children against the family itself. The state sets children free and the family holds them back: that's their view. Children's rights is a carom shot in the struggle against patriarchy. Making children "responsible" is freeing them from personal authority. For Hillary's gang, a quintessential act of human liberation is a 13 year old girl having an abortion without parental notification, much less approval.

It is not hard to see where that leads: to further enfeeblement of the one institution in our society that can stand against crime and moral decay. For all her palaver about families and children, Hillary seems not to have understood the tragic lesson of the black family, which has become a laboratory showing the evil wrought by the malign symbiosis of a devalued patriarchy accompanied by intrusions of the therapeutic state. In her view that family is best which governs least. It should be something like a round the clock version of day care. Any expectations for something more than this are on the one hand sentimental and on the other dangerous because intimacy is both unpredictable and carries the burden of unequal relationships. What would Hillary and friends substitute for those "fantasized" family values they claim to view with nostalgic fondness but actually scorn? Programs. Programs architected no doubt by Marian Wright Edelman and the ubiquitous Children's Defense Fund.

Hillary makes one wish for a Clintonectomy even before the administration takes power. Yet what we face now in her accession to power was bound to happen sooner or later. The culture war has been going on for a long time and the Left has been winning. Yet even as they march into the nation's Capitol, they still like to pretend that they are a counter culture under assault by low-browed, reactionary American nativism. This is a self serving fantasy. The Left *is* the cultural establishment. This is bad because it means they have power. It is good because it means they must defend what they do and say — defend the payoffs to interest groups, the projects in cultural deconstruction, the obscene tinkerings with sex and gender, the quotidian inequities and spirit-killing double standards, the manufacturing of racism through the promulgation of rules about blood quantum and background that resemble the Nuremburg Laws. All these things they have hitherto done by hidden agenda in the mad laboratory of the university, those islands of repression, in Jeane Kirkpatrick's phrase, existing in a sea of freedom. Now the sea has shrunk and the islands have grown larger, becoming a land bridge stretching all the way to Washington.

The culture war is this generation's Cold War. In the formative period of that other conflict there was much discussion of what strategy to use against totalitarianism – containment or rollback (with the Left, of course, pushing a minority position for capitulation). As it worked out, through a combination of luck and fortitude, containment turned out to be rollback. As those present at the creation saw, if the West had the courage to hold the Soviet Union in check, it would eventually collapse of its own hideous internal contradictions. The same is true of the empire of political correctitude. It seems like a formidable juggernaut. But like Communism, it is against nature, as well as equity, and the people of this country, who might not have been able to prevent it from taking over the academic culture, will not tolerate it as a national regime.

Those of us linked only by a mutual loathing of the smelly little orthodoxies are now the real counter culture and we had better start acting like it.

January, 1993

Gays March On The Pentagon

by Peter Collier & David Horowitz

Bill Clinton came to power in a time of crisis among the nations of the world. The nation of Bosnia was under genocidal siege. The nation of Somalia was occupied by U.S. forces. The nation of Iraq was being bombed. The nation of Russia was being strangled by hyper-inflation. But Clinton could not focus on the plight of these nations during his first and most important days in office. The only nation he cared about was Queer Nation.

And the first enemy he chose to confront was the U.S. military. By forcing the issue of gays in the military as the first item on his presidential agenda, Clinton showed a disquieting lack of the one quality, political savvy, that he was supposed to possess above all others, and the one quality that we, his constituents, were supposed to be able to count on. But this was not just an anomaly of ineptitude. Clinton raised the issue of gays for the same reason that he stocked the administration with his wife's politically correct appointees. At the same moment that he was selling himself as a common sense centrist during the recent election, he was selling his soul to the special interest groups that have deformed his party over the last twenty-five years. As the furor over gays in the military erupted, homosexual activists made it clear that they knew that the crux of the issue was not morality but payoff. In rallies and public statements they pointed out that gays and lesbians had supported Clinton at a higher rate even than blacks, and now their time had come.

Clinton's astonishingly banal statement that he intended to be the first president to "lead" on a "civil rights" issue shows not only how much a prisoner this alleged pragmatist is of the myths of the Sixties, but how perversely those myths have been deformed over the last quarter century. That decade which the President has courted with embarrassing unctuousness since announcing his candidacy might have begun with the notion of "making America better," but it ended with a commitment to "bring America down" (in the words of that eloquent theorist Abbie Hoffman). And this is the aspect of the Sixties identity that is at work today promoting gays in the military. From Act Up to Queer Nation, from the pro-Castro head of the Armed Services Committee, Berkeley Congressman Ronald V. Dellums, to ranking member Patricia Schroeder, the crowd that is pressing the confrontation with military tradition is a crowd that has been defiantly opposed to the military mission over the past quarter century. Does Ron Dellums or Pat Schroeder lie awake at night worrying what the impact of this or any policy will be on the effectiveness of America's military shield? Of course not. Both regularly proposed cutting America's military by half during the height of the Cold War with the Soviet Union; they both proposed that America's role in the Cold War was generated by paranoia and nativism rather than by the threat posed by an imperial aggressor. When the Red Army was invading Afghanistan Ron Dellums was denouncing the Carter White House as a place of "evil" and as the principal menace to world peace. The only enemy Pat Schroeder ever saw on America's horizon were Navy fliers guilty of sexual harassment.

It is endlessly suggested by spokesmen for gays in the military, from the President on down, that the issue is simply a matter of "fairness" and "equity." It is no different, they insist, from Harry Truman's decision in 1948 to end racial segregation in the military. That analogy is, of course, deeply insulting to black soldiers in the same way that the trendy parasitism of other self identified victim groups who compare their travails to slavery is insulting to the black experience. Black soldiers could not escape their pigmentation. Gay soldiers are homosexuals only when they are having sex. And all the fatuous sophistry about the inescapable stigma of "biological orientation," much of it inserted into the debate on gays in the military by Clinton himself, cannot overcome this fact.

Only an administration that conceived of its relationship to public opinion as being the same as the relationship between Sally and Phil and Geraldo and their audiences could expect the American people to believe that the issue of gays in the military was simply about fairness. (If fairness in dealing with homosexuals in public were an issue, gay Congressmen Barney Frank, whose gay lover allegedly used Frank's home for a prostitution business, and Gerry Studds, who confessed to statutory rape with a Congressional male page, would have been subjected to the same inquisition as Bob Packwood faces for lesser, heterosexual offenses). Clinton himself kept trying to drive the point home by repeating in a kind of mantra meant to soothe the passions he had aroused, it is not what you are that matters, but what you do.

This is indeed an appropriate philosophy for all the civic institutions of America but the military. (Institutions like the university, for instance, where who you are is regularly trumped by what group you're from). Unlike these other institutions, the military exists not as an engine of social change (whether for better, or, as in the case of the university these days, for worse). It exists as an effective fighting machine to protect this country from its enemies.

If the issue were simply one of civil rights, why stop at gays? Why deny other minority groups that have been traditionally excluded from the military? The disabled for example. Surely it doesn't take more than two hands to operate a computer and fire a missile. Is an American in a wheelchair less of an American for that? Should he/she be denied the right to serve his/her country? Why is the President content with half measures? If the military exists not to protect America but to liberate American society from racism, sexism, homophobia, ableism and other politically incorrect blemishes, let's not equivocate. Let's have a plan to integrate the entire rainbow into the military mission.

Theoretically, the military could find a place for almost any able-bodied or differently abled citizen — if it did not have to consider the cost, or the effect of such a policy on the military mission. But the military mission is precisely the factor that is paramount in these concerns. This is, after all, an institution that exists to make war, not love.

It is for this reason that the principal rationale for the present policy on gays, which is backed by the entire U.S. chain of command, is the threat to military effectiveness of integrating overt homosexuals into the armed forces. This threat is not reflective of a phobia, homo or otherwise. It comes from a recognition of the nature of the sexual bond — one of the most powerful and uncontrollable factors in human affairs. The military command believes that the introduction of the sexual factor into its fighting units would have an incalculable and potentially disastrous impact on military effectiveness. Unit cohesion, the ability of individual soldiers to weld themselves into a unified force prepared to die for each other and kill an enemy, would obviously be called into question if sexual forces were allowed to operate between the individuals within the unit — forces which allowed servicemen to see themselves as lovers and sexual competitors rather than soldiers whose only job was achieving their objectives.

Sexual attraction is a threat not only to combat cohesion and effectiveness but to ordinary military discipline and order. That is why segregation still prevails in the military between women and men among enlisted personnel in the areas of housing and hygiene, but also across a whole spectrum of military assignments and pursuits. Even with this segregation, the inclusion of women in the military has had a demonstrably negative impact on military effectiveness. To cite just one fact, the rate at which women were undeployable (that is, failed to fulfill their military assignments) in the Persian Gulf War was four times that of males. The principal reason was pregnancy. Thanks to the previous pressures of feminists like Ms. Schroeder, there were no dishonorable discharges for these pregnancies as the military code mandates.

It would be possible, of course, to end the existing segregation: to put women and men in the same quarters, for example, and then try to regulate the interactions between them in a manner that is conducive to military order. But no one in his/her right mind would propose this as a feasible possibility. Instead, everyone ranging from the President to feminist organizations is as happy with gender segregation (hypocritical though this is at the abstract level at which these critical issues are publicly discussed) as they would be dismayed at the suggestion of comparably segregating all-homosexual military units. Yet they blithely propose a solution that would not work between men and women for men of radically different sexual orientation. We are supposed to believe that open homosexuals — for whom, after all, sexual behavior is the key to identity — could be easily integrated into units in which heterosexuality is not only the dominant orientation but also elemental part of the fighting elan.

In the background of such an assumption can be heard the totalitarian clicking of the word processors turning out the manuals for an effort in sensitivity training that will make the Normandy Beach landings look easy by comparison.

Homosexual men have distinguished themselves as honorable, even heroic soldiers in the service of this country. Yet they have done so only after agreeing to submerge their homosexual identity in the identity as serviceman. Only a generation like the present one, infected by the malicious cliches of the Sixties, would consider this some sort of psychological mutilation. Only a generation like the present one would claim that the central issue in bringing gays into the military is civil rights and not behavior. We are witnessing a power play here. There is a reason that the President and his gay advisors have chosen to make their stand on this ground. As Dennis Altman, gay historian of the gay liberation movement explains in *The Homosexualization of America*, "The greatest single victory of the gay movement over the past decade has been to shift the debate from behavior to identity, thus forcing opponents into a position where they can be seen as attacking the civil rights of homosexual citizens rather than attacking specific and (as they see it) antisocial behavior."

In the present debate the Pentagon brass have been portrayed as Neanderthals trapped in bigotries of the past. In fact, the Generals are probably the only ones thinking realistically in this case. They know that the rules against open homosexuality have not only protected morale but also, by closing a dangerously volatile issue, protected those homosexuals who have chosen to serve in this volunteer army. They know that the military has been one of the few institutions in America relatively untouched by AIDS, and that such a status is absolutely critical to the military mission. (Under the new dispensation it would be hard to imagine that men would give their wounded comrades mouth to mouth resuscitation, let alone try to haul their bleeding bodies to safety). They know too that simply lifting the ban on homosexuals is only the first step in a process that would soon make the military into a political battleground involving agitation for quotas of homosexual officers, demands for benefits for domestic partners, and remaking of military hospitals to be able to handle the panoply of diseases that result from practices like "rimming" and "fisting" which have made gay medicine into a petrie dish where exotic cultures grow.

To ascribe this knowledge to the Pentagon brass is not to grant them clairvoyance. After all, the generals of the gay movement have already made clear that this is exactly the sort of blitzkrieg they intend to wage. Inclusion of gays in the military is the beginning. The members of the homosexual power structure have already said that they will oppose any exclusion of gays from combat units or ships or any situation where their identity-behavior may be thought to affect military effectiveness in a negative way. "That's unacceptable," Tanya Domi, director of the civil rights project of the National Gay and Lesbian Task Force told the *New York Times*. "We stand absolutely opposed to any segregation of gay men and lesbians in the military." So the prospect now is that wherever gays are present, military objectives and activities will come under the jurisdiction of the Equal Employment Opportunities Commission and the courts, and the scrutiny of the whole battery of legal experts and lawyers marshalled by the National Lawyer's Guild Military Law Task Force, the ACLU Gay and Lesbian Rights Project and other left wing organizations, which have historically demonstrated their unrelenting hostility to the U.S. military and its purposes in the first place.

The gay activists have also made it clear that they intend to implement the entire agenda of affirmative action mischief in the military. Here is a letter to superintendent of West Point from a Clinton volunteer (and Act-Up member): "Lifting the ban is not enough... We intend to sue in Federal court as soon as the ban is lifted to insure compensatory representation in the service academies. In particular we intend to get a ruling mandating a set number of places for homosexuals in the Air Force Academy, the Naval Academy and West Point." There is more. In the current reformulation of what constitutes civil rights, for example, AIDS carriers and sufferers are postulated as a protected minority, whose rights must be observed. Thus, Ernesto Hinojos, Director of Education for the Gay Men's Health Crisis, has already announced: "Being positive for the human immunodeficiency virus, which causes AIDS, does not mean someone is unfit to serve."

Obviously the intent here is not making the military fair and equitable but remaking the military altogether. Queer activist Frank Browning, author of a new book called *The Culture of Desire*, concedes that this is the case: "I agree with Colin Powell that admitting gays into the military will have a negative impact on military effectiveness. The difference between us is that I think that this is a good thing."

It is little wonder that, reflecting on the furor over gays in the military and extreme positions by gay activists like those cited above, the respected *Washington Post* columnist William Raspberry has observed that it is neither a dislike of homosexuals or a desire to exclude them from institutions like the military that is driving the opposition to the Clinton policy. It is more a reaction against the radical and even apocalyptic character of what its proponents believe is a liberation agenda. "I'm guessing that if lifting the ban meant only that homosexual service personnel would no longer have to lie, no one would care very much," Raspberry writes. "But the fear is that something else would change, in unhealthy directions...There seems to be some larger fear that lurks just beyond our ability to define it—a sense that we may be about to release some deadly cultural genie."

Exactly right. Over the last two decades, Americans have become familiar with this "cultural genie." This one is a far cry from the pleasant blue fellow in *Aladdin.* It may be hard to define its shape, but we know it by its works. In the early seventies it established public sexual gymnasia as "liberated zones" of the gay revolution. When a series of epidemics (some, like hepatitis B, quite deadly) swept through these zones, public health authorities who allowed themselves to be convinced that there was a civil rights issue at stake turned a blind eye to the physiological mayhem in deference to the demands of the same activists who are proposing to deconstruct our current military traditions. The sexual "bath" houses, which were the breeding grounds of the epidemic, were declared off bounds to public health officials who might have closed them, by the same civil rights vigilantes who have now descended on the military. When AIDS began to cut a deadly swath through the gay community, these activists rewrote the book on public health, blocking testing, reporting, contact-tracing and other tested epidemiological procedures in the name of privacy and other civil rights. Instead of proven methods for fighting an epidemic, we have AIDS "education" that fails to stress the dangers of anal intercourse (the source — if the government's HIV hypothesis is correct — of transmission in more than 95% of the sexually spread cases) and we have condoms. The recent tragic death of Arthur Ashe, who contracted AIDS through a tainted transfusion, is a reminder of yet another triumph of gay disinformation. During the early days of the epidemic, when screening tests were ineffective, blood bank officials attempted to discourage potential gay blood donors, and groups like the San Francisco Coordinating Committee of Gay and Lesbian Services issued policy papers asserting that donor screening was "reminiscent of miscegenation blood laws that divided black blood from white."

What have been the human and public costs of political correctness in the battle against AIDS? Has anybody attempted an accounting? The unleashed cultural genie has accomplished other works. High on the list was transforming the public arena regarding sexuality, making the bizarre and repellent part of the Muzak of our lives. America would acknowledge extreme forms of homosexuality in the public arena. It would be forced to sit in on seminars in "fisting" at universities. It would be forced to act the unwilling voyeur and admire, for example, the "water sport" of one man urinating into another's mouth as high art. It would be forced to accept these behaviors as normative and teach their authenticity in elementary and secondary schools, where children who were not yet sure how to brush their teeth would learn how the polymorphous perverse use a dental dam.

It would be short-sighted to understand the critical mass now mobilized behind admitting gays in the military simply as a product of the Clinton Presidency, although this administration is well aware of the debt it owes gay groups who fueled its campaign with $3.4 million in contributions. The current debate is rather the final step in a twenty-year-old agenda. It was in 1972 that over 200 gay organizations put together their 12-point "Gay Rights Platform." One point was "Federal encouragement and support for pro-homosexual sex education courses in public schools; prepared and taught by gay men and women, presenting homosexuality as a valid, healthy preference and life-style." Another was "Repeal all laws governing age of consent." But right up there near the top, in number two position, was "Permit homosexuals to serve in the Armed Forces." The genie brings with him a package deal.

The homosexual power structure sees the issue of gays in the military as the tip of an iceberg whose lower depths it is quite willing to describe. "This isn't about just the military," said David Mixner, Clinton's adviser on gay issues, after the President was forced into a temporary compromise. "This is about homophobia in America. It's the beginning of a two-year, a three-year fight in 11 states [where various initiatives affecting gay rights are on the ballot] ... and in school-board rooms around the country." The agenda is not about civil liberties; it is about transformation. As lawyer-activist and Clinton volunteer Bob Wightman told *Newsweek*, "When Bill Clinton lifts the ban, he is going to push national acceptance of homosexuality. It's not just going to push people out of the closet in the military—it's going to push people out of the closet all over the country. It's going to be OK to be a homosexual."

OK? That's not the word for it.

February, 1993

LUNA BEACH By Carl Moore

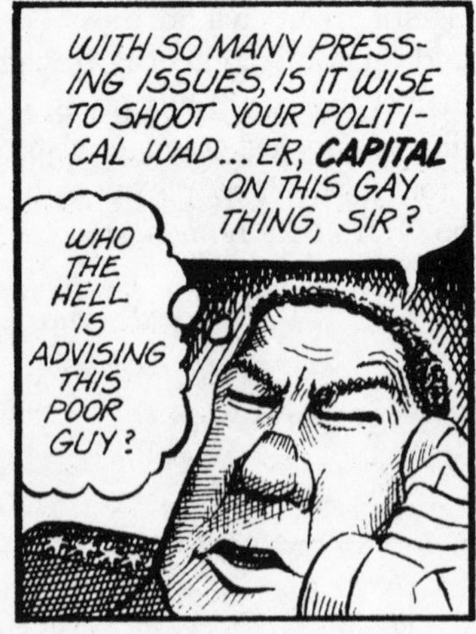

Tailhook Witch-Hunt

by David Horowitz & Michael Kitchen

According to Navy Lieutenant Paula Coughlin, a helicopter pilot and aide to Rear Admiral John W. Snyder, she had no idea that she would be walking into sexual hell around midnight on September 6, 1991, when she went up to the third floor of the Las Vegas Hilton to visit the hospitality suites at the Tailhook Association's annual convention. But as she entered the hallway of the hotel, she immediately found herself in a sea of leery male faces swollen with sexual energy. A taunting chant arose, "Admiral's aide! Admiral's aide!" A man bumped her from behind, grabbing both of her buttocks and lifting her up off the ground. Then, as she spun to confront this attacker, someone else grabbed her from behind. She felt hands going down the front of her blouse.

Paula Coughlin was not the only victim of this bacchanal. Ensign Elizabeth Warnick said that she entered a hotel room after an invitation and was immediately jumped by three naval aviators who grabbed and blindfolded her, threw her on the bed and began ripping her clothes off. With heroic effort she managed to kick at the men, get herself free and escape from the room.

The scandal known as "Tailhook" which erupted two years ago, after Paula Coughlin told her story about what happened that night in Las Vegas, would eventually shake the American military and the culture that supports it more than any event since the trial of Lieutenant William Calley for the My Lai massacre two decades ago. Just as Calley's trial became a symbolic event for a military haunted by losing the war in Vietnam, so the Tailhook scandal was a symbolic moment for a profession still trying to accommodate to the requirements of a gender-integrated force. These requirements had already created a revolution inside the military, yet critics claimed that women still were "second class" participants, restricted from combat and thus from the careers that conferred the highest rank and esteem. When Tailhook, the annual bash of the Navy's and Marine Corps' elite "top guns," seemed to have turned into an orgy of wholesale sexual harassment and assault it also appeared to have proven everything the critics said, presenting a picture of the male military culture which was not only resistant to change, but morally degenerate and out of control. When Navy brass instituted a "cover-up" in the wake of the revelations of

Coughlin and other victims of Tailhook, it was taken as proof by politicians and the public at large of the existence of an Old Boy Network that would stop at nothing to protect its own. Critics of the military like Representative Patricia Schroeder said that heads would roll, and roll they did.

Two years and many military careers later, these images of sexual barbarism and cover-up are still firmly fixed in the American mind. Perhaps they always will be. But as the Tailhook investigations have been completed and the trials and court-martials of alleged criminals have begun, a very different picture of what took place that fall weekend is beginning to emerge. That the late evening hours of Friday and Saturday nights on the third floor of the Las Vegas Hilton constituted a mob scene which to some extent was out of control is beyond dispute. That some $23,000 worth of damage was done (albeit most of it the result of stains on carpets) cannot be doubted. That there was in fact public lewdness and sexuality, some drunken brawling, and a general groping of females by intoxicated military personnel has been proven. Some civilian women who strayed into the third floor party unsuspectingly were indeed verbally and physically abused and there were perhaps one or two cases of real sexual assault.

All this notwithstanding, however, the Pentagon investigation, conducted by civilian federal agents and involving several thousand interviews with witnesses and detailed reports on the night's activities in every single one of the 26 hospitality suites, shows something else as well: that many victims who were identified as victims in the press and even who are identified as victims in the Pentagon report, do not consider themselves victims; that many who do consider themselves victims, including the chief accuser, Paula Coughlin, were willing collaborators in the sexual frivolities that spilled over into the abuse of innocents; that when the party was over, and Coughlin and her cohorts appeared to advance a cause, it was not the cause of duty, honor, country, but a gender cause that sees the military as an enemy to be defeated by a war of social attrition.

From the beginning the Tailhook scandal had the air of a public burning rather than a dispassionate inquiry into the facts of the case. Before a single participant in Tailhook was given his day in court, the Secretary of the Navy and six admirals, including the commander in charge of the Navy's own investigation, had been sacked and had their careers terminated, 4,000 Navy and Marine Corps promotions were held up, and the entire male enlisted corps was required to attend a million hours of sensitivity training.

The tangled chronology of investigation began with Paula Coughlin. She did not report her assault to the Hilton security staff or to the police the night it allegedly occurred, but the next morning she did file a complaint with Admiral Snyder. After reading it, Snyder did not regard the complaint as warranting any action (a judgment that would cost him his career).

After several weeks without a response to her complaint, Coughlin wrote to Vice Admiral Richard M. Dunleavy and Dunleavy notified his superior, Admiral Jerome Johnson, the Vice Chief of Naval Operations. On October 11, 1991, the head of the Tailhook Association sent a letter to squadron officers who had attended the bacchanal rebuking them for the excesses at the Hilton. "Let me relate just a few specifics to show how far across the line of responsible behavior we went," his letter said "....We narrowly avoided a disaster when a 'pressed ham' [naked buttocks] pushed out an eighth floor window...Finally, and definitely the most serious, was 'the Gauntlet' on the third floor. I have five separate reports of young ladies, several of whom had nothing to do with Tailhook, who were verbally abused, had drinks thrown on them, were physica lly abused and were sexually molested."

This letter was leaked to the *San Diego Union* on October 29, triggering a full-scale inquiry by the Naval Investigative Service (NIS) and producing the national scandal that has determined the dynamics and shaped the meaning of the case ever since.

Two thousand one hundred witnesses were summoned for questioning about Tailhook by agents of the NI—100 more in fact than the number of those actually registered for the convention. Many were subjected to mandatory lie detector tests and other star chamber methods of interrogation that would not have been allowed under a civil investigation. And when this exhaustive dragnet identified only 26 assault victims, the small number was taken as a sign of the Navy's willingness to "whitewash" the problem.

A clamor went up from gender radicals demanding a larger body count. If 4,000 men attended Tailhook, the reasoning went, there had to be more culprits. Summoning the Joint Chiefs before the House Armed Services Committee, longtime foe of the military Patricia Schroeder interrogated them in a voice dripping with sarcasm: "Is the bottom line [that] most of you think you could do without women?"

As a result of the pressure, the head of the Naval Investigative Service, Rear Admiral Duval Williams, was removed from his command. According to the subsequent Pentagon report, one of the admiral's sins was to comment, according to his female special assistant Marybel Batjer, "That, in his opinion, men simply do not want women in the military." His other two sins, according to the report, were his reluctance to interview admirals who had attended Tailhook and "his repeatedly expressed desire to terminate the investigation." A key testimony to this allegation was a female agent's claim that "Admiral Williams said that NIS did not have 'a fart's chance in a whirlwind' of solving this investigation."

Two days after the submission of the initial Navy Investigative

Services Report, the Secretary of the Navy, whom the Navy report had failed to place at Tailhook even though he had been present on the third floor, was summarily cashiered.

Embarrassed by the Tailhook publicity and feeling itself vulnerable to increased budget cuts and the downsizing policy of the Bush Administration, the Pentagon brass simply capitulated to the pressure of powerful legislators, like Schroeder, who controlled its purse strings. On June 24, 1992, a second investigation was ordered, this time by the Pentagon.

Federal agents normally accustomed to tracking white collar crimes were dispatched by the Inspector General's office of the Defense Department to investigate not only the Tailhook convention but the naval investigation itself. Their bottomline assignment was clear: to produce a more satisfactory result.

In this second effort, 22,000 man-hours were allotted to the investigation of the first investigation alone. Instead of being criticized, the star chamber methods of the failed Navy investigation were intensified. Eight hundred more witnesses were interrogated. Immunity was given freely in exchange for incriminating testimony. At least one senior Marine officer was put on notice by investigators that if he did not cooperate he would be audited by the IRS (and subsequently was). Other officers were told if they did not comply, their names would be given to the media.

These techniques of intimidation paid off. This time 90 assault cases were identified, including 83 women and 7 men. (The male assaults were the result of brawls.) Penalties assessed for these and other charges ranged from fines to dismissal from the service to possible prison terms.

These ongoing inquiries have adversely affected more careers than any similar investigations since the 1950s. Like the McCarthy hearings of that era, they have created their own drama with their own heroes and villains. And as was the case then, the morality play also has a political text.

The heroine the media came to fix on was Lieutenant Paula Coughlin, aide to Rear Admiral John W. Snyder. Coughlin's complaint that she was sexually assaulted during the Saturday night revelries at the Las Vegas Hilton was the smoking gun that led to the investigations and the incident that dramatized the public scandal surrounding them.

On the same day that the Pentagon began its investigation, Coughlin herself surfaced on a television show, revealing herself ready and eager to step into the role of a military Anita Hill, and to play her part in the unfolding "rights" drama. In fact, the Hill-Thomas hearings had begun the very month of the Tailhook party and Anita Hill was—by Coughlin's own account—her role model and inspiration as she cast herself as scourge of the Navy. For its part, the press was more than willing to facilitate her new career as an icon of feminist courage and progress. Coughlin's name was soon enshrined in Women of the Year stories in the national media and canonized in feminist political circles. Commander Rosemary Mariner, a prominent feminist naval officer (and herself a lifetime member of the Tailhook Association) compared Coughlin to Rosa Parks, the pioneer of the black civil rights movement: "When one individual has the courage not to accept something that's wrong, it inspires other people to have the courage to stand up."

But like Anita Hill's story, Coughlin's has proven problematic, to say the least; a story whose hasty stitching begins to unravel under close scrutiny. In the same way that Hill's presentation of herself at the time of the hearings as a Bork conservative with no hidden political agendas has been effectively refuted by David Brock in *The Real Anita Hill*, Coughlin's presentation of herself as a morally outraged whistle blower with no ulterior motives in making her charge has been undermined by the testimony (including her own) given to government interviewers.

Far from being an unsuspecting bystander who stumbled into the raunchy, raucous, intoxicated, and sometimes sexually explicit atmosphere on the Hilton's the third floor on the night of September 6, Coughlin was returning to a scene with which she was already familiar. She knew that the wild party was part of a tradition that went back more than a decade and she had been to Tailhook, herself, six years earlier, in 1985. The sexual aggression she encountered this time was neither new nor unexpected. According to the Pentagon report: "Throughout the investigation, officers told us that Tailhook 91 was not significantly different from earlier conventions with respect to outrageous behavior." The report lists the Tailhook traditions that "deviated from the standards of behavior the nation expects of its military officers" including the Gauntlet, ballwalking (exposing the testicles), "sharking" (biting the buttocks), leg-shaving, mooning, streaking and lewd sexual conduct.

Lieutenant Paula Coughlin was an active participant in at least two of these traditions—the Gauntlet and leg-shaving. Leg-shaving is described in the Pentagon report in these terms: "Most of the leg shaving activity at Tailhook 91 occurred in the VAW-110 suite. A banner measuring approximately 10 feet long and 2 feet wide reading, FREE LEG SHAVES! was posted on the sliding doors of the VAW-110 suite in plain sight of large portions of the pool patio. According to the witnesses and the officers involved, the leg shaving was a rather elaborate ritual that included the use of hot towels and baby oil, as well as the massaging of the women's legs and feet. The entire process took between 30 and 45 minutes per shave. Other activities often accompanied leg shaving. For example, officers in the VR-57 suite reportedly licked the females' legs with their tongues to ensure 'quality control.' Several witnesses observed nudity in conjunction with leg shaving. Three instances were reported where women exposed their breasts while being shaved in the VAW-110 suite. Witnesses related that some women wore only underwear or bikinis during leg shaving, or pulled up their shorts or underwear to expose the areas they wanted shaved."

Some of the women volunteers were strippers who bared their breasts and then demanded money to remove their underpants. "One uncorroborated witness reported seeing a female naval officer having her legs shaved while wearing her whites." That woman, according to one of the Tailhook defendants, was Lieutenant Paula Coughlin.

This accusation was made to the Pentagon team (which suppressed it) and to the press by Lieutenant Rolando Diaz, a Puerto Rican E-2C Hawkeye pilot. A sixteen year veteran, Diaz had been recently selected for promotion to Lieutenant Commander. Diaz had previously attended Tailhook 90 where he performed leg shaving without incident. For his 1991 leg shaving (he gave a "bikini cut"), Diaz has been charged by a courts-martial with disobeying the order of a superior commissioned officer who allegedly ordered him not to shave above the mid-thigh. He has also been charged with conduct unbecoming an officer.

Diaz told the Pentagon investigators and the press that he shaved Coughlin's legs twice during Tailhook 91 in the VAW-110 suite. On Friday, September 6, Diaz claims he shaved Coughlin while in uniform, and the next day—i.e., the day of her harassment—while she was in civilian clothes. Diaz did not ask any money for his service but requested that customers sign his banner. Diaz says that Coughlin signed the banner thus: "You make me see God. The Paulster."

The banner is now official evidence held by the Inspector General's Office. Diaz's attorney, Colonel Robert Rae has said that if needed, he will call in handwriting experts to identify Coughlin's script.

Diaz had reported this incident during his official interview with Pentagon investigator Special Agent Patricia Call. This part of his testimony was not included in Call's report. Similar omissions from the investigators' reports, damning to the male participants and protective of female participants were widespread, according to officers who were interviewed.

Paula Coughlin also participated in the Gauntlet, the most notorious Tailhook ritual. The earliest reported existence of the Gauntlet was contained in a Navy commander's testimony that he heard the term in the early 1980s when it referred to the hallway outside the hospitality suites as it filled with drunken officers who had overflowed the rooms. Another officer thought "the practice started in 1983 but was not termed a Gauntlet until 1986." At this time Tailhook conventions were mainly stag affairs and as women walked through the hallway, officers would call out ratings of the women who passed through. A large proportion of the women who attended the earlier Tailhook conventions were groupies and prostitutes. Wives generally did not attend and the Las Vegas setting was treated as a port of call away from home. The Pentagon report notes that this was the first Tailhook after the Gulf War and was treated as a kind of victory celebration by the aviators.

One rationale for the Tailhook behavior, states the report, "that of returning heroes, emphasizes that naval aviation is among the most dangerous and stressful occupations in the world. During Desert Storm, for example, the US Navy suffered six fatalities, all of whom were aviation officers...Over 30 officers died in the one-year period following Tailhook 91 as a result of military aviation related accidents. Others were found to have died in nonmilitary plane accidents, in vehicle crashes and, in at least one incident by suicide."

As women were recruited to the armed services and became more of a presence at Tailhook, the behavior began to change and become even more sexual. According to the official report, touching was for the most part consensual and the women involved were "aware of and tolerant of the consequences of walking through a hallway lined with drunken male aviators." The aviators would loudly call out either "clear deck," "wave off," "foul deck" or "bolter," indicating the approach respectively of attractive females, unattractive ones, senior naval officers or security personnel.

Any approaching females not turned away by these loud and raucous ratings would be warned of what lay ahead by another of the rituals associated with the antics of the Gauntlet—men pounding on the walls and chanting on their approach. Moreover, the dangers of a walk on this wild side were well known. According to the Pentagon report, "indecent assaults" dated back to at least the 1988 Tailhook convention. These assaults included breast, crotch and buttocks feels and efforts to put squadron stickers on the "tail" areas of the women.

By 1991, these activities had clearly gotten out of hand. One female Navy lieutenant told the investigators that her squadron mates had warned her, "...Don't be on the third floor after 11:00 p.m." Apparently she disregarded their advice, because she told the investigators that between 10 p.m. and 10:30 p.m. on Saturday night the hallway was transformed from "a quiet place with 20 people" to "an absolute mob scene." On the other hand, the Pentagon report on this mob scene states:

"Our investigation revealed that many women freely and knowingly participated in Gauntlet activities. A significant number of witnesses reported that women went through the Gauntlet and seemed to enjoy the attention and interaction with the aviators. Those witnesses, both men and women, generally stated they could tell the women were enjoying themselves because, despite being grabbed and pushed along through the crowd, they were smiling and giggling. Some of the women were observed going repeatedly through the Gauntlet. Many women who went through the Gauntlet told us they did so willingly and were not offended by the men touching them."

Paula Coughlin was one woman who claimed to be offended, enough to go to her superiors and eventually the public, and whip up a national outrage against her male comrades in arms. Yet, as an attendee at Tailhook previously, she knew beforehand what the ritual entailed. Moreover, the evidence shows that she purposefully showed up on the third floor of the Hilton when the dangerous hours had begun.

That Saturday morning, Coughlin attended a Tailhook symposium at the Hilton, as Admiral Snyder's aide. That evening, she went to the group's banquet wearing what she described to investigators as "a snazzy red silk dress" she had bought from Nieman Marcus. After dinner, accordi ng to her own testimony, she left the Hilton, went back to her own hotel (the Paddle Wheel), changed into a tube top, short denim skirt and "little black cowboy boots," and went back to the Hilton and up to the third floor where the hospitality suites were located and where sometime around 11:30 p.m., when she claims to have been assaulted, the Gauntlet was reaching its frenzied pitch.

It is hard to believe that Paula Coughlin strayed into the hallway carnival unsuspectingly, or that she did not have a hidden agenda in putting herself into a situation where she knew she was going to be "harassed."

According to Coughlin, as she entered the hallway, the men started chanting "Admiral's aide! Admiral's aide!" and Marine Corps Captain Gregory J. Bonam bumped into her from behind. "He grabbed both my buttocks and lifted me off the ground almost," she testified. She spun around and their faces were within six inches of each other. "What the fuck are you doing?" she asked him. She immediately noticed his eyes and his burnt orange shirt with the monogram "Boner" across the chest, she testified. Then somebody else grabbed her from behind, and Bonam forced his hands down the front of her blouse and squeezed her breasts. When Bonam let go, she turned and faced him. "He had his hands across his chest," she testified, "with his chest out proud and he smiled."

At the trial, Bonam denied assaulting Coughlin and testified that he had spent most of the evening out of the hallway in a suite nicknamed the "Rhino Room" in honor of his squadron's mascot. His attorney produced a photograph taken that night showing Bonam dressed in a green "Raging Rhino" shirt—not the orange shirt that Coughlin remembered.

Paula Coughlin was not the only "victim" with problems in sustaining her testimony in the legal proceedings. Ensign Elizabeth Warnick had accused Navy Lieutenant Cole Cowden of holding her "down on a bed, pulling off her underwear, kissing her thighs and touching her pubic area," and attempting with two other officers to gang rape her.

Giving more detail, Warnick told the Pentagon investigators that she had a dinner date with Lieutenant Cowden and arrived at his room at 7:00

p.m.. The door was ajar, so she knocked and entered. As she stepped into the dimly lit room, three men grabbed and blindfolded her, threw her on the bed and began to take her clothes off. But she was able to kick one of them off and fight her way free from the other two and flee the room. She did not report the incident or talk about it to anyone.

The reason that she kept silent was that the story was made up, or embellished so as to transform its meaning. Under repeated interrogations, Warnick changed her story considerably. In the new version, she sat down on the bed with Cowden, who began to kiss her. She responded and they moved to more heated necking and she helped him take off her stockings. While they were on the bed she felt the presence of a second man and they began a 2 v. 1 (fighter lingo for a threesome). For a while, according to Warnick, it "felt good." Then she became uncomfortable and kicked Cowden off the bed and fled the room.

As it worked out, even this version of the story was false. Warnick's motive in lying, as she admitted under oath, was to deceive her fiancee and prevent him from knowing that she had cheated on him at Tailhook. Warnick had told investigators that she was disgusted with Tailhook after her experience at the previous convention. But under oath she admitted she had engaged in leg-shaving and allowed Cowden and others to drink "belly shots" of liquor out of her navel and had had sex three times with a Lieutenant Commander (whom she also falsely accused of sexually harassing her). Excerpts from the transcript are revealing:

> *Defense Atty: Now, you indicated already that you lied on your initial account of having been assaulted?*
>
> *Warnick: Yes, sir.*
>
> *Defense Atty: You also indicated you lied about having sex with Lieutenant Commander X?*
>
> *Warnick: Yes, sir.*
>
> *Defense Atty: Initially you denied having consensual sex with Lt. Cowden at Tailhook '90?*
>
> *Warnick: Yes, sir.*
>
> *Def. Atty: Is that a fair summary of your testimony?*
>
> *Warnick: Yes, sir.*

As a result of the exposure of Warnick's perjury, all charges against Cowden were dropped.

Far from being unique, the complicity of "victims" like Warnick and Coughlin were the rule at the Tailhook bacchanal, marking the ideological fault lines of the ensuing scandal as a witch-hunt driven by political agendas. The initial hysteria whipped by the politically correct winds of the time allowed vague accusations of "sexual harassment" to become imprinted as facts of "sexual assault" on the nation's pliant consciousness. But as the investigations have moved into various military courts, the flimsy evidentiary base has crumbled, producing a dissonance not unlike that which arose when Senator Joseph McCarthy would emerge from a Senate cloakroom claiming that there were 247 or 81 or 23 Communist agents in the State Department, depending on who was asking and with how much specific knowledge. Thus press accounts of Tailhook will mention 175 or 140 or 83 officers as having been involved in "assault" or "sexual misconduct" or "conduct unbecoming" during the Las Vegas party, while the bottom line is—after nearly two years and $4 million of investigations—the Pentagon has felt on solid enough ground to bring only 3 charges of assault.

There are really no surprises in this result, as the Pentagon's official report makes clear. There were, for example, 100 Hilton security guards on duty during Tailhook and 12 present and patrolling on the third floor during the Gauntlet revelries where the scandal-making incidents occurred. The exhaustive summary of the Pentagon investigation lists and describes each intervention by the Hilton staff. The security officers "stopped three aviators from carrying off a wall lamp they had torn from a wall;" they "broke up a large crowd of aviators who were chanting at a woman in an attempt to encourage the woman to expose her breasts;" they stopped an intoxicated naked male who had walked out of room onto the pool patio and returned him to his room; they responded to "incidents involving public urination, physical altercations and aviators expectorating ignited alcohol." In another incident, a security officer was walking with a woman on the pool patio when she was "grabbed on the buttocks." The report then states: "The woman verbally confronted her attacker but the security officer, at the woman's request, took no action."

The Pentagon summary then describes "the most significant incident reported by a security guard." Hearing a commotion, the security guards approached a crowd of men in the hallway and "witnessed a pair of pants being thrown up in the air." On closer examination they saw an intoxicated woman naked from the waist down lying on the floor of the hallway. The security officers assisted her and reported the incident to the Executive Director of the Tailhook Association, "warning him that improper conduct by attendees had to cease or the hotel would be forced to close down all activities in the hallway."

There was, in addition, an assault reported by two women who also reported the matter to the Las Vegas police. The police had referred them back to hotel security because the women refused to return to the third floor and attempt to identify their attackers. *This was the only report of an assault made that night by any alleged victim either to hotel security or to the Las Vegas police*: "The security officers told us that, excluding the aforementioned incidents, no women reported being assaulted nor did any of the security officers witness any assaults."

Later, under pressure from Navy and Pentagon investigators many participants at Tailhook claimed to have witnessed "indecent assaults," which were not reported at the time. In a section of the report titled "Victims," the claim is made that in the four days of Tailhook "at least 90 people were victims of some form of indecent assault," including 83 women and 7 men. According to the report, 68 of the assaults took place on Saturday evening, and, except for one, all of those took place on the third floor. The report adds the astonishing fact that 10 of the women were assaulted at previous Tailhook conventions, 8 were assaulted more than once, 4 on more than one occasion that evening, and that 9 "did not consider themselves to be a 'victim,' even though they had been subjected to indecent assault." In an intriguing footnote the report explains, "We have used the term 'victim' to describe any individual who was subjected to a nonconsensual indecent assault," even when the victim does not consider themselves victimized.

Lacking a real criminal dimension, the only way Tailhook could be made to appear an epoch-making scandal was to use the strictly military charge of "conduct unbecoming an officer" to inflate the number of total offenses into "140 acts of assault and indecent conduct." But eventually, when it came time to prosecute, this method of raising the body count did not hold up in court.

Thus Lieutenant Cowden, alleged attacker of Ensign Warnick, was charged with "conduct unbecoming" on the basis of a picture the Inspector General's office found of him with his face pressed against a woman's breast. His tongue was sticking out and her hand was behind his neck, apparently pushing his head down. IG agent Peter Black tracked the woman down and interviewed her in Las Vegas. During the interview, the woman told agent Black that she did not consider herself to be a victim or to have been assaulted. She told Black that she did not want Cowden to get in trouble for the picture. Ignoring the woman's expressed views, Agent Black had her sign a statement that he wrote to include all the elements that would make a sexual assault case.

The cross examination at Cowden's court-martial proceedings revealed the lengths to which the government agents were prepared to go in order to produce culprits:

> *Defense Atty: That first statement by Ms. M., who wrote that?*
>
> *Agent Black: I did, sir.*
>
> *Defense Atty: Did she tell you that she didn't consider that an assault?*

Agent Black: Yes, sir.

Defense Atty: Did she tell you that she didn't appreciate the government telling her whether or not she's been assaulted?

Agent Black: That I don't remember , sir.

Defense Atty: You explained it to her that it was an assault whether or not she considered it to be an assault. Correct?

Agent Black: That's correct sir.

The Defense Attorney, Lieutenant Commander Jeffrey Good, then turned to the woman's own statement, producing an even more chilling look at the mentality of the government's agents:

Defense Atty: Have you read her subsequent statement that she provided?

Agent Black: Yes, sir.

Defense Atty: It's a lot different than her first statement.

Agent Black: Yes, sir.

Defense Atty: So, the statement that you wrote out [made it seem that Cowden's behavior] constituted an assault even though the woman clearly told you that she had not been assaulted?

Agent Black: Yes, sir.

Defense Atty: Now, looking at the second statement, it's pretty clear that she hasn't been assaulted. Correct?

Agent Black: In her view, yes, sir.

Defense Atty: Whose view is important here, the view of the victim or the view of you?

Agent Black: Well, I would answer that question, sir, by saying that...

Defense Atty: No, the question was whose view is important. If you're talking about an assault, a woman has been assaulted, whose view is important?

Agent Black: In this instance, the government['s].

Thus, in the Tailhook investigation, it appears, the United States government has taken the position immortalized by Lavrenti Beria, the head of Stalin's secret police, who said "You bring me the man, I'll find the crime." This of course is merely a particularly brutal way of expressing what has become the cardinal principle of the new feminist jurisprudence, which maintains that where gender is concerned, the crime is in the eye of the accuser, and, when the accuser won't accuse because of false consciousness or some other defect, it is in the eye of the government.

Almost as illuminating as the government's prosecution of Lieutenant Cowden was its failure to charge Lieutenant Diaz with "conduct unbecoming" for shaving the legs of Lieutenant Coughlin, an infraction he freely admits. Diaz is indeed facing a court-martial for leg-shaving but on a different legal ground. As the *San Diego Union* reported the story, "Rather than charge Diaz with conduct unbecoming an officer— a charge that might also have been made against Coughlin and the two other female officers identified by the Pentagon inspector general as having had their legs shaved —the Navy took a different tack. Diaz was charged with disobeying an order from a Navy commander instructing him not to shave a woman's legs above the knees."

What the *Union* failed to add was that if such an order had indeed been given (Diaz denies that it was) it would itself have been an illegal order, since it had no bearing on military duties, and military orders must relate to military purposes. (You can't be ordered to mow a superior's lawn, let alone shave a leg below the thigh.)

Thus the charges based on "conduct unbecoming" reveal the political nature of the entire Tailhook prosecution. No charges of "conduct unbecoming" have been levelled at any females, even though culpable activities like leg-shaving, belly shots and public sex could not have taken place without the willing participation of female officers. Lieutenant Elizabeth Warnick has not been charged with perjury nor faced with any disciplinary measures for lying under oath, let alone with any "conduct unbecoming" charges for her participation in belly shots and the "lewd behavior" which made her male partners culpable. Nor has Lieutenant Coughlin. Nor has any other female been faced with disciplinary action for levelling false charges or (as in the case of one female Navy lawyer) parading around the entire evening topless.

"The agenda of the Pentagon Inspector General did not include looking at the misconduct of women," a senior naval officer told *San Diego Union* reporter Greg Vistica, the journalist who broke the Tailhook story. "It was a conscious decision," the officer added, "to punish male aviators for misconduct. That was the direction, and investigators were not going to get sidetracked by the misconduct of women."

The Navy brass was going to try to appease the feminist attack by showing the nation that it would prosecute sexist men. As Acting Navy

Secretary Sean O'Keefe said in unveiling the Pentagon report at a press conference on September 24: "I need to emphasize a very, very important message. We get it. We know that the larger issue is a cultural problem which has allowed demeaning behavior and attitudes toward women to exist within the Navy Department. Over the past two and a half months, the Navy Department has pursued an aggressive campaign to address this issue."

To prosecute the women involved in the Tailhook party would have been to puncture a fatal hole in the feminist myth driving the investigations in the first place—that all women on the third floor were victims. Before the appearance of the final report, Elaine Donnelly, a former Pentagon official and head of the Center for Military Readiness, complained to the then Navy Secretary Dalton about the selective prosecution of male officers but received no redress. She later commented, "The apparent double standard at work here is both demoralizing to Navy men and demeaning to military women....I am disappointed...that you apparently have no intention of issuing a general statement of principle that prosecutions must be conducted fairly, without regard to rank or sex of the person who allegedly engaged in improper conduct at the Tailhook convention."

The reason for the Pentagon's disregard for the doctrine of fairness lies in the origins of the second investigation by the Pentagon's Inspector General, which was specifically tasked with finding out why the first Navy investigation didn't come up with the requisite number of criminals. Barbara Pope, an Assistant Secretary of the Navy, threatened to resign in the middle of the 1992 presidential election campaign unless all of the commanding and executive officers of squadrons who attended Tailhook were fired. Rather than stand up to this latter-day McCarthyism in which the officers would be assumed guilty before trial, Secretary of Defense Dick Cheney acquiesced to the Inspector General's witch-hunt, which would increase the body count of the Navy probe.

"I have been a Navy prosecutor, and I worked in the state's attorney office. I've been on both sides, but I have never seen the likes of this ever, anywhere," commented defense counsel Robert Rae of the suppression of evidence and extralegal methods used by the government investigators in their attempts to come up with a "body count" that would appease feminists like Barbara Pope and Pat Schroeder. "People are charged with felony offense-level charges with no evidence or evidence patently insufficient and totally without any credible testimony."

Commander Jeffrey Good, the lawyer for Lt. Cowden, concurred. "The reports of interview are shoddy and can't be relied on," he told *The*

Washington Times. "I think Tailhook is a mountain out of a molehill from what I have seen. There certainly was some misconduct there, but I think it's been blown out of proportion and I think the Navy is overreacting with these prosecutions."

What Tailhook really represents is another skirmish— along with the clash over gays in the military—on the most important battlefield of the new diversity. Until now, the military has been the only institution to remain immune from the malevolent influences of radical social reevaluations. But all that is changing.

The Pentagon report is fully aware of the culture war that enveloped its investigation. The report notes that the 1991 Tailhook convention was affected by the victory in the Gulf War, the downsizing of the military which would most affect the junior officers involved in the Tailhook excesses, and the growing debate initiated by ranking Armed Services Committee member Schroeder about women in combat. A GAO report, not mentioned in the Tailhook summary, estimated that 90% of the "sexual harassment" charges in the military as a whole stemmed from resentment over double standards and the role of women in previously male preserves.

The double standards present in the Tailhook investigations are, in fact, merely extensions of the double standards that have come to pervade the military in the last decade, as a result of pressure from feminists like Schroeder. These range from double standards in performance tests at all the military academies except the Marines' to double standards in facing death. Women failed to be ready for battle at a rate three to four times that of men during Desert Storm (mainly as a result of pregnancy) and, in one notorious instance, 10% of the female sailors aboard the Navy ship *Arcadia* became pregnant after leaving port in California for the Gulf, thus avoiding the risks of actual combat. Not one of these women was court-martialled.

This debate was in the air in Las Vegas in September, 1991. According to the testimony of one Navy commander, Lieutenant Paula Coughlin became embroiled in an argument with him on Friday night of Tailhook over just this subject. Coughlin, it was well known, was chafing under the restrictions that prevented her from piloting a combat helicopter. During the argument about women in combat, Coughlin angrily told the commander that "a woman getting pregnant was no different than a man breaking a leg." Five weeks before Tailhook, Paula Coughlin herself was lobbying on Capitol Hill for a repeal of the restriction on women in combat.

If Coughlin felt she didn't get the best of the argument on that Friday evening in Las Vegas, the subsequent scandal which her actions triggered changed the dynamics dramatically. In her new persona as a national heroine she told the Los Angeles *Times*: "I look at many of these guys—who still don't get it—and I think to myself: 'It *was* their Navy. It's soon going to be my generation's Navy.'"

Nor was the issue of women in combat only on Coughlin's mind at Tailhook, although she may have been the only one there who acted on her convictions. The conflict over the policy recently proposed by Congresswoman Schroeder and others to breach the wall barring women from combat by allowing them to fly combat aircraft was, according to the Pentagon investigation, "the single, most talked about topic" at the convention. At the "Red Flag Panel" of the convention where the issue of women flying combat aircraft was discussed, the issue "elicited strong reactions from attendees." These included cheers and applause when one male officer forcibly stated his personal objections to women in combat and complaints from the women when a male Vice Admiral failed to provide "sufficient support" for their position. One female aviator complained to Pentagon investigators that immediately following the Flag Panel, she was "verbally harassed by male aviators who expressed to her their belief that women should not be employed in naval aviation. They also accused her of having sexual relations with senior officers while deployed on carrier assignment."

Instead of allowing this dispute to work itself out within the military community, with the possibility of restoring single standards for both genders and thereby eliminating much of the male resentment, the Tailhook scandal tipped the scales in favor of the feminists. In the wake of Tailhook, and the Clinton electoral victory, women were allowed to fly combat planes by an executive order of the new Secretary of Defense, a victory achieved by scandal rather than by demonstrated competence.

Meanwhile the trials continue. Symbolic of the tragedy of Tailhook is the case of Commander Robert Stumpf. An 18 year veteran in the military's most dangerous and demanding profession, he has been Commander of the Blue Angels, the Navy's elite flight demonstration team. An F-18 pilot and Gulf war hero, Stumpf received the Distinguished Flying Cross for his heroism in Desert Storm. He came to Tailhook to receive the Estocin Award for the best fleet FA-18 squadron in the Navy. But he found himself removed from his command without a single charge being filed against him. His crime was to have been in a private room (not on the third floor) in which, after he left, a stripper performed fellatio on an aviator.

Commander Stumpf is like the thousands of victims of the witch-hunt that scarred our country several decades past. But there is one difference. The vast majority of those who lost their jobs because of McCarthyism were supporters of a police state which was their country's enemy. The crime of Commander Stumpf was to serve his country and risk his life, as a male, to defend it.

October, 1993

But Is It Art?

by K.L. Billingsley

When Elizabeth Sisco, Louis Hock, and David Avalos began prowling the streets of San Diego and buttonholing strangers and talking to them with animation, some observers, used to various forms of urban malaise, may have thought they were just another trio of panhandlers practicing their craft. Not so, they were *artists* and what they were practicing was *art*, conceptual art, which in this case involved handing out crisp new $10 bills to illegal aliens. These immigrants were puzzled by the handout—in effect a sort of reverse panhandling—but delighted to cash in. Some doubtless thought that *gringolandia*, billed as a bastion of oppression by the same Hispanic activists who want them to come here, wasn't such a bad place after all. But some of the peasant laborers from Oaxaca and Michoacan were surely *muy confundido* when it was explained to them that they weren't just getting a ten-dollar handout but participation in a genuine *obra de arte*, kind of like what Diego Rivera had done back home. It is not hard to imagine the conversations that took place in the migrant camps later on. *"Me dieron diez dolares. Y soy artista tambien!"* Like Russian comic Yakov Smirnoff, the lucky *indocumentados* may have exclaimed, "What a country!"

The project was called "Arte-Rebolso/Art Rebate" and received a $5,000 grant from Museum of Contemporary Art in San Diego as part of a border exhibition called "La Frontera/The Border." That, in turn, is part of a four-year project called "Dos Ciudades/Two Cities," which received a healthy $250,000 grant from the U.S. tax-paying public—not through the State Department, or some other agency dispensing foreign aid, but through the government agency that supports art in America, the National Endowment for the Arts (NEA). The $10 bills, said Sisco, "are like the bucket of paint that a muralist would go out and purchase, like the slab of bronze a sculptor would use." The project was supposed to show that the "immigrants were linked with the rest of the economy through a chain of dollars," thus making a larger political point that illegal aliens contribute to the community. But underneath the jabber about art-as-politics (and vice versa) the fact remained: the federal government was serving as a sort of welcome wagon for illegal aliens.

On September 3, as news of the giveaway was being reported in the major media, Museum of Contemporary Art director Hugh Davies stated that he stood by the artists. "We believe we have done nothing wrong," Davies said. "We do not intend to back away from that position." The next day the NEA withdrew its backing of the project, prompting Davies to say that he would not interfere with the one last handout that Sisco, Hock and

Avalos planned. But he would do some "budget shifting" so that federal funds would not be used. Someone else's money will now be sent, as the *New York Times* editorialized over the incident, "straight down the gurgler," which was probably the only fitting receptacle for the project in the first place.

It was hard not to see this giveaway of taxpayer money along the California border as a metaphor for an arts-industrial complex that is out of control. Somewhere along the line, the notion that free artistic expression constitutes the right to a government grant has become the Magna Carta of that increasingly strange entity called the "arts community." (As onetime NEA Director of Public Affairs Marvin Liebman notes, "It's not a community of artists, but of administrators, an art bureaucracy [that is] self-perpetuating and elitist.")

The NEA, whose current budget is in the region of $180 million, receives about 18,000 grant applications each year but only approves about 4,000 grants. Most of those that the NEA rejects each year go back to the drawing board and start again, except for a vocal minority who, with the full support of the "arts community" believe that to deny them a grant—particularly if their "art" is pro-homosexual or anti-normative—is to "censor" them.

The arts community has effectively propagated the myth that anyone opposing public funding for the activities of *merdistes* like Sisco, Hock and Avalos—and their kissing cousins on the opposite coast, Holly Hughes, Tim Miller, and Karen Finley, whose "art" consists of smearing their bodies with odd substances and exposing various orifices—of goose-stepping behind Jesse Helms. This has been their most successful piece of disinformation—a rhetorical work of art. "The NEA is not an entitlement agency," the agency's former publicity director Jill Collins points out. "When you take government funding, an NEA or a government subsidy, there are strings attached. It is not free. To earn an NEA grant should require excellence of a person's art. It's not designed to be a welfare agency nor an entitlement. It's an award."

This is so self-evident that it has the force of a proof in geometry. When episodes such as the giveaway of public monies to illegal aliens comes to light the reaction of any rational person is obvious: why doesn't someone do something? But this is easier said than done. Anne-Imelda Radice discovered this during her brief tenure as head of the National Endowment of the Arts. In return for attempting to apply the rules of common sense to the public support of the arts, she ran afoul of the arts community and suffered what one observer accurately described as "drive-by slander and moral knee-capping."

An avid Renaissance scholar, Radice earned a B.A. in Art History from Wheaton College in Massachusetts, an M.A. from Villa Schifanoia in

Florence, and a Ph.D. in architectural and art history from the University of North Carolina. Paying her dues in the arts bureaucracy, Radice served as Executive Director of the National Museum of Women in the Arts, Assistant Curator of the National Gallery of Art, and as the Architectural Historian of Capitol Hill. Before moving to the NEA, she worked at the creative arts division of United States Information Agenc y. But while she had a resume Jane Alexander would envy, she had a couple of problems—her party affiliation and (an irony given the current hypertrophied debate about sexuality) her sexual preference.

Radice's father, a medical doctor, was an active Republican and she followed suit, joining the liberal wing of the Young Republicans in college and working on the campaigns of people like Margaret Heckler and Edward Brook. She also became a lesbian. Radice was a supporter of George Bush in 1979 and after Bush was finally elected, White House personnel asked Radice if she would be interested in a post at the USIA. Radice's sexuality was never an issue with the Bush people. They did not ask and she did not tell. For Radice, one's sexual life was a private matter.

From her various arts posts, Radice had watched with alarm as the National Endowment for the Arts careened out of control. In the Endowment's early days administrators like Nancy Hanks and, later, Frank Hodsell had carefully scrutinized NEA philosophy and exerted considerable control over the kinds of work rewarded with grants. In a private review process, they would call applicants and tell them that certain things just wouldn't fly. "A lot of things were thrown out," says former NEA administrator Jill Collins, "and nobody made a big deal out of it."

But by the end of the 70s there had been a change in the arts community. It had made the transition from being antiestablishment and gently subversive, which has been the dominant mentality of artists at least since the Romantic movement, to being anti-American. By the mid-1980s the "arts community" had become completely politicized and mobilized against that segment of American culture which was alarmed about questions of values and morality in public life, and, worse yet, which had given Ronald Reagan and George Bush 12 years in office to do something about these issues. This community believed that art had to "challenge" certain evils—notably those evils embodied in the unholy trinity of sexism, racism and homophobia which are thought by some right-thinking artists to characterize American social life. It was looking for a confrontation.

Around 1990, between the departure of Frank Hodsell and the arrival of John Frohnmayer, the Robert Mapplethorpe and Andres Serrano issues hit the fan and gave an opportunity for the culture war which had been taking place in guerrilla fashion for so many years to be joined in a pitched battle. Serrano was clearly a creature of the arts community. He knew that a portrait of Lenin, Stalin, or Mao Tse-Tung framed in poodle excrement, for example, would not be likely to secure a grant, whereas immersing Jesus Christ in urine might do the trick. Mapplethorpe's models pissed into each other's mouths, fisted each other, and put various impedimentia into each other's anuses. And the photographer constructed images from these encounters which he knew were not merely abstract forms.

When it emerged that the NEA had been funding such high culture, Senators Alfonse D'Amato and Jesse Helms complained on the Senate floor. This provoked the showdown the art community had been hoping for. And the power of this establishment was such that the conflict was fought exactly on their terms—free expression versus repression. Caught up in the polarization, the National Endowment of the Arts pretended that it was defending the First Amendment, although the organization knew that it had been pushed into a danger zone by the radical fringe it had been placating, a fringe which did not care about the possible damage which might be done to this agency and was quite willing to bite the hand that had been feeding it public money. To be attacked by the likes of Pat Buchanan and Jesse Helms fed its sense of victimhood and fueled its sense of righteousness.

"The NEA didn't understand," says Anne-Imelda Radice. "The feeling was that it would blow over. It didn't. Mapplethorpe was the beginning. When the NEA did not respond [to public outrage] it really opened the door." But for some people inside the Endowment, Radice says, the Mapplethorpe affair served as "a wakeup call."

When John Frohnmayer was going through the confirmation process, the NEA formed an independent commission to, as Radice puts it, "combat errors at the endowment." This commission made suggestions on the diversification of the panels that made decisions on the awarding of grants, and recommended that the number of possible grantees for any category exceed the amount of money available so the organization would pick the best candidate instead of just giving away the money to artists in effect hand-picked by the panels.

"If only Frohnmayer had taken their suggestions...," Radice says wistfully, her voice trailing off into the speculative realm of the what-if. But he didn't. The Portland lawyer was supposedly an outsider who would set things right with the agency, and during the early skirmishes in the culture war whose Gettysburg the NEA would shortly become, the Oregonian tried to be tough. Frohnmayer demanded return of NEA grant monies for a questionable AIDS exhibit in New York, for instance. But when this provoked fierce protests from the "arts community" he quickly backed down.

When the *Washington Post*, *Los Angeles Times* and other papers filed suit to have the NEA's review process opened to the public, Frohnmayer settled before it went to court. It was no longer possible for NEA brass to conduct private negotiations with grant applicants. It was at that point, says Jill Collins, that the "artists" said "let's see how far we can go with this." As for Frohnmayer, he quickly learned the way things work in D.C. As Jonathan Yardley of the *Washington Post* put it: "As so often happens to those who come to Washington and assume positions of importance in public agencies; he became a representative not of the people he was supposed to serve but of the interest group over which he was supposed to preside." He further permitted himself, said Yardley, "to lose all sense of the distinction between rights and privileges" and came to believe that NEA subsidy is a "right" to be enjoyed "by any artist who passes muster within the closed circle of the endowment's various advisory groups."

Yardley of the liberal *Post* found himself in agreement with Wes Pruden of the conservative *Washington Times*, who wrote that "the 'red flag' was thrown up by the artists, who were taught by John Frohnmayer that the way to guarantee a grant is to make the 'art' so offensive to the taste of those putting up the money that the NEA dare not turn it down for fear of being accused of abusing the First Amendment."

A prime example is the work of Joel-Peter Witkin, who has received, count'em, four NEA fellowships since 1980, including one for $20,000 in 1992. A master at *abbatoir* chic, Witkin is a kind of Nikon-equipped Jeffrey Dahmer cum Dr. Kevorkian who has photographed the armless, legless and headless bodies he wheedled first out of the medical facilities of the University of New Mexico and then, when that institution found out to ends to which he was putting their cadavers, from sources south of the border.

Witkin has persuaded his undead models to pose nude with crucified dead monkeys, to suck on an eel, to hammer an eight-inch nail through one nostril, and to masturbate on the nose of white plaster man in the moon. Witkin's works include *Testicle Stretch with the Possibility of a Crushed Face, Woman Castrating a Man* and the unforgettable *Arm Fucking* (which he probably should have called *Sphincter Stretch with the Possibility of Reconstructive Surgery).*

But Witkin's masterworks have used as their preferred materials pieces of dead bodies. For *Le Baiser* or *"The Kiss,"* Witkin cranked up his Black & Decker and proceeded to saw the head in half. (Puns about "cutting edge art" are irresistible.) He then photographed the two halves together, touching at the mouth, a neat conceit joining necrophilia, homosexuality, and an inert form of auto-eroticism. One critic said that Witkin reminded her of the mutilator "Buffalo Bob" in the film *Silence of the Lambs*, except that "at least that guy made something out of his victims." As if to quiet such criticism, Witkin, in another work, chiselled a quarter section out of another severed human head and made a planter out of the remainder.

"Bad art fixated on body parts is not more worthy of government patronage than bad art fixated on the flag, or a bowl of fruit, or a pot of flowers," opined Wes Pruden, who added that this was something

Frohnmayer failed to grasp. He gave out grants to body-oriented "performance artists" like Karen Finley and Holly Hughes, and to homosexual dadaist Tim Miller. Trying to please everyone, Bush's NEA man wound up pleasing no one. In his run for the presidency, Pat Buchanan took aim at Frohnmayer as a facilitator of filth.

Shortly after Frohnmayer gained confirmation, Radice accepted a post at the endowment. "My first goal as the Senior Deputy Chairman," she says, "was to shore up the Chairman." This proved a daunting task. Not only was Frohnmayer lacking in knowledge about art but, Radice says, "he was very disrespectful to the political appointees." When people tried to help, they would only get "beat up."

According to Radice, Frohnmayer's motive was "fear of the arts community" and his standard line was, "We've got to support the arts no matter what." He didn't understand, says Radice, "that he was part of an administration, that he was not CEO of his own private art foundation."

As Dave Barry has observed, when you run out of arguments or nothing else seems to work, the easiest tactic is to compare your opponents to Nazis. Frohnmayer resigned under fire in February of 1992 and in a National Press Club Speech likened his dismissal to Hitler's annexation of the Sudetenland. On May 1, Anne-Imelda Radice took over as acting head of the agency. Within days her troubles began.

Radice vetoed a grant for an exhibition at MIT's List Visual Arts Center. Though it lacked images of bullwhip suppositories and urinary marksmanship, the exhibit included plenty of penises, vaginas, and assorted body part s, by which the creators evidently intended to shock the puritanical, heteronormative public. Outraged by the decision, Katy Kline and Helaine Posner, director and curator of the List Center, explained that these body parts were "metaphorical expressions of a spiritual malaise" in America. The rock band Aerosmith chipped in some of their millions to forestall the arrival of a Dark Ages of censorship, and the exhibition went forward.

Yet if Art had been saved, a new villain had been born. It was Radice. On May 12, she vetoed NEA funding of a similar display at Virginia Commonwealth University's Anderson Gallery on similar grounds: that it did not meet the Endowment's standards of artistic excellence. These exhibits, it should be noted, were not singled out. That year the NEA received 433 grant applications in the special exhibitions category and approved only 167.

Radice also rejected NEA funding for three homosexual film festivals, also on the grounds that they did not meet artistic standards. The flicks included *Nice Girls Don't Do It* by Kathy Damond and starring masturbation, dildos and urination. *No Skin Off My Ass* starred nipple piercing skinheads licking boots and toilets and giving each other fellatio and Nazi salutes, backdropped by a Nazi soundtrack.

Radice removed John Killacky, a Minneapolis gay, from another term as chairman of the solo performance panel. She recommended rejection of the famous "Scarlet O" pornographic videotape, which showed lesbians working on each other with dildoes and which an NEA panel had neglected to examine but wanted to fund. "Some of the people on the panels are really off the edge, left type people," Radice says. "Very radical. Anything goes." As it turned out, even Frohnmayer wanted to turn down "Scarlet O," whose chief special effect was a dildo. Radice also rejected NEA funding for the Names Project AIDS memorial quilt because she thought it violated fund-raising guidelines.

Radice discovered that some organizations were using NEA funds for blatant political lobbying, which NEA policy forbids them to do as a condition of receiving a grant. The agency had known about this for years, says Radice, but "looked the other way." A dance newsletter from an NEA funded group consisted of, what else, a bunch of crotch shots plus specific political messages, including names and phone numbers of various senators. "Any such thing I came in contact with was defunded," Radice says.

In the early going there was some editorial support for Radice. "The new interim head of the Endowment has begun on a promising note," said the *Wall Street Journal.* For Jonathan Yardley of the *Washington Post,* Radice had "acquitted herself well." The *New York Post* spoke of a "new broom" at the NEA and pointed out that there is "no divine right to government subsidies" for so-called "cutting edge" artists who "have a disproportionate influence" on the NEA's peer review panels. "When the liars, perverters and bunko men come after her, as they will," wrote Wes Pruden, "we hope she's ready for them." They did and she wasn't.

One straw in the wind came when NEA gravy-trainer Jon Robin Baitz wrote to the Endowment protesting that getting a grant with Radice in control was "like being given the thumbs up by the Vichy government in France during the Second World War." Baitz bravely showed himself willing to put taxpayers' money where his mouth was by donating his $15,000 NEA grant to two organizations Radice had turned down. "I will not be complicit with faux-moralist sharpies of the Right," he huffed, "nor with the psychosexual hysterics in the cultural sacking of this country, which has once again become a favorite conservative pastime."

Soon the rest of the *soi-disant* arts community, accustomed to rubber-stamp approval from their colleagues in the arts bureaucracy, took aim at Radice. And when they did so, it was not only her actions as Acting Head that the radicals in this community took aim at, but also her sexuality. Apparently Radice's lesbianism did not qualify for fair treatment under the sensitivity guidelines of diversity and multiculturalism. In short order they decided to "out" her.

On May 14, representatives of Queer Nation and ACT-UP gathered outside NEA headquarters at 11th and Pennsylvania Avenue handing out posters of Radice labelled "Absolutely Queer." An accompanying statement by Queer Nation's Margaret Cantrell said that "Washington's queer political circles have been buzzing" over Radice. "It has been known for many years that Ms. Radice is a lesbian."

Queer Nation gave a highbrowed rationale for "outing" Radice: "She is a well known public figure" and because "straight people who say they don't know anyone who is gay find out that they do and that queers are everywhere." Further, "gay and lesbian teenagers are killing themselves at record rates because they have no queer role models," and "AIDS is being ignored by our government because our government doesn't care if a bunch of fags die."

When told that Radice had been "outed," gay Republican Marvin Liebman, a former administrator in the NEA, blurted "those idiots!" Liebman found Radice "a rather nice woman" but says that NEA staff didn't like her party affiliation. "If she had been a Democrat they would have loved her, and if she had been a Democrat she probably would have come out." The fact that she was a Republican who had once served on Dan Quayle's staff and who, while making no secret of her sexual preference, believed that sexuality was part of one's personal life, placed her beyond the pale. As one observer remarked, "the campaign against Anne Radice was as vicious a piece of homophobia as I've seen."

On May 15, 1992, the Women's Action Coalition, a purported advocate of "sensitivity," and defenders of the "right to privacy" wrote to Radice blasting her "eagerness to act as a decency czar." The "alleged controversy provides the religious right with an opportunity to promote 'traditional values,' a neat euphemism for their agenda, which combines white-supremacy, misogyny and homophobia in one neat package." Then it got threatening, lapsing into the dialect of a Mafia enforcer: "Let this letter serve to tell you, Imelda, who we are: The Women's Action Coalition, we are watching YOU and we will take action."

For Donna Minkowitz, writing in *The Advocate*, "Radice's position is a sign of new gay political power: Suddenly we are a community conservatives want to tokenize and divide—not simply ignore." Minkowitz quoted Rochella Thorpe, a colleague of Radice at the Museum of Woman in the Arts, that "everyone on the staff knew Radice was a dyke." Gregory King of the Human Rights Campaign Fund, (HRCF) a gay political group in which Radice and her lover served, said that "we are certainly treating her as the enemy."

In a "Dossier" piece, titled "Not Even Worth an Outing," *The Advocate* also called Radice "Helms' favorite hatchet." President George Bush, the piece said, "has a new doormat homosexual who could give his administrations' self-hating blacks and male-identified women a serious run for their money." Vivian Shapiro of the HRCF called Radice "a lesbian from hell." Further, the "Dossier" continued, "Bush's lesbian Clarence Thomas has always had the politics of a Neanderthal." The *Bay Times* called Radice "A Lesbian Even Bush and Helms Could Love," and a "queer Clarence Thomas."

After calling Radice a "decency czarina," Robert Bray of National Gay and Lesbian Task Force met with her to discuss her policy on art produced by homosexuals who comprised a disproportionately large part of the arts community and of NEA largesse. Radice denied she was "homophobic" and said that such accusations hurt her. But after the meeting, Bray told various gay publications that Radice wanted only "Norman Rockwell lookalikes" and that "it's clear to us that she's willing to sacrifice gay and lesbian art to save the NEA." Bray did not mention that her first week in office, Radice had defended the Todd Haynes gay film *Poison*, which had been the focus of complaints by Rev. Donald Wildmon.

"It's a shame that people were revealing her sexuality strictly in a political context," says Michelangelo Signorile, author of *Queer in America* and one of the initiators of the "outing" strategy. "She should have been outed whether or not she was doing any positive or negative things for the gay community." Yet Signorile believes that it was "unfair [of gay critics] not to mention the *Poison* film."

Radice did find some support. "The homosexual thought police," said The *New York Post*, "are attempting to enforce ideological conformity in an attempt to put forward the notion that there's a monolithic homosexual view of the world, that certain gay groups 'speak' for all gays and lesbians." The *Post* found "a particularly totalitarian sensibility at work here. It holds that anyone in a public post who dares to disapprove of a gay 'cause'—from funding Mapplethorpe to keeping the bathhouses open—has no right to privacy. The radical groups will use whatever means they can to enforce homosexual group-think."

But for the most part, reaction from the prestige press differed little from that of the *Advocate* and other gay organs. For example, Los Angeles *Times* art critic Christopher Knight blasted Radice first "as a conservative Republican" (as though the entire Western Hemisphere would instantly recognize this fact as the unforgivable sin). "Second, she is an insider in the Washington maze. And, finally, she is an open lesbian." Radice, wrote Robert Pincus of the *San Diego Union-Tribune*, "is a... bureaucrat in the Orwellian mode."

"It was clear to me," says Radice, "that there were a bunch of folks out there who didn't like the fact that a Republican woman was in charge of an agency, a woman who had a private life as opposed to a public life." The outing and the ongoing attacks that followed had the objective of making her life miserable and ultimately of removing her from the NEA. She continued to receive threats in the form of anonymous phone messages: "We're going to get close to you. We're going to hurt you." And: "You better not go after the artists because we're going to go after you." Compounding the problem, the *Washingtonian* magazine published where she lived. For a while Radice had a U.S. Marshal protecting her, which made her job still more difficult.

Hostile staffers began to wear "Arrivederci Radice" buttons. But Radice, as a Washington veteran, had never been under any illusions that she would be a permanent fixture. She resigned last January when the Clinton Administration took office and is now working for a television company. Though she had plenty of grounds to do so, she did not publicly protest that her departure had been the result of storm-trooper tactics on the part of homosexual radicals.

Bill Clinton's acting director of the NEA was Ana Steele, who recently reversed Radice's rejection of the grant to the gay film festivals. The tax dollars of Kansas plumbers are now flowing to the promoters of *No Skin Off My Ass.* Steele also authorized a $252,000 settlement to performance artists Holly Hughes, Karen Finley, Tim Miller and John Fleck, a payoff approved by Attorney General Janet Reno.

During her tenure, Radice rewrote Endowment grant guidelines to make them more democratic and "more open to people outside of the [in] group." Under Ana Steele, all those guidelines have been called back. Radice also launched a new process to make it easier for lay persons to become NEA panelists, which Steele also reversed. "Supervision over programs has returned to fiefdoms," Radice laments. "It's back to business as usual, or worse."

Like union patriarch Samuel Gompers and his heirs in the education establishment, the creed of the arts community may be summed up in one word: "More!" For example, in its threat to Radice, the radical Women's Action Coalition said it believes "that the NEA DOES need reform: it should be greatly expanded. A larger budget and a broader, more courageous vision is required." The Clinton Administration has just the woman for the job, actress Jane Alexander, who testified in 1990 that it was not appropriate "to try to regulate or judge what is obscene."

Yet this is the end of a chapter but not of the book. The controversy over the NEA can only become more serious as the arts community, feeling that it is in the saddle again, strikes out at values and public morality with renewed vigor. As this happens it is inevitable that more and more people will call for the abolition of the NEA and of the state supported art of grave robbers, excrementalists, and homo-McCarthyites.

November, 1993

PC Kidnappers

by K.L. Billingsley

On the morning of May 9, 1989, eight-year-old Alicia Wade awoke complaining of pain deep in her midsection. Her father, 37-year-old Navy enlisted man James Wade, and her mother Denise, took the girl to the NAVCARE facility in San Diego where initially she either couldn't or wouldn't explain what happened. The doctor found that the child's anal and vaginal regions had been torn in a sexual attack and would need to be surgically repaired. When informed of this, both parents showed great distress and began to weep uncontrollably. The NAVCARE doctor immediately called the local Child Protection Services.

CPS immediately suspected family involvement for two reasons: the rapist, they believed, had not removed the child from her room, and Alicia did not immediately complain of pain. The CPS worker interpreted the hours the Wades had spent at NAVCARE as a delay in reporting the crime and thus an additional sign of guilt.

Though shaken by what had happened to their daughter and also by the hints of accusation they felt coming from authorities, the Wades cooperated fully in an interview with Child Protective Services. They could not hide the fact that they were overweight, which child welfare authorities often take as evidence of general neglect. They did not hide the fact that Denise Wade had been molested as a child and that James was a recovering alcoholic who twice blacked out while drinking in foreign ports. They did not know that they were waving "red flags" that further substantiated suspicions toward family involvement in the crime. They had no idea that authorities were already beginning to build a case against them and were taking particular aim at James Wade who, was a walking bull's eye because he was a white middle-aged male and a serviceman in addition to his other defects.

The Wades were more interested in the facts. During an evidentiary exam at the Center for Child Protection (CCP), their daughter Alicia calmly told the physician that a man came through her window, claimed to be her "uncle," took her out in a green car and "hurt her." They would have had a better notion of the ordeal ahead of them if they had known that on the space on the medical form for "chief complaint in the child's own words," the examining doctor ignored Alicia's testimony and wrote only that the child showed "total denial."

Alicia provided a detailed description of the attacker's clothing, color of hair and eyes, even a pimple on his face. James Wade, a genial Missourian, cooperated fully with the police, who collected evidence including smeared fingerprints and a partial footprint outside Alicia's window. Wade submitted to a polygraph and a "rape kit test" which included a semen sample. He did not know enough about the murky legal realm he had entered to request that the sample be compared to Alicia's semen-stained panties, which police seized but did not examine.

After a long interrogation and numerous accusations by the police, James Wade said, "You're so sure I did it, but if I did I sure don't remember it." Child-welfare workers, who soon began to direct the examination of the Wades, repeatedly lifted this line from its context and construed it as an admission of guilt, not an expression of frustration, shock or anger. They were not interested in the fact that four of Alicia's friends who lived within a four-block area of the Wade home had also recently been sexually attacked and in each case the attacker had entered through a bedroom window. Five days after the rape of Alicia, in another Navy housing project, five-year old Nicole S. was abducted through a window and attacked. Some two weeks after the attack on Alicia, police confirmed that someone attempted to break through the bedroom window of the Wade's six-year-old son Joshua. All these episodes notwithstanding, James Wade was the prime suspect in the rape of his daughter.

While Alicia was being prepared for surgery, guards forcibly removed Denise Wade from the hospital. The surgeon was outraged that the mother was not present. Alicia was crying for her parents but investigators from the Department of Social Services (DSS) forbade the parents to speak to her. In spite of a request by the Wades, no one explained what was happening to the girl, whom social workers packed off to a therapist and placed in a foster home. In the argot of the child-abuse industry, what had happened to the Wades is called a "parentectomy."

At this point the Wades were unaware that their ordeal was part of a national syndrome which began in the 1970s with Walter Mondale's Child Abuse Prevention and Treatment Act and has gained momentum in the last few years with the proliferation of feminist ideologies about the evils of patriarchy and politically correct thinking about the nuclear family as a *locus classicus* of sexual oppression and violence. Fueled by state monies, the child protection system has since grown to immense proportions, like the monster Woody Allen describes in *Sleeper* with "the body of a crab and the head of a social worker."

In *Wounded Innocents: The Real Victims of the War Against Child Abuse*, Richard Wexler examines the national child protection system and documents a number of horror stories. Parents have been charged with child abuse for being late to pick up their children at school, letting them eat breakfast at McDonald's too often, or for not letting children watch television after 7:30. In this Wonderland world, the operant principles have less to do with the Constitution than with the maxim of Lavrenti Beria, Stalin's chief of the NKVD: "You bring me the man, I'll find the crime."

Wexler shows how the statistics which assert the existence of a national epidemic of child abuse are based on reported cases in which some 60 percent of reports are bogus, amounting to one million false accusations each year nationwide. In the police state atmosphere of child protection, informers remain anonymous. And the accused remain branded with a scarlet A even after they have been cleared of wrongdoing. It is a system rife with abuses and filled with the arrogance of power, yet the child police continue to assure us that child abuse is an "American tradition" for which the only remedy is massive and aggressive intervention by the state.

The case of the Wade family magnified all the intrinsic defects of the system. The following account is based on original interviews with the victims, public officials, and some press accounts from an excellent investigative series in the *San Diego Union.* Its primary source, however, is a number of highly detailed reports by the San Diego County Grand Jury, which has been investigating the child protection system since 1988. All told, the Jury received testimony from hundreds of witnesses from all areas of the system: the judiciary (Superior Court and Court of Appeal), defense bar, appellate bar, public defenders, Family Court, Center for Child Protection, District Attorney, and a number of victims. The jurors also spent many days observing court proceedings, visiting "receiving homes" for children, and attending Juvenile Justice Commission meetings. The Jury also received testimony from some social workers who wanted to blow the whistle on corruption. Such workers had to testify without notifying their superiors, lest they suffer retaliation.

One institution in which the Wades found themselves enmeshed was San Diego's Center for Child Protection. The Director is Dr. David Chadwick, who has been described in the local press as a "definitive zealot" for a system ruled by politically correct thinking. Chadwick once told a state legislative committee that his organization performed evidentiary examinations not in a disinterested search for the facts but "in order to prove abuse." Reporters at the *San Diego Union* found a number of instances where Chadwick's Center "diagnosed molestation when other medical authorities insisted there wasn't any."

Through Chadwick's agency the Wades learned the lesson of "denial." In denying that James Wade had raped his daughter, the couple was not seen as asserting innocence that could be adjudicated by a review of the facts but rather as being "in denial." And "denial," as the San Diego County Grand Jury noted, is taken by the system as evidence of guilt, a tactic the child-police share with the KGB and other professional witch-hunters.

"Denial" is the child protection system's version of perpetual motion, an incantation that makes the presumption of innocence disappear. Richard Wexler records the following classic exchange between a caseworker and a woman named Susan Gabriel, whose husband Clark had been accused of molestation.

Caseworker: We know your husband is guilty, you've got to force him into admitting it.

Gabriel: How do you know he is guilty?

Caseworker: We know he's guilty because he says he's innocent. Guilty people always say they're innocent.

Gabriel: What do innocent people say?

Caseworker: We're not in the business of guilt or innocence, we're in the business of putting families back together.

Gabriel: So why not do that with us?

Caseworker: Because Clark won't admit his guilt.

If, as was the case with Denise Wade, the wife should be so stubborn as to support her accused husband, she is adjudged to be co-dependent and "accommodating his denial." And if the child denies the charge, this is considered merely part of the "child-abuse protection syndrome." As the San Diego Grand Jury later reported, Alicia Wade's only "denial" was that her father was the attacker. The possibility that Alicia was telling the truth and that James Wade was innocent never entered the minds of the child police.

Once enrolled in the Kafkaesque Center for Child Protection, the Wades soon found themselves in the hands of social workers. Most members of the profession (about 70 percent in San Diego) are female and, according to both victims and longtime observers of the system, many come to their job seeing themselves as liberators, rescuing the innocent from an oppressive, male-dominated dungeon called the family.

Social workers are not required to record their interviews, and their statements, often used in court, frequently include hearsay evidence and are not made under penalty of perjury. After sifting mountains of evidence the San Diego Grand Jury found that social workers "lie routinely, even when under oath." And there were "numerous instances" in which social workers disobeyed court orders. Everything is on the social worker's side. They simultaneously acquire evidence for the prosecution and "provide services" to the family of the accused. Families enter the process eager to cooperate but are soon horrified to find their statements distorted, taken out of context and used against them.

In the Wades' case, for example, a social worker told the couple early on that if they showed any emotion (under the circumstances a perfectly natural response) they would not be allowed contact with their child. When they complied, the same social worker then accused them of being "unconcerned" about their daughter, using this allegation against them in court.

Jim Wade found himself "horrified by the absolute power over the lives and freedoms of an individual American that these individuals are allowed to exercise." All of the Department of Social Services reports about the Wade family failed to include anything positive. They did not mention that Wade's drinking was not a source of problems, and that he had not been drinking the day of the attack. There was no reference to his Navy record, which, except for his weight problem, was described as "superb" and "excellent." Reports also ignored Denise Wade's day-care business, which ran with no problems, and no one bothered to interview parents of the children she cared for. Reports further failed to mention that Alicia was an A student, who had just been named Student of the Month at her grammar school. There was no mention of family participation in community and church activities.

In a videotaped interview, Alicia was asked with whom she would feel most safe. "My mom, dad, and brother," she answered. The transcript of the tape, however, chopped the reference to the father. A child-protection official later acknowledged that he never bothered to review the video.

Feminist cliches and anti-family zealotry are not the only forces that drive this system. Here, as in political abuses, the Watergate rule applies: follow the money. Therapists who fail to back up the social worker can quickly find themselves cut out of court referrals. And referrals applying to military families are particularly lucrative because they are backed by the fathomless funds of the Civilian Health and Medical Program of the Uniformed Services (CHAMPUS). San Diego County pays court-appointed therapists $40 an hour but CHAMPUS springs for nearly double: $78.60 for 45 minutes of psychotherapy. The Wades went to therapy twice a week.

Alicia's therapist was Kathleen Goodfriend of the La Mesa Village Counseling Group, who worked on the case entirely without supervision. Like the social workers now pawing through the Wades' lives, Goodfriend ignored the evidence and assumed more or less automatically that Jim Wade had been the attacker, although his daughter continued staunchly to deny this in their sessions. Receiving more than $11,000 in state monies for this case alone, Goodfriend began relentlessly to brainwash Alicia Wade, now totally isolated from her family, pressuring her into naming an "acceptable perpetrator." That is, her own father.

The Grand Jury eventually subpoenaed Goodfriend's notes, which contained many comments about how Alicia "liked" her therapist. But Alicia's own testimony makes it clear that the child wanted only to go home. The Grand Jury was also alarmed that Goodfriend taught the child about masturbation "without any parental input or apparent interest by the child."

While Goodfriend worked on Alicia's mind, the Wades' social workers were working on her future. They rejected Alicia's grandparents, aunts and uncles, the pastor of the family church, and the father's attorney as possible custodians for Alicia because of their "allegiance with the parents." One social worker told Alicia's grandmother not even to waste her time coming to San Diego because her son James was guilty of raping Alicia, who would not be coming home to anyone in the family. Instead they were sticking the girl in a secret foster home and the social worker and Goodfriend would be controlling all access to it.

Children are put into foster homes as quickly as possible because that act opens the floodgates of federal funds. Foster parents receive $484 a month for a child from ages 5 to 18, almost twice the amount a welfare mother receives for her own offspring. Special care cases can bring up to $1,000 a month. All funds are tax free. Some foster parents are concerned and caring. But others are entrepreneurs in what the San Diego Grand Jury called "the baby-brokering business." They depend on the good will of social workers to get and keep the little human beings who keep the government checks coming.

Alicia Wade's second foster mother — for unexplained reasons the girl was traumatically removed from the first foster family where she was placed — believed her story about a man coming through her window. She sought to testify that the child not only had no fear of her father but desperately wanted to return home. This outraged social workers, who promptly yanked Alicia from that home and reported an "infraction" to the foster care licensing department. The social workers then placed Alicia in a third foster home. This one had a difference: the foster parents were trying to adopt a child through the "fast track" program. Alicia was offered as an obvious candidate.

By now the Wades knew they were in a hostage situation. To get their child back, they had to fully cooperate with accusatory bureaucrats who assumed their guilt from the start.

James Wade willingly submitted to polygraph tests. One of these was inconclusive but he passed two others and the examiner found no intent to deceive. Then there were some 700 sexual questions to get through, part of a battery of tests that includes the Thorne Sex Inventory, the Multiphasic Sex Inventory, the Sexual Attitude Scale, the Sexual Opinion Survey and the Contact Comfort Scale. Here are some of the 300 "true and false" questions:

"I have occasionally had sex with an animal."

"I get more excitement and thrill out of hurting a person than I do from the sex itself."

"I have become sexually stimulated while feeling or smelling a woman's underwear."

"I have masturbated while making an obscene phone call."

"Younger women have tighter vaginas than older women."

"Sometimes I have not been able to stop myself from fondling one or more of the children in my family."

"I have performed oral sex on a child."

And then, near the end of the test, a light touch: "I have fantasized about killing someone during sex."

Virtually all men accused of child abuse in San Diego must then endure a stretch on the penile plethysmograph. In this procedure, a therapist places the accused on a booth and shows him how to wire his penis to a mercury strain gauge. Then the therapist lowers the lights and starts a procession of erotica that can include child pornography, all the time watching dials that measure erection. During the video portion of his test, the operator stops the pictures, asks the subject how he feels, and waits until his organ "hits baseline" before he starts again. (A San Diego social worker who administers the test has composed kiddy-porn audio tracks, with vignettes of fathers performing oral sex on their daughters.) At the conclusion of the test, an electronic machine spits out a "phallometric score."

Operating a penile plethysmograph is a lucrative business, with some therapists charging $1,000 per session. Those backed by military insurance find themselves booked for more sessions than others. One tester claims to be able to use the device to provide "orgasmic reconditioning" to help the subject "learn to become sexually responsible." He is currently trying to talk the Navy into letting him treat the Tailhook offenders. Specialists are developing a version for women that measures the engorgement of the labia along with a gauge that takes the temperature of the vaginal area.

Penile measurements were part of an inquisition which is different from the Salem witch hunts or the Moscow show trials in that the accused must pay cash up front to be degraded. The Wades found themselves required to accept all kinds of "services," such as counseling, therapy, parenting classes, and " abusers groups." Though taxpayers shoulder much of the cost, the system bills many of the charges back to the family through a scheme called "Revenue and Recovery." The out-of-pocket costs to the Wades, before being billed for foster care, were $260,000, not the kind of spare change a Navy man keeps around. Wade was fortunate to have insurance; many others don't.

Once stuck in the court system, moreover, the Wades found themselves at a constant disadvantage in trying to establish their innocence. Unlike the prosecution, they had no money to pay for expert witnesses. (Jim Wade later pegged his legal fees at $125,000, and his insurance did not cover these costs.) When the Wades realized the deep anti-family animus of the system, they struck a plea bargain by pleading no-contest to a charge of "neglect," part of a deal that would eventually return their daughter home. But after the bargain was struck, the county said that, based on the recommendations of Kathleen Goodfriend, Alicia would not be returning home.

The Wades' attorneys argued that the parents should have moved to have the plea overturned and requested a jurisdictional trial. The Department of Social Services countered that if they tried that tactic, the DSS would also seize their son Joshua and put their family "further behind the eight-ball." This threat constituted an offer the Wades couldn't refuse.

Later on, as part of its review of the Wade case, the San Diego Grand Jury found that the entire juvenile system was characterized by "confidential files, closed courts, gag orders, and statutory immunity" and had "isolated itself to a degree unprecedented in our system of jurisprudence and ordered liberties." Said former court referee William Burns: "Any time you have secrecy you have the seeds of corruption...the people who are behind closed doors can to any damn thing they want. And in Juvenile Court, they do." Evidence contrary to the system's position, the Grand Jury found, is "either excluded or ignored" and more than 98% of the system's petitions are granted. (During proceedings in the case at hand, for instance, the prosecution objected to Alicia's own detailed description of her attacker as "hearsay" and the court sustained the objection.)

From October 1989 until June 1990, Alicia had no contact with her parents. While the court proceedings dragged on, devastating the Wades financially and emotionally, social workers determined that Alicia was "adoptable" and that a "parental rights termination hearing was appropriate."

All this time the eager Kathleen Goodfriend was still interrogating Alicia. One of her therapeutic tactics was to say that she knew the father was the attacker and that it was therefore "okay to tell." But the child persisted in her detailed story about the intruder. Alicia continued to speak positively about her father, saying to social workers, "I love my parents and want to see them." As the date for a twelve-month hearing approached, Goodfriend stepped up her efforts, setting up a kind of tag-team system by ordering the foster mother also to pressure the child to "disclose."

Thirteen months of isolation and brainwashing eventually took their toll on the child. In late June of 1990, the nine-year old girl succumbed to the pressure. At a hearing later on, she said she couldn't hold out any longer. The record makes it clear that she did this to get the therapist off her back.

After the "disclosure," all questioning of Alicia stopped. Goodfriend's "therapy" had achieved its goal. The foster parents immediately whisked Alicia away on a month-long trip to Disney World, an obvious reward for delivering the goods on her parents, as well as a diversion to keep her from recanting. At this point Denise Wade, whose social worker had been pressuring her to leave her husband, had to be hospitalized to prevent suicide.

In December, James Wade was finally formally arrested on the charge of raping his own daughter and found himself staring down the barrel of a 16-year prison term. The Torquemada in his inquisition would be Deputy County Counsel E. Jane Via, whose legal philosophy was summarized in the comment, made in another court case, "Just because we can't find evidence that this man molested that child doesn't mean that he is not guilty."

Via had perfected one of the child abuse system's key strategies: winning by attrition. Her collaborators in social services farm out the children she is trying to extricate from their families to pet foster parents and delay reunification until the child bonds with the new parents. Then they use this bonding, backed by testimony from friendly therapists, to block family reunification and justify adoption. According to one investigator, the child-police tell foster parents to take the children on long and frequent vacations. Then they turn around and accuse the true parents of not seeing their children enough as grounds for adoption. It was Via who tried to justify removing Alicia's brother Joshua from the Wade home.

Via's zealous pursuit of James Wade involved an irony which soon acquired crushing weight. Before handling the Wade case, Via was the Deputy District Attorney who prosecuted the man authorities now believe was the one who assaulted Alicia. Via was thus fully aware that Albert Raymond Carder had been molesting girls in the Wades' neighborhood, and that his modus operandi involved entering a window, committing the crime, and then leaving without a trace. In the case of Nicole S., attacked five days after Alicia, the attacker drove a white truck, which was not consistent with Alicia's testimony about a green car. But it emerged that at the time of the attack on Alicia, Carder did indeed drive a green car, which he reported stolen not long afterward. The stolen car report was never given to the detectives, who apparently never ran a vehicle check on Carder.

Via ordered blood samples to be taken from Carder, whom she eventually tried and convicted. But later, when Via transferred to the office of the County Counsel and began to prosecute James Wade, she denied that she had ordered these blood samples and that there could be any connection between the cases of Nicole S. and Alicia Wade. (The Grand Jury later found Via's actions incomprehensible and recommended that the state investigate her for possible conflict of interest and ethics violations.)

In the pre-trial maneuvering, police finally re-examined Alicia's semen-stained panties two years after the attack and determined that they could be tested. It took months for DNA tests to be completed but they finally confirmed that James Wade could not have been the man who attacked Alicia. It was a clear exoneration, but the District Attorney's office, where Via had previously worked, required that the tests be repeated, and the Department of Social Services continued to prohibit contact between father and daughter.

Convicted sex offender Albert Raymond Carder, on the other hand, was in the five percent of the population whose genetic profile matched that of the stains. His shoe size matched the print taken outside Alicia's window. But even this powerful evidence was not enough for the child-police. Once they could no longer deny third-party responsibility for the attack on Alicia, they simply changed tactics and tried to link James Wade with Carder in some sort of bizarre conspiracy. Worse, the system marshaled its considerable resources to ensure that, however strong the evidence of Jim Wade's innocence, Alicia still did not return to her family.

The Grand Jury later identified a "race against time to arrange for Alicia's adoption prior to the availability of the DNA results." When the result of the evidence was known, Jane Via strenuously resisted a defense motion to delay a hearing that would terminate the Wades' parental rights. Cooperating with Via, Court referee Yuri Hoffman showed himself willing to have Alicia adopted even when James Wade's innocence had been established.

In November, 1991, two and a half years after his ordeal began, the DA's office dropped rape charges against James Wade. Then judge Frederic Link issued a rare "true finding of innocence" for the embattled Navy man, which prosecutor Cathy Stevenson unsuccessfully opposed in court. Wade petitioned the court to have the original neglect charge, which had been part of a desperate plea-bargain, set aside to clear his name and free the way for Alicia's return. Wade said that the declaration of innocence was like getting out of jail. But as it worked out, his troubles were not over.

As a result of his ordeal, Wade had become an outcast in the community and so had Alicia's brother Joshua, one neighbor having forbidden his children to play with "the son of a pervert." There were what Wade later described as "sleepless nights, accusatory stares, the unending tears, the strain on our family, the doubts planted in the minds of our friends." The legal fees, says Wade, "robbed me and my parents of our life savings." And, of course, there was the absence of their daughter during a crucial formative period in her life.

But politically correct Jane Via did not believe that the Wades had suffered enough. Via argued that the finding of innocence for the parents "didn't matter" because the original petition was not sexual molestation but neglect, which still provided sufficient grounds for Alicia's adoption. The Wades appealed to the Grand Jury for help, and it was only through their eleventh hour intervention that Alicia escaped being adopted away forever.

On November 23, two and a half years after the attack, Alicia Wade was reunited with her family. The system that purportedly operated in her best interest returned the girl home using a medicine to which she was allergic, without the glasses she wore when taken from her parents, and with no record of an ophthalmologist's check-up. Two days later, on Thanksgiving Day, Alicia turned ll.

The Grand Jury found that the Wade case, which they said did not even need to be in the system, was far from unusual. In the San Diego area alone, the jurors found 300 cases with similar elements. No system could be without errors and mistakes, but the Jury was disturbed by the fact that rather than attempting to correct these problems, "the system appears designed to create or foster them, to leave them untested and uncorrected, and ultimately to deny or excuse them, all in the name of child protection." The jurors described the system as out of control, with no checks and balances.

Faced with the overwhelming weight of the evidence, several agencies the Grand Jury criticized, including the Department of Social Services, admitted the problems and began to undertake reforms, including an emphasis on family reunification. The District Attorney's office was another matter. San Diego District Attorney Edwin Miller is a board member of the Child Abuse Prevention Foundation, and the former head of his child abuse unit, now a local judge, is Harry Elias, married to Kee McFarlane, whose interviews with children were the basis for the McMartin pre-school molestation case, the longest and costliest trial in American history. Miller's office justified its handling of the case and defended the vindictive Jane Via, but at least admitted that mistakes had been made. On the other hand, County Counsel Lloyd Harmon, Via's other boss, admitted no misconduct, nor even the possibility of injustice. Harmon's response to the Grand Jury, incredibly enough, maintained that the Wade case "was handled in a thorough and professional manner and with due concern for the rights and interests of all parties."

While the child police circled their wagons, the Wade family languished in debt and tried to deal with the emotional fallout of its ordeal. Yet, except for Court Referee Yuri Hoffman, none of those who had attempted to ruin the Wades' lives stepped forward to apologize. No form of compensation was offered. And as far as can be determined, no one was fired or even severely disciplined over the Wade case. In December of 1992, more sophisticated DNA testing found a 100% match between the blood of convicted molester Albert Raymond Carder and genetic markers in the semen evidence in the Wade case. But as of the first of the year, the DA's office had still not filed rape charges against Carder, probably because to do so would be to acknowledge the legitimacy of the suit James Wade had filed against the County.

What happened to Jane Via? It was more business as usual, the tragedy of James Wade not having altered her attitude or procedures. In November of 1992 Via represented the Department of Social Services in the case of Gavin O'Hara, whose daughter had been seized by a social worker and placed in the custody of the social worker's sister. O'Hara had been told that his being a Mormon and presumptive believer in patriarchy made it more likely that he would abuse the child. The social worker and her sister, testimony showed, had discussed taking the girl from him before she was even born. When Yuri Hoffman awarded custody to the natural father, Via went ballistic and petitioned for a new hearing based on the therapist's belief that the child was suffering "separation anxiety." It was the old attrition game she had played with James Wade, but this time the court was having none of it. Judge Richard Huffman said that a "dumb system" had "brutalized" a child and sarcastically put Via down, to the undisguised delight of people in the courtroom.

And the therapist-masturbation instructor Kathleen Goodfriend? It would seem that brainwashing a child for more than a year to get her to accuse her father of a crime would at least disqualify someone from getting court referrals. But Juvenile Court is still providing Goodfriend with a steady supply of lucrative clients. When asked if Goodfriend's performance in the Wade case might merit some kind of censure, the official response was that a therapist "was innocent until proven guilty," precisely the presumption of innocence the system denied to the Wades.

Jim Wade retired from the Navy and moved to his parents' farm in Missouri. There he hopes to heal the wounds and build a new life among the same people with whom he grew up. He has filed a suit against San Diego County. "I just want to be able to pay my parents back the money they gave me to fight this thing," he says. Slow to anger, Wade nonetheless tells anyone who asks, that he believes the child protection system is filled with "pimps and parasites living off the miseries of others."

Wade's ordeal was dramatic, but don't check the listings for a movie of the week. The story was optioned and shopped around Hollywood, but there were no takers. "The reason the networks turned it down," says Wade, "was that they didn't want to show anyone getting off [on a child-abuse charge]. They got the wrong message because that isn't what it was about."

Jim Wade has also undertaken a mission to warn others about the system. He has appeared on the "Larry King Show" and other programs but he cites the op-ed piece he wrote for the *San Diego Union*, right after his family was united, as best representing what he wants to say: "Take heed, citizens of San Diego and all Americans. There is a creature running amok in your midst which can steal your children, your financial future and, very possibly, your personal freedom, as it did mine."

January, 1993

PC Goes To Church

by K.L. Billingsley

Faye Short had no doubt when she became a heretic. It was in 1980 when she was mingling with the sisterhood at a district event of United Methodist Women. It was a time when the battle for the Equal Rights Amendment was raging. Short had done considerable reading on the pros and cons of the controversial measure. She had her own thoughts about it, but did not think she would find the church sponsoring either side. Then she spotted a table displaying materials on ERA and checked it out. As she perused the offering she noted something strange: all the material was pro-ERA. Short found this puzzling. After all, this was not a NOW rally but a function of her church.

Short knew that individual Methodists held widely differing opinions on ERA, just as they did on taxes, gun control, welfare, economics, nuclear weapons, abortion, and many other issues. There was no specific biblical text on ERA, just as there was none about the speed limit in Alaska or what policy the U.S. should adapt toward Col. Qaddafi. The Methodist tradition allowed for reasoned discussion and of course differences of opinion on such questions. Feeling that if the church was going to render unto Caesar it ought at least to do so even-handedly, Short asked why the display didn't include any material from the other side of the ERA debate.

"We don't have any," she was told, "because this is the view that the Women's Division takes, so we are only presenting pro-ERA material." In other words, Big Sister knows best. Those in charge of the Women's Division evidently believed that they possessed deep insights, intelligence, and moral clarity far beyond those of the church-going rank and file. This disturbed Short. She did not like the notion of an elite that had taken it upon itself to enlighten the heathens whose weekly contributions in the offering plate supported such missionary activity.

In this moment, Faye Short had embarked on a journey, although she did not know it at the time, that would take her through the politics, dogmatism and ideological rigidity that now rule political activists inside the Methodist church. In the years ahead, she would discover by direct experience that the church's social-issues hierarchy, what George Weigel calls the *lumpenreligentsia*, does not take kindly to those who oppose their politically correct position. She would see that the teachings of Christ have been elbowed aside by the teachings of Marx. She would see that for the activists who had created a social agenda for the church,

Methodism was now a place for right thinking rather than a place to think good thoughts.

If Faye Short and her husband Dennis, both in their 40s, are different from other Methodists it is because of an ongoing involvement in the internal workings of the church. Faye was born in La Grange, Georgia, and grew up in Florida, where she studied at Southeastern College in Lakeland. She worked in personnel administration in Massachusetts and Atlanta while Dennis completed his graduate work. Dennis studied at Gordon Conwell Seminary (Reformed) and graduated from Columbia Seminary (Presbyterian) in Decatur, Georgia.

The Shorts were far from being social reactionaries. During his seminary days Dennis served as youth director and associate pastor in a Wesleyan church. While living in Boston as newlyweds, the couple worked weekends at an inner-city day-care center. Dennis is now a dean of academic support services at a technical college and a part-time United Methodist pastor. The pair have now been with the United Methodists for nearly 20 years and are currently living in Georgia.

Over the years, Faye was involved in adult, youth, and children's ministry, and held offices in various Christian Women's Clubs. In the late 70s, she became a district officer, conference officer, and president of a local unit of the United Methodist Women. She never thought that the UMW was an ad hoc gathering of tea-grannies busy transporting covered dishes to church socials. She knew the organization boasted over one million members and wielded considerable money and power.

The overall budget of the United Methodist Church for 1990 was $2,967,535,538. (The kind Methodist lady who provided this information conceded that it was a large sum but revealingly shrugged it off as less than "the phone bill at the Pentagon.") The Women's Division is the strongest and wealthiest branch of the Methodists' General Board of Global Ministries, whose income in 1989 was $123 million. The WD functions as the flywheel of board social policy because of a decision made during the 60s when the Methodists ruled that half of the World and National divisions' boards must be women, and further, that 40 percent of the General Board staff must be women, with additional quotas for higher echelon positions.

The Women's Division is the official policy-making body of the United Methodist Women and has assets of over $90 million. In 1992 the UMW gave the WD $37,926,300 to spend on its projects.

Initially, Faye Short was proud that the dedicated women volunteers of the Methodist Church raised this much money for the Lord's work—ministry, relief, and philanthropy, the sort of thing one expects a church to do in service to God and neighbor. But while some of the money went to these purposes, she found that there were other expenditures which seemed rather strange. Also, as she got more deeply involved, she was perplexed by the fact that those in charge held such narrow views about who ought to get their charity and sometimes took such pains to ensure that the rank and file did not find out.

In some cases, WD workers omitted the addresses of recipient groups. Sometimes staffers even used codes to identify recipients. Here is where some of the money people put in the church collection plate actually wound up:

The UMW gave $3,000 to the Coalition for a New Foreign and Military Policy (CNFMP), one of the Left's most strident bullhorns, a consistent demonizer of U.S. policy and a public-relations agency for Marxist dictatorships. After CNFMP disbanded in 1989, the following year Methodists gave $4,000 to the Central American Working Group, which carried on CNFMP's work. A grant of $23,500 went to the Interfaith Center on Corporate Responsibility, a rigidly anti-military and anti-capitalist group.

The Antonio Valdivieso Center, a propaganda oracle of the Sandinistas, picked up $16,099. In 1990 the Inter-religious Task Force on El Salvador, a consistent defender of the Salvadoran Communists of the FMLN was delighted to land $9,000 from the Methodist Women, especially after their boys had lost their colonial bankroller from the Soviet Union. Also in 1990, United Methodist Women gave $7,000 to the Institute for Policy Studies, the American Left's most lavishly funded intellectual bunker which churns out the opinions for leftist mainstays such as Richard Barnet and Saul Landau, a Castro groupie who produces the dictator's promotional films. That same year the North American Coalition for Human Rights in Korea got $3,000 from the Methodist women, although this group's newsletter says it is not possible to conduct "full analysis of the human rights situation in North Korea" (Amnesty International has no such difficulty) and calls the North Korea invasion of the south a "myth."

Other leftist organizations have received grants from UMW, which has supported still other groups with "in-kind" contributions such as the use of meeting space. These recipients include the African National Congress, the Pan-Africanist Congress of Azania, SWAPO, the Christian Peace Conference (for years a Soviet front group) and even the Venceremos Brigade. In 1989 they even gave $1,000 to *The Nation*, the Dead Sea Scrolls of the Left.

Such activism was an outgrowth of the 60s. Before then, the Methodists, like other Protestant churches, strongly opposed Communism and largely supported the bipartisan policy of containment. While maintaining the primacy of their spiritual mandate, the churches also played a brave and important role in the civil-rights movement. The Vietnam War marked a turning point, with spokesmen for the churches not only opposing American involvement with the zeal of Spanish flagellants but often parroting the propaganda of the NLF.

Impoverished Asians who attend church meetings for the food are known as "rice Christians." In the 60s the Protestant leaders became rice Marxists, panhandling crumbs of political enlightenment from KGB-influenced ecumenical "peace" agencies with whom they cooperated. During the 70s and 80s the church agencies locked the entire leftist foreign agenda into place by giving it a name: "liberation theology." In retrospect—a retrospect actually never officially undertaken in an inventory of its commitments by the church—this movement liberated nothing and no one.

As the Marxist movements it had supported went down to defeat, the Methodist Left looked to America for its next set of commitments—spreading the gospel of political correctness and redeeming the heathens from their theological and especially their social traditionalism. Environmentalism, Columbus-bashing, and homosexual and radical feminist advocacy became the new causes.

This trend had actually begun in 1972, when the Women's Division gave $10,000 to eight women's liberation action groups and proclaimed its purpose to "bridge gaps between church women and the women's movement." UMW's *Response* magazine began to publish feminist radicals such as Mary Daly and Rosemary Radford Ruether, a sense of whose writing is given by her 1985 work *Women-Church*:

> *We say that the temples of patriarch have disfigured and hidden our true Mother and Teacher and replaced her with a great mechanical idol with flashing eyes and smoking nostrils who spews out blasphemies and lies. What does this idol say? How speaks this monstrous robot of the temples of patriarchy?*

At the 1992 UMW assembly Dr. Hazel Henderson invoked Gaia, Greek earth goddess, who, before troublesome human beings came along, "managed the biosphere very well by herself." A book on the UMW's 1991 reading list was *Revolutionary Forgiveness* by the Amanecida Collective. According to the group,morality requires that we confront those people and policies which proclaim "sexual relationships between men and women, heterosexual marriage, and nuclear family constellations are normative for society."

Faye Short found herself a stranger in a strange land. She was in constant disagreement with the radical feminism, fundamentalist pantheism, liberation theology, and the demonizing of capitalism and American policy she found in official Methodist publications. She was not a political activist by nature. In fact, speaking and organizing were difficult for her. But she wanted to support her church and the people who depended on it for real spiritual sustenance rather than the ersatz fare of the Women's Division. And so she quit her part-time job and decided to devote a few years of her life to getting deeply involved in church policy-making.

Before Short became a conference officer in 1984, the denomination sent her to New York for what was billed as a session of training but turned out to be largely indoctrination. The trainees found themselves wined and dined and taken on tours of the United Nations and the "God Box," the National Council of Churches headquarters on Riverside Drive. The Methodists are the largest-member denomination of the NCC, which Short would eventually come to see as a sort of interlocking directorate of church social agencies where the *nomenklatura* of religious political correctness plan their strategies.

The training sessions turned out to be a kind of sensitivity encounter with questions asked which required a visible response such as standing up or raising a hand. For example, there was a "Litany for Mission," which mingled traditional Christian concerns with partisan advocacy of ERA and abortion rights. At each table of trainees, a professional staffer carefully monitored the response. "It was obvious if you disagreed," Short says. "It was coercive. I was like a sore thumb."

Theressa Hoover, longtime head of the Women's Division, told the trainees that there would be times when they would find Women's Division policies out of line with general thinking in the church. She reminded the inductees that they had, in a sense, "signed a contract with the Women's Division." She told them that if they felt that they could not support WD policies perhaps they should step aside. But Short's loyalties lay along different lines.

"At conferences I would raise questions from another view," she recalls. "It would create quite a bit of concern. People said 'Don't rock the boat, you are breaking the team spirit.'" These people, she says, had accepted the premise that women must accept what was called the United Methodist Women's "line of movement," otherwise they would lose their position and not be considered for roles higher in the hierarchy. "Privately they would come and agree with me," Short says, "but publicly very few stood with me."

Short was reading voraciously on social issues. Her notes had filled a number of notebooks. In discussions—they were never arguments if she could help it—she would marshal her facts and suggest that everybody in the church might not agree with the official "line of movement." She used the Methodist Book of Discipline, for instance, a massive official manual of faith and practice, to underscore the issue of whether or not the denomination's official position on homosexuality was incompatible with Christian teaching. And Short pointed out that in advocating liberation theology, the WD had reversed the Methodists' order of Scripture, tradition, reason, and experience in matters of faith.

After Short had been in office for a year, the chairperson of the nominating committee came to a regional school of missions. She followed Short around like a detective and eventually took her aside. "You've probably noticed that I was here and that I was following you," the woman said. "I was told that you were a troublemaker. But I found nothing of that. You get along beautifully. When you ask questions, you do it in a very courteous way. I don't see any problem." The woman failed to say who had given her the assignment. Short thinks it was someone in the denominational hierarchy.

According to official policy, the Methodists' Service Center enjoys "sole right of display and sale of literature" in all meetings sponsored by the Women's Division. Short found that the approved fare included "mission studies" and other materials put out by the Friendship Press, the publishing arm of the National Council of Churches which has been consistently sympathetic to left wing dictatorships around the world. The UMW makes more use of these "studies" than any other group, and Women's Division staffers must approve the content before they are adopted. Among others given the seal of approval are the following:

Fire Beneath the Frost by Peggy Billings, a former UM staffer. Her view of the Korean War summarizes Billings' political outlook: "The Soviets chose to utilize the People's Committees that the United States had spurned. Apparently there was less violence and less resistance to the Soviet takeover in northern Korea than to U.S. control in southern Korea." Furthermore, Billings faults the U.S. for choosing "repression, not reform. The constabulary was increased and converted into a national police force. Several right-wing youth organizations were formed, modeled after the Hitler *jugend* for the purpose of intimidating workers."

China: A Search for Community advances the idea that China is "the only truly Christian country in the world, in spite of its absolute rejection of all religion." Another book, *China: People-Questions*, widely used at UMW functions for years after its 1975 publication, says that "a violent revolution and bitter civil war were necessary to sweep away the decay, exploitation and backwardness of old China." This work also includes the following classic passage: "While liberation turned the whole society toward socialism, the Cultural Revolution deepened and continued that process. *Mutant social growths were identified and unceremoniously uprooted.* And, the Chinese conclude, there will be more cultural revolutions in the future as their society moves along a socialist direction." (emphasis added) The editor of this volume was Michael Chinoy, now CNN's man in Peking.

Mary Lou Suhor of the pro-Castro Cuba Resource Center edited a *People-Questions* book on Cuba also approved by the Methodist women. In it she writes: "Cuba could not have grown in domestic stability or international prestige without the help of the USSR, to which Fidel Castro has acknowledged a deep debt, moral and financial." The idea that Cuba owed a "moral debt" to the Soviets bore the distinctive signature of the politics the Women's Division supported.

By the rules of some UMW conferences, spiritual growth retreats are the only events where women may display materials other than those certified by the Service Center. Before attending one of these retreats, Short went to a Methodist bookstore and picked up some books which she believed "showed a different perspective." They were Dee Jepsen's *Women Beyond Equal Rights*, *Let Justice Roll Down* by black minister John Perkins, and Michael Novak's critique of liberation theology, *Will It Liberate?*

Although Short said she merely wanted to broaden the dialogue, the presence of these books bothered Marie Cofer, UMWs conference president, and other officers. But they didn't want to debate the books' content. Rather, in the best PC style, they wanted the offending volumes banished from the premises lest contrary facts and opinion cause any of the sisters to question the infallibility of official policy.

Short describes the UMW's April 1986 quadrennial assembly in Anaheim as the most volatile political event she ever attended. Speakers included Nigerian Amba Oduyoye, who called lobbying Congress "a particular experience of faith." Elsa Tamez from the Latin American Bible Seminary in Costa Rica accused "North American soldiers" of committing widespread rape and child molestation in Central America. Peggy Hutchinson, a stalwart of the sanctuary movement, linked the CIA with Nazi torturers. Dr. Mamphela Ramphele, from South Africa, accused the U.S. of underwriting apartheid. Janice Love, professor at the University of South Carolina, blasted Ronald Reagan's bombing of Libya. And so on.

This anti-U.S. hatefest gave Short a desire to let rank and file Methodist women know how their money was being spent. She wrote an article for *Good News* magazine, published by one of the Methodists' traditionalist caucuses. In it, she questioned the belief expressed by some speakers that the U.S. government "loves war and advocates exploitation," and, after exploring some of the anti-American and anti-democratic rhetoric of the assembly, said she came away from the event not knowing whether she had attended a church function or a "left-wing political rally."

At the next conference meeting, she was "roasted alive" for her incorrect thinking. The article was evidence of her guilt. How could she have done such a thing, the other members of the Women's Division asked, implying that she was a Judas who had betrayed the group. They demanded that she appear before full nominating committee with the full text of her article.

Short was then warned that there would be a strong move to unseat her, although she couldn't discover who was behind it. But it was clear that the move came from on high, not the rank and file members of the Conference, with whom she remained popular. Rather than going through a disruptive and rhetorically violent floor fight to keep her position, she decided to step down. In her final presentation, Short expressed her sadness that a part of the church would no longer be represented. When she finished the audience gave her a strong ovation. There was clarity in this dramatic moment: all who had heard her understood that Short's sin was having challenged the leftist social and political dogma which the ideological fundamentalists of the Women's Division regarded as holy writ.

Short had left the United Methodist Women, but she could not keep silent about what she had seen. She knew that there were thousands of other UM women who shared her concern that their church had abandoned its spiritual role and was worshipping at the altar of partisan politics. She had been working with the Good News organization, Methodists who had established a task force monitoring Women's Division activities. She accepted the invitation of this group to direct the Evangelical Coalition for United Methodist Women, which she describes as a "renewal network." While concerned with social issues, the coalition stresses traditional Christian theology, spirituality, evangelism, and worship—activities, unlike political activism, which only the church is equipped to pursue.

Her antagonists reacted wrathfully. Women's Division Deputy Secretary Theressa Hoover sent a letter saying that the Coalition was a group to be avoided. Short's group wound up on the denomination's blacklist of "unofficial" organizations, along with the respected *United Methodist Reporter*, publications put out by the Institute of Religion and democracy, and even *Reader's Digest*, because of it has published articles on the KGB infiltration of the World Council of Churches.

Yet this counter-offensive did not slow the growth of Short's Coalition. The organization does not solicit members, but it has experienced steady growth, a trend which confirms what other surveys have shown—a growing gap between the still traditionalist rank-and-file church members and the more leftish denominational leaders. Even the Methodists' Bishop and chief spokesman Melvin Talbert acknowledges that such a gap exists, although he says, in a theological Yogi Berraism, that "the perception is not as real as reality."

The reality is that conservative and traditionalist religious groups and denominations are growing, while all the mainline churches have been steadily losing members since their radicalization began in the late Sixties. Methodist leaders may feel good about the fact that their church counts Hillary Clinton as a member, but the fact is that they are out of step with their members and certainly with their founder John Wesley.

In fact, George Will has suggested that what America needs is a new version of this founder of Methodism, who "rode Britain's rural roads and city streets, evangelized the underclass, exhorting pride and combating family disintegration through behavior." That is also what Faye Short's Evangelical Coalition for United Methodist Women is promoting. But current Methodist and other Protestant leaders have other ends in mind, which is why there is a culture war in the nation's churches.

At their moment of membership crisis (and a time of spiritual crisis for their flock) the chaplains of the Left are crowing about their new access to the White House. In late March they held a 45-minute closed door meeting with Bill Clinton in which they pledged to support his administration, particularly the economic package. Rev. Joan Brown Campbell, General Secretary of the National Council of Churches, said, "Yes, Mr. President, we will walk with you on this journey," adding later on with self congratulation that "the President sees us as a resource."

Methodist Bishop Melvin Talbert carried coals to Newcastle by describing Bill Clinton as "a man of great integrity and spiritual strength." This remark contrasted greatly with the Bishop's earlier remark during Desert Storm that President Bush was "the real aggressor in the Gulf."

Meanwhile, the leaders of the United Methodist Women, awash in money from the pockets of churchgoers who would be shocked at some of their ideas, continue to function as the left wing of the Democratic Party at prayer despite the brave efforts of dissidents like Faye Short. Here are excerpts from a litany used at a March 1993 UMW "worship" service:

> *—Women and people of color make up a disproportionate share of those in our society who have difficulty accessing the health care system.*
>
> *—Since the military coup in Haiti, thousands who supported the deposed government have been harassed, tortured, or killed, Thousands have fled from the persecution, seeking asylum in the U.S.*
>
> *—Global media, controlled by a few media conglomerates, is defining what does and does not exist in an unprecedented way. Driven by the needs to serve the cultural demands of world markets, they are unable or unwilling to serve the cultural and social needs of the people.*

This may sound like a rough draft from some left-liberal position paper or an editorial from *The Nation.* But for its composers it's the equivalent of Psalms. After each stanza of this litany, the political cadre repeat, "As United Methodist Women, we use our faith in the struggle for justice."

May – June, 1993

PC at the New York Times

by Barbara Rhoades Ellis

Some time ago I read an extraordinary review in the NewYork *Times Book Review* of James Kincaid's *Child-Loving: The Erotic Child in Victorian Culture.* In the book, Kincaid says that "the real criminal is not the pedophile but the prescribed attitude to pedophilia," that "denying the child access to sexual feeling is also a way of maintaining unchallenged what are clearly traditional views of gender, family and authority," and that "pedophiles, such as may exist, are gentle and unaggressive."

In a saner world than ours now is, a reader might be forgiven for wondering how any historian or sociologist could take so benign a view of adults who prey on children, or be so misinformed as to think them gentle. Kincaid is not an expert in the field, however, but rather a professor of English Literature. This odd work stems from that strange world of college literature departments, where command of an arcane phraseology and set of doctrines is sufficient preparation for all kinds of topics formerly thought to require real empirical knowledge.

Even more astonishing than the book, however, with its notion that we can't know lust until we lust after children, or that parents who fear pedophiles are just afraid of the power their children may acquire, is the fact that the *Book Review* editor had obviously taken great pains to find a reviewer who shared these attitudes so completely that he might have written the book himself. Walter Kendrick (author of *The Secret Museum: Pornography in Modern Culture* and of course also an English Literature professor) commended Kincaid for giving us the good news about those gentle pedophiles who commit "very few crimes," and especially liked the idea that we are all pedophiles—the problem, of course, being that you are I are repressed pedophiles who need to demonize the unrepressed ones to propitiate our own guilt and fear. The editor signalled her agreement with the headline: "We Have Met the Pedophiles and They Are Us."

Some *Times* readers may have been startled: a national institution, the nation's "newspaper of record," cheerleading for pedophilia and PC absurdity? But the sad fact is that this kind of thing is no longer a surprise: most will long since have realized that the *Book Review* has become a lobby for political correctness. When a book deals with one of the hot-button issues in the culture wars, the choice of reviewers is ruthlessly partisan: pro-PC books are protected by assigning them to ideological clones of their author, while books that object to any aspect of PC ideology are given to the very people the book criticizes, who then respond with predictable animosity. In this way the *Book Review* promotes political correctness and stifles critical voices; alone among the mainstream media, it gives a national platform even to PC's lunatic fringe, with its mindless bourgeois bashing and freakish sexual attitudes.

The editor's thought process is transparent. How do you ensure a respectful review of feminist eminence Gloria Steinem's *Revolution From Within*? Since Steinem is the former editor of *Ms*, the book goes to Deidre English, former editor of *Mother Jones*: a close match. Susan Faludi's *Backlash* is the work of a journalist with a sour view of any criticism of feminism, so let's find another like her: the equally sour Ellen Goodman, who thinks the infamous Antioch sex code has "the plot line just about right" while the rest of the country is roaring with laughter. Neither book fared particularly well in reviews, and even feminists attacked Steinem, but the *Times* protected both from a negative review.

PC extremists are similarly protected. Marilyn French has a paranoid vision of "today's male-dominated global society, with its underlying aim of destroying, subjugating, or mutilating women." She even fears that "new reproductive technologies can make women obsolete" and that "men are well on their way to exterminating women from the world." The *Times* not only met the challenge of matching this degree of fantasy in its reviewer, but went one better. Reviewer Isabelle de Courtivron agreed with French that "the world is irremediably paralyzed by a global war between the sexes," but thought it "quite feeble" [!] that she did not urge women to take up arms in response or suggest "an equally brutal response in self-defense."

This zeal to protect a PC book is in stark contrast to what happens when orthodoxy is challenged. Again, the editorial thought process is transparent. Dinesh d'Souza's *Illiberal Education* criticized university administrators, especially at elite institutions, for cooperating with radicals to transform liberal education and make it victim-obsessed. Who better to give the book to (if you want it trashed) than a feminist professor and administrator responsible for the academic program at one of the institutions criticized: Nancy Dye, Dean of the Faculty at Vassar. Shelby Steele's *The Content of our Character* argued that affirmative action, though designed to improve the racial situation, had actually made things worse, and that black concern with victimhood was self-destructive. Who would likely be provoked to an angry response? Clearly, a black radical professor like Patricia Williams, and so the book went to her. Thomas Sowell's *Inside American Education* is an indictment of the educational establishment and its liberal political support; the *Book Review* neatly managed to find someone who combined both reasons to be offended—former liberal Democratic congressman and President of NYU John Brademas. Agree with them or not, these books by D'Souza, Steele and

Sowell have established themselves as major contributions to a national debate. Yet each time, the *Times* made sure that they got nastily dismissive reviews.

Sometimes the intent is clear but the execution incompetent. Robert Hughes attacks all sides in the culture wars in his scattershot *Culture of Complaint*, but he is scathing about victimologists, and so the review went to feminist English Professor Linda Salomon. Yet Salomon seemed fearful of taking on so formidable a figure as Hughes and stayed well clear of the specifics of his argument, only huffing in general terms about the "cultural phony war" and chiding him for criticizing Afrocentrism instead of letting further work separate the wheat from the chaff. This weak rejoinder is the last refuge of one who is losing an argument.

David Brock's *The Real Anita Hill* is another case of clearly hostile intent but lame result. Brock's book made a strong case that Anita Hill had been lying, and it caused enormous concern to feminists who had been busy making Hill an icon. Signe Wilkinson, cartoonist for the Philadelphia *Daily News*, seemed a bizarre choice for this book, but the intent is clear enough from the title of her collected *Abortion Cartoons on Demand*. She could be expected to be anti-Thomas (and therefore pro-Hill) because of Thomas's potential vote on abortion was the underlying issue in the Thomas-Hill confrontation, and so Wilkinson's allegiance was not in doubt. Like Salomon, Wilkinson might have the right attitude, but she was unable to find persuasive arguments against Brock. As if to make up for its failure, the *Book Review* later printed two angry letters attacking Brock.

Neither a protective review nor an adversarial one is necessarily objectionable in itself. Book reviews have two main functions: to inform the reader about the content of new books, and to initiate a discussion and evaluation. Editors can differ legitimately in the relative weight they give these different purposes. The problem with the *Times*' pattern of choices is that they reflect neither a consistent attitude to reviewing in general, nor a desire to maximize the usefulness of the review for each particular book, but simply the bitterly partisan ideology of the review editor: books on one side of the debate are carefully protected, those on the other side are savaged.

It is not always wrong for a review editor to be guided by a viewpoint. Journals like *The Nation* or *Commentary* have a characteristic point of view, one which their readers seek. (*Heterodoxy* does too.) But the New York *Times* is, or should be, a very different case—its readership has no ideological restriction. It is a national, not a sectarian resource, and it ought not to behave like *The Nation*.

How can this bigotry have infected the *Book Review?* The case of Allan Bloom indicates both the magnitude of the change and its time frame. In 1987, Bloom's *Closing of the American Mind* was reviewed by , managing editor of the *New Criterion*, certainly a "protective" choice, but probably a wise one. Bloom is a maddeningly inconsistent thinker, at one moment shrewd, original and thought-provoking, the next plain silly. An adversarial review would have run the risk of picking on all that is silly in Bloom, easy to do and not very useful. Bloom's latest book, however, was treated differently. The *Times* gave the book to Katha Pollitt, associate editor of *The Nation*, with results the editor could easily foresee; Pollitt is snidely dismissive throughout. Bloom had died quite recently, and this was surely an occasion for a serious appraisal of his work and influence. How spiteful it was to let Katha Pollitt loose on Bloom for his obituary. (Contrast this with socialist Michael Harrington's swan song, given to Paul Berman for a predictably effusive review, though both were members of the *Dissent* editorial board.)

There had been previous episodes of intrusive ideology in the *Book Review*, notably in the early seventies when then-editor John Leonard gave over the entire contents of one issue to a single piece by Neil Sheehan on Vietnam. But what happened to the *Book Review* after the Kimball review of Bloom marked a cataclysmic departure from the status quo. The key to understanding the break with the more or less even-handed tradition of reviewing that had, up until a few years ago, been honored by the *Times* lies in the story told by Nan Robertson in her *The Girls in the Balcony: Women, Men and the New York Times.* Central to that story is The Lawsuit, a legendary event in *Times* history. The paper had always been staffed largely by men, but by the early seventies it had a small number of highly talented women who were routinely ignored for promotions to managerial status that sometimes went even to the men that they had trained. The incensed women filed a lawsuit, and the *Times*, though insisting that it had never discriminated against women, was too sensitive about its liberal credentials to want a prolonged court battle; it settled, promising to begin hiring women managers.

So far, this was first wave feminism; the issue was equitable treatment for women who already held jobs in which they had proved themselves. But here, as everywhere else, the victories won by equity feminism soon degenerated into quotas, and worse still, sensitivity-feminism. The highly experienced women who brought the suit did not benefit from it, and instead, in a supreme irony, the new women managers sometimes had less experience than either the women who had been passed over or the men who had been promoted over their heads.

Robertson is uniformly sympathetic to all the women involved but inadvertently shows us something of the nature of second wave feminism in an incident that occurs in the last few pages of her book. In April 1991 the *Times* ran a story naming the woman who accused William Kennedy Smith of rape (and who had already been named on network TV). The morning the story appeared one of the new women managers "was so incensed that she charged downstairs from her eighth-floor office and burst into [executive editor Max] Frankel's conference room, where a meeting was going on....[and] told them the story was an outrageous smear—sexist, class-ridden...." Who was this person who, though fairly new to the newspaper, stormed into the executive editor's suite to harangue him with her radical feminist views? She was the editor of the *Book Review*, Rebecca Sinkler.

Sinkler had been a Vassar girl, dropping out when she got married at age 20. Eventually she finished her undergraduate degree as a reentry student and got her first job at age 39 as an unpaid intern at a small local newspaper in Philadelphia. Some ten years later she was taken on by the New York *Times* as deputy editor of the *Book Review*, and soon thereafter (January 1989) was its editor. It was now that the decisive change in the *Book Review* took place. Was nobody in the top management awake and taking notice? Indeed they were. Robertson's book gives us a chilling pointer: Arthur Sulzberger, Jr., who recently succeeded his father as Publisher (no affirmative action here) "considers himself a feminist... [and] is an ardent fan of the writer Marilyn French." Yes, Marilyn French, she who tells us that men aim to destroy, subjugate or mutilate women. Heaven help us. No wonder it often seems that fringe feminism is in charge at the *Book Review*.

Becky Sinkler feels free to enforce all aspects of PC dogma. Literature professor Edward Said's *Culture and Imperialism* is given not to someone who might question its one-dimensional view of western colonial oppression, or just to a historian, but to another English professor who is working on—what else?—"a study of imperialism and the novel." More egregiously, *M.I.A. Or Mythmaking in America* by Bruce Franklin (60s Maoist and editor of Stalin's works) is given to and reviewed appreciatively by a soulmate, SDS founder Todd Gitlin. Richard Slotkin's *Gunfighter Nation*, a book which warns us of the racism and imperialism in our infatuation with Western movies, is reviewed by Peggy Pascoe, also author of a revisionist book on the American West, who praises it but wishes Slotkin would go further and include sexism in the list of the Western's sins. Frank Browning's *The Culture of Desire: Paradox and Perversity in Gay Lives Today* is given to Charles Kaiser, also at work on a history of gay life, and so the writer and reviewer have no trouble agreeing to the silly proposition that homosexual desire among men (like every other PC obsession) "presents a threat to conventional arrangements of power and identity in society." All of these books are protected from commentary on their glaring weaknesses by reviewers who are their ideological twins. With matchmaking skills like these, Ms. Sinkler is wasted in journalism—she should run a dating service.

My favorite example of Sinkler's thought process is the April 4, 1993, feature essay on the east German writer Christa Wolff. Whom do you get to write on an author with a history of sanctimonious, humorless advocacy of the virtues of socialist regimes, who instead of accepting responsibility for the damage she did is now scrambling desperately to salvage her reputation after the course of events made her look foolish?

Todd Gitlin. Just so.

Yet when Stanley Lebergott writes a book on the blessings of free markets, it is given to Robert Kuttner, who is working on, you guessed it, a book "about the virtues and limits of markets." In case somebody missed the point, Sinkler chimes in with a childish headline: "The One With the Most Toys Wins: an economic historian reassures the acquisitive." This, one hopes, embarrassed Kuttner.

Sinkler's main obsession is of course campus radical feminism and the associated "discourse" that sustains it.

It is this that regularly takes the *Book Review* to the outer edge of PC dementia. She carefully protects even the goofy work of Mary Daly (see "Ten Wackiest Feminists on Campus," *Heterodoxy*, May, 1992), giving her *Outercourse* to—naturally—another radical feminist professor of Religious Studies. Sinkler manages to find a reviewer who will reassure us that Judith Herman's *Trauma and Recovery* (where the terrors of war for men are equated with the "domestic captivity" of women, their subordinate position being enforced by male violence) is "not a polemic" but a "grave, measured, sophisticated book." And she finds one who will swallow Anne Campbell's silly claim (in *Men, Women, and Aggression*) that the difference between men and women with regard to violence and aggressiveness has nothing to do with physical factors (e.g., testosterone) and is simply a matter of different attitudes (socially-constructed, of course), men being taught to use violence to control women.

Sinkler even manages to find a protective reviewer for Robbie Davis-Floyd's outlandish *Birth As An American Rite of Passage*, a paranoid rant about doctors and hospitals as a sinister conspiracy against women that aims "to integrate birth—a female, sexual, intimate, unpredictable and natural process—into a misogynistic and technocratic society whose central tenets include 'the necessity for cultural control of natural processes, ... the validity of patriarchy, [and] the superiority of science and technology.'" Davis-Floyd makes self-caricature a high art, but it is almost comic to see her book given to the author of *Maternal Thinking: Toward a Politics of Peace*, Sara Ruddick, who, as expected, finds much to admire: "I share Ms. Davis-Floyd's suspicion of technocratic values, and can imagine the act of giving birth becoming an occasion for philosophic and political as well as personal transformation. And I admire, without qualification, the generous critical, passionate spirit that animates this book." Most women are just glad to have a healthy baby, and their parents, who are old enough to remember a time when almost everyone had a relative who had died in childbirth, are glad to have their daughters alive; nature can indeed be a bit "unpredictable."

Susan Bordo's *Unbearable Weight: Feminism, Western Culture and the Body* evidently has a new take on the social pressure against obesity: "The widespread fear of women's fat, she argues, is a symptom"—here it is again—"of the fear of women's power." PC seems to have found a new version of ergo bibamus, the universal conclusion that can be drawn from any factual premise whatever. Who could take this caricature of argument seriously? Yet Sinkler found someone who did. Maud Ellmann, author of *The Hunger Artists: Starving, Writing and Imprisonment,* thought the book "excellent."

The matching of author and reviewer sometimes shows real delicacy. Carol Gilligan is a member of the feminist establishment who tries to combine a grim, victimized-woman orientation with an aura of judiciousness and maturity. That sounds like a description of Carolyn Heilbrun, and so she is the reviewer for Gilligan's new book. Heilbrun in turn is similarly protected when two books of hers are given to Claremont English Department chair Wendy Martin, and UCLA feminist Barbara Packer, both members of the inbred circle. Both love the way Heilbrun runs down the institution of marriage, but Packer is especially animated: "If women covet the male role in life or in fiction, it is because the female role is something no sane person could want [!]. Ms. Heilbrun is easily the most savage critic of marriage since William Blake." Yes, that really is meant as a compliment.

Gerda Lerner is well-known for railing against that historical conspiracy, the patriarchy, and her *The Creation of Feminist Consciousness: From the Middle Ages to 1870* continues in the same vein: "Men's power to define what is political and what is not, what is historical and what is not...has left women adrift in an eternal present." Yet again, the reviewer (Katherine Gill) is also at work on a feminist historical study, and so Lerner gets lavish praise and escapes serious questioning.

Sinkler has managed to make the *Book Review* a place where, just as in Women's Studies Departments, no reality check operates to slow radical feminism's slide into ever greater unreality. The only serious criticism permitted for books with PC themes is that they are not PC enough. *No Man's Land* by Sandra Gilbert and Susan Gubar is too heterosexually-oriented for our old friend Walter Kendrick. Joanna Weinberg is lukewarm on Elaine Showalter's *Sexual Anarchy*, though Showalter is praised for her stress on homosexuality and homophobia. Martin Duberman's history of the gay movement *Stonewall* is not radical enough on gay rights for Sara Evans. Joseph Dudley's *Choteau Creek* is a memoir of the life of his grandparents ("quiet, common American Indians") but reviewer Sherman Alexie wants "political and social examination"—in other words a different book, not about how Indians lived, but about how they were oppressed.

The Myth of the Goddess, by Anne Baring and Jules Cashford, tells the now familiar PC daydream of how the religion of the goddess was pushed aside by a patriarchal god who brings repression and violence, but for Mark Taylor that's not up to speed on PC doctrine. The authors fail to see, he tells us, that societies fabricate notions of gender, and they "mistake cultural constructions of gender for natural laws of sexuality."

(What Taylor himself can not see is that PC doctrines are contradictory on this very point, always wavering between relativism and absolutism.)

Sinkler outdoes herself when violence against women is a book's theme. In the July 5, 1992, issue she printed two consecutive reviews—the first of Judith Levine's *My Enemy, My Love*, the second of Marilyn French's *The War Against Women*—linking the two with headlines that made a single sentence. The first read "Women Have Always Hated Men...," the second "...And With Good Reason." Levine's book tells us that "man-hating is everywhere, but everywhere it is twisted and transformed." (Some women think they like men.) The chosen reviewer (Cyra McFadden) naturally agrees that this is an unpleasant truth.

Sinkler obviously loves the postmodern jargon of university cultural radicals, and the dated French thinkers that are central to it. As usual, she conspicuously loads the dice when that strain of French thought is at risk. Tony Judt's *Past Imperfect: French Intellectuals 1944-56*, is a scathing account of the irresponsibility of Parisian intellectuals in the postwar period. Follow the familiar editorial thought process once more. Since the people whose ox is being gored by Judt's book are those whose investment in French thought is greatest, John Sturrock, best known for his *Structuralism and Since: from Levi-Strauss to Derrida*, is the man for this job. Sturrock's zeal to protect Sartre is no less than his editor's, but his excuse for Sartre's Stalinism is embarrassingly foolish. The function of an intellectual is just to be one, he says, and intellectuals are not responsible for the real world consequences of their ideas. What a wonderful thing it must be to be certified as an intellectual and so be absolved from all responsibility. The millions of victims of the murderous Third World Marxist leaders who learned their ideology in Paris might not let Sartre (or Sturrock) off so easily.

James Miller's new book on Foucault—the most important god in the PC pantheon—presented Sinkler with a difficult situation. Miller seems on the surface to be pro-Foucault, but he does damage to Foucault's reputation with the new information he reports: Foucault had cruised the San Francisco gay bathhouses and leather bars with delight and abandon long after he must have known he had AIDS, spreading death as he went. Here it was not the author but his material that had to be undermined. Sinkler needed to find a reviewer more devoted to Foucault than Miller: once again, Isabelle de Courtivron. She commends Miller for "dismissing cliché-ridden concepts about specific erotic practices" and for understanding that, "this was the last frontier in Foucault's search for a singular and potentially transformative kind of 'truth.'" Cruising gay bathhouses and infecting people with a deadly disease is a bold intellectual quest? Is there no limit to the idiocy of the politically correct—or to Ms. Sinkler's tolerance for it?

When a need to protect PC shibboleths drives the choice of reviewers to this extent, other factors—like knowledge and intelligence—

can not get their due. Many of these reviews are just poor by any standard. It is not hard to imagine provocative and interesting adversarial reviews; for example, Andrew Hacker (author *Two Nations: Black and White, Separate, Hostile, and Unequal*) reviewing Shelby Steele, and while we are about it, why not Steele reviewing Hacker? But Patricia Williams is barely able to state Steele's position correctly, and Brademas on Sowell gives no idea of the scope of the book's argument. Nancy Dye may have Sinkler's confidence as a predictable "no" vote on D'Souza, but the best she can do is accuse D'Souza of using unrepresentative anecdotes; the real argument of his book is not met. A cartoonist chosen because she is ideologically safe is not up to the task of evaluating Brock's argument, nor is an obscure radical feminist an intellectual match for the ebullient Robert Hughes. English on Steinem and Goodman on Faludi do not begin to approach the quality of the reviews of those books in other national journals.

Another consequence of narrow sectarianism in choosing books for review and people to review them is that much appears in the *Book Review* which does not deserve national exposure, while much that does is absent. Books like those by Daly, Kincaid, Bordo or Davis-Floyd deserve to stay in the obscurity of the campus PC fringe from whence they emerged and to which they speak. The same can be said of reviewers like Kendrick and de Courtivron, yet these two are regulars who return even after their first efforts should have appalled an editor with any judgment. Meanwhile Sinkler protects the nation from incorrect thoughts by omitting from the *Book Review* works like Robert Edgerton's *Sick Societies*, a fine book and a devastating answer to PC's beloved cultural relativism, or George Ayittey's *Africa Betrayed*, a well-researched account equally devastating for Afrocentrists, or Herman Belz's *Equality Transformed*, which Nathan Glazer called "by far the most thorough account of the tortured history of affirmative action in employment that has ever been written," or Rita Kramer's excellent *Ed School Follies*. How could anyone think that such books are less deserving of attention than the dotty work of Kincaid and Mary Daly, or that these two deserved a full page while major books by D'Souza and Sowell got a bare half page each?

Front page feature articles by campus radicals (for example, Annette Kolodny, Todd Gitlin) have become commonplace, but writers like Ronald Radosh or Roger Kimball have all but vanished from the Book Review, where the spectrum of opinion now runs (with rare exceptions) only from moderate left to loony left.

Sinkler did her best to avoid Rush Limbaugh's *The Way Things Ought to Be*, but that became too embarrassing when the book climbed to the top of the *Times* own best seller list, and she was forced to change course. Not big enough to admit her error, Sinkler spitefully gave the belated review to, of all things, a TV Critic, the Times' Walter Goodman, who, as he candidly admits, was openly partisan, having already been in a war of words with Limbaugh. Goodman's review is on the high intellectual plane that Sinkler doubtless expected: Limbaugh, he says, alternates between "slobberings of sincerity and slaverings of invective." Sad to think that such small-mindedness is at work in a (formerly) great national institution.

Is it possible that this pattern of choices is just an unconscious thing, without malicious intent? Certainly not, for the issue comes up all the time in book reviewing. Two friends who have reviewed for the *Times* have told me of incidents in which editorial staff piously told them that (in the one case) protective reviews by people who had any kind of vested interest in a book must be avoided, and (in the other) that it would not do to have a predictably adversarial reviewer. But on both occasions, a politically incorrect review was what this display of piety seemed to be trying to avoid: insult was added to injury as the *Book Review* used noble principles that it routinely violates as an excuse for enforcing its narrow little ideology.

Close to a thousand books a year are reviewed in the *Book Review*, and inevitably the occasional exception can be seen: Frank Kermode's omnibus review of a number of books dealing with the PC controversy comes to mind, as does a feature essay by Camille Paglia—though the second book by this now surely major figure received only a brief note, not a review proper. The general pattern, however, is clear, and it is overwhelming.

No other publication has the *Book Review*'s power to make or break a book. As a source of news and opinion on new books it has no rival. It is a national scandal that a publication with this unique position rigidly enforces a politically correct orthodoxy, protecting or destroying books accordingly, and acting as a mouthpiece for even the craziest and most irresponsible aspects of PC radicalism.

We should all look to see what comes next. Since Brock's book went to a feminist, will the upcoming Jane Mayer/Jill Abramson defense of Anita Hill go to Tom Sowell or Walter Williams? If Steinem's book went to a fellow feminist editor, will Christina Sommers' forthcoming critique of radical feminism go to Lynne Cheney? Not likely. The *Times* management has decided to donate the *Book Review* to the cause of political reeducation.

November, 1993

Shooting The Messenger:

THE REVENGE OF THE AIDS ESTABLISHMENT

by Michael Fumento

In February, the *New York Times* reported on the findings of a report of the National Research Council, part of the National Academy of Sciences: "The AIDS epidemic will have little impact on the lives of most Americans or the way society functions, the National Research Council says. In a study made public today, the Council said AIDS was concentrated among homosexuals, drug users, the poor and the undereducated..."

The *Times* treated this information as if it were somehow new, but if you had read *Commentary* magazine back in November of 1987, you already knew it. That's when my article, "AIDS: Are Heterosexuals at Risk?" appeared. In it, I explained that despite what virtually everyone was saying at the time—from the head of Health and Human Services to the Surgeon General to all the AIDS activists to virtually every newspaper, magazine, and television station in the country—there had been no heterosexual breakout of the disease.

AIDS, I explained, was a disease essentially of homosexual men and of intravenous drug abusers and their partners. To the extent heterosexuals where getting the disease they almost always black or Hispanic, and almost always victimized by bad needles. Since AIDS was not a generalized disease, I argued, it was wrong to spread the hysteria of heterosexual breakout and waste resources trying to prevent infections that would never occur.

It wasn't necessary to wait for the National Resource Council report to know that it has proven the case. According to the most recent federal Centers for Disease Control and Prevention (CDC) data, AIDS cases overall increased only 3.5 percent in 1992 from the year before, while cases increased only five percent from 1990 to 1991. Cases attributed to heterosexuals increased 17 percent, compared to 21 percent from 1990-1991. The increase in female cases declined from 17 to nine percent. Cases diagnosed among teenagers were exactly the same as the year before, while those among persons aged 20-24 actually declined slightly.

Just before releasing the 1992 figures the CDC announced that for the second time it was revising downward its estimate of future AIDS cases. You probably didn't hear about that, either. Major newspapers like the Los Angeles *Times,* sensitive to homosexual activists invested in AIDS hysteria, completely ignored the downward revision. But it happened all the same.

Generalized infection data, such as that of military recruits and blood donors, continue to show low infection rates. Only some specific studies, such as those done at sexually transmitted disease clinics in inner-cities, have shown infection increases. That, too, is as I predicted.

To get some perspective on this heterosexual breakout predicted with the regularity of a metronome over the past several years, consider these facts. More white women were killed in automobile accidents by January 15 of last year, and more white women died of breast cancer by January 7, than were diagnosed with AIDS on the basis of presumed heterosexual contact during the entire course of the year. One fact which is not in dispute is that it is more difficult for a man to get infected by a woman than vice versa, so it will be no surprise that the risk for heterosexual men is lower yet.

In saying that I first disputed the likelihood of a heterosexual AIDS epidemic, I'm not simply tooting my own horn as some sort of soothsayer or genius. Quite the opposite. All I did in 1987 was to look at the data, talk to the experts, and reported my findings fairly and objectively. No, the real story isn't that I did what I did, but the degree to which I and my statistics were forced to go it alone these past six years, and the six years of bad AIDS policy that resulted because of the staying power of the myth of heterosexual AIDS.

After the *Commentary* piece appeared I expanded the thesis into a book. One paragraph in a letter I recently received sums up what happened to it:

> *Reality hit home when I tried to purchase The Myth of Heterosexual AIDS last November. Not only was I unable to locate a single book store in Houston carrying the book, but your publisher removed Myth from print. I then began researching the subject matter and soon realized that there is widespread collusion and conspiracy to discredit you and your book. The news media is playing a major part in what I now feel is deliberate and intended deceit, distortion, and misrepresentation on the entire subject of AIDS. Sound like right-wing paranoia? If so, it would be very curious that the charges were documented in the liberal Washington Monthly in its March issue.*

My trouble began long before there was a book, when publisher after publisher rejected the manuscript, not because there was a basic disagreement with the facts, but because, as one editor put it, "I'm not convinced that [the] argument or the cause of curing AIDS for those who have it or are prey to it is best served by publishing this in book form." Or, as another stated, "I'm afraid I feel the book community is terribly overloaded on this subject, and also on Michael Fumento's point of view on this subject." At the time, there were over two hundred AIDS books in print, not one of which had anything approaching "Michael Fumento's point of view."

After Joe Queenan published an article in *Forbes* on the troubles I was having, the homosexual activist group ACT-UP picketed the magazine, demanding that publisher Malcolm Forbes "retract" the article. Forbes did so, calling my views "asinine."

Members of the media gleefully reported this and absolutely nobody came to Queenan's defense. Shortly thereafter, Queenan quit. Forbes then died and a book came out soon thereafter by *Wall Street Journal* reporter Christopher Winans suggesting that Forbes caved in because he was a closeted homosexual who wished to remain that way.

ACT-UP doesn't fool around. Even as my book was in galleys, activists began writing to stores and demanding that they not carry it. To a great extent, they succeeded in their smear campaign. Waldenbooks, the largest chain in the country, would not carry *The Myth of Heterosexual AIDS* until I described this policy during an appearance on C-Span's "Bookends." Leslie Kaufman, in last month's *Washington Monthly* article, wrote that, "Mike Ferrari, Walden's buyer, is reputed to have told representatives selling the book that he didn't want it for political reasons."

Shortly after my book was finally published, a group of 30 physicians in the states of Washington and Oregon realized they couldn't find a single store in either state that carried the book. They reported this to a Seattle, Washington, TV station, KING, which in a televised report noted that it contacted 80 different stores, also without finding the book. Indeed, only one store had ever carried the book; it sold out quickly and the store didn't reorder until after KING contacted them. One university book store in Seattle claimed to have over 350,000 titles, including every single AIDS title in print. Except one.

At the same time that my book was being suppressed, I was fired from my job as an editorial writer at the *Rocky Mountain News*. The stated reason was that I had "made too many phone calls." The man responsible for this indefensible charge, managing editor Michael Finney, had just weeks earlier responded to pressure from a feminist group by announcing an affirmative action plan, scheduling sensitivity sessions for white males, and publicly expressing his sorrow at being a white male. It wasn't too difficult to figure out what led to my firing.

Many reviewers were also inclined to smear the book. While the book received excellent reviews in medical journals such as the *Journal of the American Medical Association* and the *New England Journal of Medicine,* I was stunned to find that the prestigious *Science* had assigned it to a linguistics professor, Paula Treichler, whose only previous writing on AIDS had been for the Marxist magazine *October,* in which she had railed against the assertion that the anus is more susceptible to penetration by the AIDS virus than the vagina, not on any scientific grounds but because it makes AIDS appear to be a "gay disease" which "protects not only the sexual practices of heterosexuality but also its ideological superiority." I was equally stunned to find that *Nature* had assigned the book to a homosexual AIDS activist, one who blatantly lied about its contents.

The bottom line was that a book which received tremendous national and international publicity, was reviewed in virtually every major publication, and was the subject of such shows as "Donahue," "Crossfire," "Today," and "CBS This Morning," sold less than 12,000 copies. And that's where the figure has stopped, because Basic Books, which usually stocks books for years, abruptly yanked it from print. Asked why the book didn't sell well, Clinton Morris, the Basic representative who sold to Waldenbooks in New York, says, "Look, it was going against everything we know about AIDS, against anything anybody who was reputable was telling us. Why buy a book like that?" Forget the issue of self interest for a moment. This was said of a book that the *Journal of the American Medical Association* had praised as "thoroughly researched, poignantly written, and a must read for anyone in learning the dynamics of the HIV epidemic or health care planning." This of a book that carried an endorsement by the former chief epidemiologist for the federal Centers for Disease Control.

The problem with *The Myth of Heterosexual AIDS* was not that it went against the grain medically or scientifically. Quite the opposite, by stressing the medical and the scientific, it made the political agenda blatantly obvious. This is the bottom line of that agenda: many AIDS activists, including gay radicals, have shown little more than a rhetorical interest in preventing the spread of AIDS. Consider what happened after *Newsday* dared allow me to review two AIDS books. Michelangelo Signorile at the now defunct *Outweek* magazine blasted the paper and its book review editor with language that would make a child pornographer blush.

Signorile declared what he thought of me ("baboon, racist, homophobic") and demanded in all upper-case letters: "WHY THE FUCK WOULD NEWSDAY HAVE SUCH A HATE-FILLED, UNTALENTED, LYING LOSER REVIEW IMPORTANT BOOKS?" Interestingly, onthe page opposite this raving were personal ads for male prostitutes.

Thus a magazine berating me for allegedly endangering the public concerning AIDS is actually making a profit off activity that clearly does spread the virus.

It has been said that homosexuals just want a quick cure to AIDS so they can go right back to the bathhouses. The statement can by no means be applied to all homosexuals, but it certainly applies to the homosexual AIDS activists. Their AIDS agenda is two-fold: to destigmatize homosexual practices, and to pump up research funds for AIDS by saying that it is a health problem for everyone which will become apocalyptic. But there is actually little room on their agenda for seeking to control new infections. Indeed, AIDS activists have jumped with joy upon hearing that various celebrities from Rock Hudson to Magic Johnson to Arthur Ashe to Randy Shilts were diagnosed with HIV or AIDS. This means more notoriety; more sympathy; more fear.

But it isn't just groups like ACT-UP and Queer Nation that have fought off attempts to actually curtail the spread of the disease. AIDS has never been fought as a disease in this country because various groups hijacked it and directed it to fly to goals they had established long before the disease arrived on the scene.

Those groups are essentially the same ones I identified in 1987, groups which carried their various agendas into the epidemic and found the disease a convenient vehicle to further them. Homosexual activists said that AIDS demanded that the nation repeal sodomy laws and teach the validity of homosexual lifestyles. Christian right groups said that AIDS demanded a sexual counterrevolution and a restoration of traditional moral values. Population control groups said that AIDS demanded the widespread distribution of condoms. The media said that AIDS demanded lurid and terrifying stories of the exploding plague that would just happen to increase sales and ratings.

One group that existed early on but which I failed to notice until they targeted me was national health insurance lobby, which said that AIDS threatened to wipe out the entire U.S. health care system and demanded that a socialized system be put in place. Donna Minkowitz, in her review of my book in *The Village Voice* (where she called it "bilge" built on "a foundation of lies") nonetheless in the opening statement of her review revealed that the real problem with *Myth*—that it busted her pet agenda of socialized medicine: "Health care is a right, not a privilege. Now that the AIDS, abortion rights, and labor movements have a good shot at making this slogan a reality, in comes . . . Michael Fumento to quell the rebellion . . ." Actually, *Myth* made no references whatsoever to national health care. But by establishing that the epidemic would never become breakout to destroy the health care system, it destroyed the argument that relied on such an apocalyptic scenario.

Finally, a new interest group in the AIDS lobby sprang up—the bureaucrats. These were the staffers at the Department of Health and

Human Services, the educators at schools and city health clinics, the pontificating professors who saw AIDS as a better way of advancement than writing obligatory books that nobody would ever want to read. My last article on AIDS in the *New Republic* prompted about 10 angry letters. The very titles of those signatories made it clear that at least eight, and possibly all ten, made their living off AIDS.

There have always been truly dedicated warriors in the AIDS struggle. I met some of them when I worked at the U.S. Commission on Civil Rights. They are local health officials and epidemiologists, outreach workers who tried to get at- risk and infected individuals to avoid sex or at least to practice safe sex, and to break their drug habits, and misguidedly or not, worked to distribute clean needles in the hope that this would at least dampen the growth of infection among addicts. But with few exceptions, these were not the "AIDS advocates" you see on the talk shows, the ones you hear about getting the awards and staging celebrity benefits, the ones quoted in *People* magazine and *USA Today*. These are the opportunists. Far from being their enemy, AIDS is their shtick.

This conflict of interest helps explain why the AIDS establishment fought so desperately to suppress a book that to this day remains the most detailed, accurate, and, yes, the most honest account of how and why people get AIDS and what they can do to avoid it. Yet the suppression of *Myth* and its author is only a microcosm of the war which the AIDS establishment has fought against other comparable efforts to reduce the number of new infections.

Consider contact tracing, urged by many public health officials, in which persons found to be infected with HIV are urged to identify their sexual partners so those partners can be notified, told the risks they face, and asked if they wish to be tested. Since it is relatively difficult to spread, AIDS is an ideal disease for such a program. Pilot studies in San Francisco, Colorado, and elsewhere have shown that contact tracing is highly cost-effective in identifying persons at high risk of getting HIV or who actually have it, and that it is effective in getting infected persons to curtail their unsafe sexual activities. Yet AIDS activists have fought against such tracing as a "violation of civil rights." (Is there not some sort of right, civil or otherwise, not to be infected?)

Homosexual activists undermined the highly successful Colorado program by forcing the state to open up anonymous testing centers. (This even though participation is by definition voluntary and no one can be forced to give the names of sexual partners.) Contact tracing is suspect to the AIDS lobby because it undercuts the entire "everyone-is-at-risk" campaign. After all, the only diseases which put truly everyone at risk are those spread by air and touch such as the flu and there is no point in contact tracing with those diseases.

AIDS activists have also hurt the campaign to curtail AIDS by drawing off money from sexually transmitted disease (STD) control programs. The evidence is overwhelming that some STDs, including syphilis and chancroid, tremendously facilitate the spread of HIV by causing small openings in the male or female genitals and thereby allowing the entry of a virus which cannot penetrate intact skin. The infection level for these two particular diseases is quite low among white, middle-class heterosexuals but much higher among inner-city blacks and Hispanics. Prior to 1987, levels of these disease were dropping in the inner-cities. But then they began to skyrocket. The cause? In my book I quoted Dr. King Holmes, a Seattle health official and chairman of an advisory board to the CDC: "When sexually transmitted disease clinics have fixed budgets, and 20 to 30 percent of those budgets suddenly has to go for AIDS control, something has to suffer. Funds for controlling those diseases have been deflected into AIDS efforts, and the other diseases have been getting worse." And those who are tempted to worry about racism ought to think of it this way: all that money used to convince the kids at all white Pleasant Valley High that they were at terrible risk of contracting AIDS was devastating the programs to control STDs that were keeping the kids at all-black Booker T. Washington Middle School alive.

Now consider the shibboleth which states, in so many words, "Until there's a cure, education is our best weapon against AIDS." The problem isn't the expression, which is basically true. The problem is that the ones using it have fought so desperately against such proper education. As I wrote in 1987, "Every dollar spent, every commercial made, every health warning released, that does not specify promiscuous anal intercourse and needle-sharing as the overwhelming risk factors in the transmission of AIDS is a lie, a waste of funds and energy, and a cruel diversion." That is as true today as it was five years ago. Yet to this day the reality of the dangers of anal sex are masked in every way: by pretending that AIDS is an "equal opportunity disease," by simply saying non-specifically that "sex" spreads AIDS, or by pretending to be specific while actually fogging the issue. I have in mind statements like this one: "Sex —vaginal, anal, and oral— can spread the AIDS virus." What is the purpose of putting vaginal before anal? It's not even alphabetical. Yet that's the order adopted in Surgeon General Koop's famous 1987 report mailed to households throughout the nation and that's the order which the media and the self-styled AIDS educators use today. The purpose of the curious word order is clear—not to offend homosexual activists who want to assault the "ideological superiority" of heterosexual intercourse.

Just as specific sex acts are not targeted for fear of offending radical gays, so rarely are high-risk groups given straight talk. Rather, most AIDS messages are designed to convince us that "anybody can get it." If breast cancer messages stated that "anybody can get it," a statement which strictly interpreted is true since men can get the disease, health officials would be outraged. Why, they would ask, when it is so difficult to get women to pay attention and have themselves checked out for cancer, are we targeting men as well? Yet, that is exactly the approach our country continues to take with AIDS. *A non-drug abusing heterosexual man in this country has a much better chance of getting breast cancer than getting AIDS*. But he is constantly told he is at risk of AIDS, told that if a star basketball player could get AIDS from a woman — or at least say he did— we're all at risk. Indeed, to the extent AIDS warnings have been directed at specific groups, those groups are often those least at risk. Last year, then-Health and Human Resources Secretary Louis Sullivan announced a new series of advertisements aimed at persons who believed themselves to be at low risk of getting AIDS, specifically heterosexuals and residents of rural areas. That heterosexuals and rural residents happen to be correct in that belief was considered utterly unimportant. Nobody in the media asked Sullivan about it and he certainly wasn't going to broach the issue himself.

Much AIDS education funding also is diverted into educational courses and other programs that have little other purpose than seeking to legitimize homosexuality. Such was the case with former New York School Commissioner Joseph Hernandez's Rainbow Coalition curriculum, which under the cover of teaching teens the deadly facts of life and love in the age of AIDS encouraged the reading of such books as *Heather Has Two Mommies* and *Daddy's New Roommate*. Such has also been the case with something called the Art Against AIDS Project, which put up posters on public transportation platforms in Chicago and other cities showing a man kissing a man, a woman kissing a woman and a man kissing a woman, with the vague message: "Kissing Doesn't Kill; Greed and Indifference Do." Chicago *Tribune* columnist Mike Royko asked what these posters had to do with preventing the spread of AIDS, saying they appeared to be little more than an endorsement of homosexual relationships. Annie Philbin, a member of Art Against AIDS, quickly fired back: "This guy clearly doesn't know the first thing beyond being a white privileged male heterosexual in this country," adding, "He is exactly, exactly the problem why AIDS is devastating this country. He's just so uninformed it's pathetic."

So you see, it's not anal sex and needle-sharing that spread AIDS, it's newspaper columnists.

But I must confess that I was not entirely unamused. For you see, Mike Royko was one of those columnists I pleaded with to write about the smear campaign against my book and by so doing hopefully save some lives. I never heard from him.

April, 1993

Ozzie and Harriet in Hell

by Jay Overocker

Back in 1989, *Fortune* writer Daniel Seligman got so fed up with reading yet another *Washington Post* story about the demise of the traditional "Ozzie and Harriet" nuclear family he did a computer search on the phrase "Ozzie and Harriet" and turned up some 80 stories just in the previous six month period. What was the context in which these two names were typically invoked? "A politician was on stage," Seligman found, "reciting the news that the traditional nuclear family — the kind symbolized by the Nelsons during their marathon stint on black-and-white TV — was dead or dying. Usual moral of the recitation: we need a government program to help the new nontraditional family — the kind where mom is a cop, the kids are on dope, and dad is nonexistent or worse."

In the three years since Seligman did his little survey, announcements of the death of the nuclear family have gotten much more intense, especially since Dan Quayle spoke out on its behalf, leading countless reporters, essayists and commentators to attack him for his regressive patriarchy.

• "The white middle class family is a fairy tale," sniffed Ellen Snortland in the *Los Angeles Times.*

• "The Reagan/Bush administrations were trying to recreate the June Cleaver nuclear family," charged Tammy Bruce, president of the Los Angeles Chapter of NOW. "The nuclear family doesn't exist anymore. The majority of families are headed by women. The economy is based on something that doesn't exist.

• "The number of kids who will grow up [in a traditional family] is miniscule," Robert Turner wrote in the *Boston Globe.*

• "Only 26% of U.S. households with children under 18 are headed by a married couple," said the *New York Daily News* in the most misleading of all the statistics slung at Quayle and at America, "[and this is] down from 31% in 1980."

What these people (and all the intellectuals whose scholarship, argumentation and revisionism stands behind them) are telling us is that the nuclear family is dead and we had best get on to the next phase of civilization by focusing on *families* rather than *the family.* This would be tragic if true, a development worthy of deep mourning rather than mere nostalgia. But the fact is that the nuclear family's death has been greatly exaggerated, usually by those who have a stake in its demise.

According to 1990 Bureau of the Census figures, 72.5% of children in the country under the age of 18 live in a home headed by a married couple. Another 21.6% live with their mothers only. The remaining 6% live with their fathers, grandparents or other guardians.

In Los Angeles County, for instance, allegedly a bellwether of breakdown, the figures are even more dramatic, with the percentage of children living with two parents ranging from 89% in white middle class areas, to 47% in impoverished and chaotic Compton. For Los Angeles County as a whole, the figure is 64%.

So why do so many people think the nuclear family has disappeared? One reason, suggests William Mattox, Director of Policy Analysis for the Family Research Council, is that many middle class, well educated feminists erroneously assume that "every one lives the same way they do." That is to say, in fast-track urban enclaves with disproportionately high rates of alienation, anomie, divorce and single parenthood.

Another, larger reason is most reporters' lack of patience with (and insight into) statistics. The *Daily News* reporter cited above, for example, thought that only 26% of children under 18 lived with their parents. What the Census actually shows, says Census Bureau information specialist Larry Hugg, is that 27% of all households consist of two parents and their children.

Well, you might say — that's still a tragic number. But attempt actually to understand the statistic. The percentage of households made up of nuclear families has certainly declined, but the reason isn't because most kids nowadays are being raised by single moms or strangers. The reason is that there are so many more households made up of widows, college students, childless married couples, empty nest couples, and gay households. If you confine your inquiry to what Mattox calls "the universe of children" (which is what you must do if your goal is to discover who is raising the children), then you discover, he says, that "70% to 75% of all kids are being raised in a nuclear family."

Then where, you might well wonder, do people like Connecticut Senator Christopher Dodd get off saying that only "one in ten American families" fit the fifties mold of dad at work and mom at home with the kids? Or how can Colorado Congressperson Pat Schroeder preach from her bully pulpit as chairman of the House Select Committee on Children, Youth and Families that "the traditional Ozzie and Harriet" family represents a mere 7.1% of all American families?

The short answer is that Schroeder uses statistics the same way the Queen of Hearts uses words — "They mean whatever I want them to mean." In order to make the percentage of traditional families (a breadwinner father, and a mother at home with children) look vanishingly small, Schroeder includes in her calculations both families with children and those without any at all. (This alone makes the problem of the nuclear family look 50% worse than it would otherwise). Further, she defines "traditional" to mean only those families where the mother does no work whatsoever outside the home. (Under the government classification, says William Mattox, even an hour's work a week outside the home is enough to cause a woman to be considered a working mother.)

But the most deceitful aspect of Schroeder's semantics is to use the phrase "traditional Ozzie and Harriet family" not according to general usage (a mother and father and some kids) but quite literally as a family *exactly like the Nelson's* with a mother and father and precisely two children (David and Ricky). Under Schroeder's definition, a family with one child isn't a "traditional Ozzie and Harriet family" and neither is a family with three or more children.

Demeaning nuclear families and the fathers who play a pivotal role in them has a history that stretches back at least to the 1960s, when feminists first started constructing the cliches which held that marriage is a "comfortable concentration camp." This was Betty Friedan's groundbreaking phrase which Hillary Clinton plagiarized in a now famous 1974 article in the *Harvard Educational Review* when she described marriage as "a dependence relationship" not unlike "slavery and the Indian reservation system."

The anti-male part of this attack was a contempt that stretched even to children of women's own wombs. Thus, in a famous 1974 article in *Ms*., a feminist related the disgust she felt when her obstetrician held up her newborn and it turned out to be a member of the oppressor class: "All I could see was cock!" The family was patriarchal and therefore a bastion of a conservative social structure.

The rantings of the radical feminist Left had an impact. As University of Southern California sociologist Carlfred Broderick points out, a spate of books soon began to appear confidently predicting the death of the nuclear family or at least asserting that it would have give way to more "flexible institutions."

Not surprisingly, says Broderick, the people hurt most by the derogation of fatherhood and the attack on the much maligned "traditional" family were the people least able to defend themselves — the children. "The hippies had this notion of the free human child, who didn't belong to his parents but was everyone's child, who had no sexual hangups and didn't have to learn the alphabet or any hard thing and why should they be encumbered with the crust of the ages. It turned out that the kids couldn't read or write or add or hold jobs. It turned out that the kids who had multiple parents didn't have any parents. They tended to be abandoned and sexually abused and drug abused. They turned out to be the saddest children of all because their parents didn't take adult responsibility for them."

Despite all the predictions about the need for more "flexible" family structures in the 60s and 70s, the family didn't disappear, not even when, in the 80s, the gay and lesbian movement lent its voice to the attack. ("You can't erase a million years of human evolution in a ten year period," says Broderick). And by the mid-eighties a widespread if fragile consensus was attempting to form around the notion that all things being equal a two-parent home was better for children than one.

But then Dan Quayle gave a speech blaming the L.A. riots on the disintegrating family structure in the inner city. Suddenly there were hundreds of intellectuals and critics — who had previously been forced to hold their tongues because of the evidence showing the salutary nature of the traditional family — who emerged from the closet to bash the nuclear family because it had once again been identified as a fortress of conservatism.

The most egregious example of such ideological attacks was an astonishing front page article in the *Washington Post,* which argued among other things that fathers were much less important than had previously been believed, new research having indicated that the education of the mother was now the most important factor in a child's prospects, and, at least for black girls, having both parents was worse than being raised by a single mom.

In the post-Quayle furor the view that the family was the fountain-head of racism and sexism once again was proposed. Family values was a code phrase for hate. "Family values and the cult of the nuclear family," wrote Katha Pollitt in a particularly obnoxious piece in *The Nation,* "is at bottom just another way to bash women, especially poor women."

As for the father, under the new dispensation, he is at best irrelevant and at worst dangerous. "...Nothing is more unsuitable to the needs of the young than 'suitable role models,'" New York writer Leonard Kriegal asserted in the *Los Angeles Times.* " The idea that role modes can make substantial contributions to the prospects of the young...is nonsense."

It's no mystery why so many poor women rely on welfare checks, argued feminist social critic Barbara Ehrenreich: they're a lot less trouble than relying on a man. "I disagree that a father's influence is positive," snapped Tammy Bruce, President of the Los Angeles chapter of NOW. "I think it is absurd to say that a boy needs a father." Abuse, she sputtered in an interview in the aftermath of the Quayle speech, "skyrockets" when a father is present in the home. The only way to keep men from passing their violent "male mind set" to their sons was to get the man out of the family entirely and give the mother a chance to raise a generation of feminist boys "who love women."

Bruce later modified her remarks somewhat, but even so, just for a second we had an uncommonly clear insight into the kind of radical feminist soul that has contempt for men, dismisses fathers, and sees the state as a husband of first resort providing the money, the childcare and whatever other social services are necessary for a woman to raise children without the benefit of either a husband or a job.

Despite these savage attacks on the usefulness of fathers, in the sociological literature evidence of the need for fathers is incontestable, says Randall Blankenhorn, President of the Institute for American Values. Boys with fathers are more mature, more outgoing, more independent, warmer, more self-confident and have better self-esteem. Girls who grow up without fathers are simultaneously more suspicious of men and more dependent on them. The most reliable indicator of whether a girl gets pregnant or a boy joined a gang isn't income or race — it's whether of not the child has a father at home.

"The data is overwhelming," says author Warren Farrell, that both sexes are more likely to become drug addicts, do worse in school on every single subject from math to literature, more likely to become delinquent, join gangs, go to prison, commit suicide and commit homocide. Children of unmarried mothers are twice as likely to end up in juvenile hall, three times as likely to be expelled from school and six times as likely to live in poverty.

As for the radical feminist notion that the easy way to make boys love women is to remove them from their father's influence, Farrell says, "We have been raising boys without fathers for 20 years in the black community, and the result is not gentle black men. The result is a society in which black men are likely to be in prison as college."

In the inner city, teen-age mothers do not get married; and almost half of the young men are arrested before they reach 18. "The black community is being destroyed by this," says UC Long Beach psychologist Kevin MacDonald. "Anyone who says single parent families are good for black people is nuts."

Even so, every time someone tries to address the issue of the family, the media elite responds not so much with an analysis of the problem as an attack on the messenger. When Dan Quayle came to Los Angeles late last May to tour a public school, a *Los Angeles Times* editorial characterized his remarks as "simplistic put downs of the evils of single motherhood." And the *Times* gleefully described a 14-year-old girl's fatuous challenge to the vice-president: "What would you prefer? A single mom, or a dad who gets drunk and beats your mom?" As if there were no other alternative.

For over 20 years now certain radical feminists have been making the case that men are wife-beaters, rapists, child abusers, murderers and plunderers of the planet — all for the purpose of delegitimizing marriage, destabilizing family, and marginalizing men. So when someone comes along and says, "Hey, wait a minute, children need fathers," it generates "real anger," says *Playboy's* men's columnist Asa Baber.

Baber got a first hand lesson in just how deep that anger really was when he took part in a debate last Mother's Day with feminist author Susan (*Backlash*) Faludi at the 92nd Street Y in New York City. During his opening remarks to an audience of 1,000 feminists, Baber noted that on Mother's Day the phone circuits are usually jammed with people calling home. But on Father's day, finding a free line is no problem. He noted, "We have to ask why there is so much less interest in fathers."

"It brought down the house," Barber says of his comment. "At first, I didn't get it. I thought my fly was open. I said, 'If you think this is funny, you are going to think this is a laugh riot: I think the fact that our fathers are so much out of the loop is a major tragedy in our culture.'"

At this point, said Barber, the audience stopped laughing and started hissing. Why, I asked him, because they thought men were useless, irrelevant and potentially dangerous?

"You got it," Baber said.

November, 1992

Separating The Men From The Womyn

by Sarah Horowitz

For years lesbians have been fighting for their own venues where they can bond with their sisters in peace. At the Michigan Women's Music Festival, for instance, the largest gathering in the country, women arrive every year to commune with nature, be with other women, and listen to singers like Holly Near. There's just one catch. You must be a "womyn-born-womyn." In other words, no transsexuals.

In 1991 transsexual Nancy Burkholder was asked to leave the festival because some festival-goers were uncomfortable with her presence. In response, the transsexuals called for a girlcott of the festival in 1992. Janis Walworth, who is not a transsexual, but supports their cause, used a different tactic. She put up a literature table on transsexual issues. She polled festival-goers on how they felt about allowing transsexuals and found that the majority were in favor. This summer Walworth brought Nancy Burkholder and three other post-operative transsexuals to the festival. According to the *Bay Times*, the transsexual women were approached by security coordinators who asked them to leave because there had been threats and they could not guarantee their safety, They were told they were not respecting the "womyn-born-womyn" policy, to which they responded that they identified as "womyn-born-womyn" even if they were women made of men.

Lisa Vogel, co-producer of the Michigan festival, says that the *Bay Times* has distorted what actually happened. "They were not asked to leave because of threats," she insists. "They were asked to respect our policy because there had been a large number of complaints. It was all a very calm interaction. They meant to make a scene, they got exactly what they planned."

Anne Ogborn of San Francisco's Transgender Nation says she always takes a deep breath before she goes into a women's only space and wouldn't think of going into a "separatist space." (Separatist lesbians insist on separating themselves completely from men.) "I've been thrown out of women's spaces, women's bars, and a massage class" Ogborn says. She was eventually allowed to take the massage class and the massage center now holds sensitivity sessions on transgender issues.

Ogborn's story is now something of a legend in the Bay Area transsexual community. She is very open about being transsexual and the issue will sometimes come up in women's groups, in the heat of another controversy. "A woman will have an issue with me and then she'll say, 'I don't feel safe with a man in the room.'" Ogborn says the rage directed towards her has an irrationality she has encountered elsewhere only in encounters with fundamentalists. She was even asked to leave a gay/lesbian support group on the grounds that she was neither a lesbian or a gay man. This befuddled the bisexual man in the group who was not asked to leave.

The mainstream community does not treat transsexuals well either. The American Psychiatric Association, which has capitulated on almost every other "deviant behavior," still labels transsexuality as an illness. A written note from a mental health professional is required in order to get the operation. (Anne Ogborn says the criteria for getting the note are sometimes based on appropriate "feminity" and sexual preference for men.) San Francisco's jails and homeless shelters put transsexuals in the men's sections. Ogborn asked me, woman-to-woman. "If you had a choice between sleeping in the men's shelter or the park, where would you stay?"

Tension between some lesbian separatists and transsexuals has been brewing for years. Lesbian writer Marilyn Murphy says, "Woman is a cultural construct more than a physiology...You can't cut it out with a knife."

One separatist stated adamantly, "Males are the oppressors of females and all oppressed groups have the right to be with each other away from their oppresors... Just because some of those boys who harassed and attacked us when we were young lesbians are now saying that they are lesbians doesn't change who they are." Another writer was more succinct in her response to a letter from a transsexual. "The problem is not simply that he had a prick—it's that he is a prick."

Transsexuals and their supporters have not been asleep during the victimization revolution. Confronted with the antagonism of the lesbian community, they have immediately charged "Transphobia!" They point out the hypocrisy and injustice of a marginalized group like lesbians excluding another marginalized group. "We demand that the straight world move beyond its fears and ignorance, can we demand anything less for ourselves?" one transsexual writes.

Some members of the transsexual community have tried to practice gender statesmanship by pointing out that the mutual enemies they share with lesbians (enemies such as Jesse Helms) were probably rubbing their hands with glee at the in-fighting. One writer made the novel suggestion that a rating board be formed, similar to rabbinic boards, which would designate "dyke safe" and "sep safe" venues. Anne Ogborn points out that taken to its logical extreme the enforcement of such a system would victimize all androgynous women and make them victims of lookism.

The great debate has inspired academics as well. Bookstores that refuse to carry racist or sexist rantings carry books by separatist writer Mary Daly (one of *Heterodoxy*'s 10 Wackiest Feminists) who has labelled transsexuals "Frankensteinian." In her book *Pure Lust,* Daly says transsexualism is a symptom of our Christian training which, through rituals like transubstantiation, teaches us to ignore our own senses.

Janice Raymond wrote a tract called *The Transsexual Empire,* in which she argues that transsexualism is a plot by men to co-opt women's space. Raymond says that "problem" is best solved by "morally mandating it out of existence." She also testified before the Health Care Finance Administration against federal funding for sex change surgery.

Transsexual Tala Brandeis left a bisexual women's rap group a number of years ago because one of the women in the group was uncomfortable with the presence of a transsexual. "I chose to leave that group but I had a strong support network. What if I hadn't had that?" Brandeis believes there needs to be space free from transsexuals but that there must also be support for transsexuals who need it. It is clear to her who the enemy is: "Anyone who defines themself as a woman and lives in the world as a woman is outside the male world. I laugh when I hear the word 'genderphobia.' It's all misogyny."

Cherche l'homme!

The Academic Zoo

Big Girls Don't Cry

by Barbara Rhoades Ellis

To celebrate her daughter's second birthday, columnist Anna Quindlen threw a temper t antrum on the pages of The New York *Times*: "My daughter is ready to leap into the world, as though life were chicken soup and she a delighted noodle. The work of Prof. Carol Gilligan of Harvard [Graduate School of Education] suggests that sometime after the age of 11 this will change, that this lively little girl will pull back, shrink, that her constant refrain will become 'I don't know.' Professor Gilligan says the culture sends the message: 'Keep silent and notice the absence of women and say nothing.'"

Always on the cutting edge of grievance, Quindlen wrote this three years ago. Today the dolorous subject of what happens to girls when they become women in Western Culture is getting the full feminist treatment, and the work of Carol Gilligan is now a fast-selling book, *Meeting at the Crossroads: Women's Psychology and Girls' Development*, coauthored by Lyn Mikel Brown.

Even Kathleen Parker, a funny and usually sensible lifestyle columnist, was impressed by Gilligan's *apercu* when she read about it in *People* magazine. "Girls have it tougher," Parker wrote. "So say researchers who already knew this, inasmuch as they are women, but apparently felt they had to prove it statistically so that others—and we know who they are—would believe it." Actually, had Parker even skimmed the book itself, she would have been hard put to find any statistics, let alone statistical proof of anything. That's one of the problems: in the current inflamed atmosphere of feminism, opinion—especially about grievances—is accorded the status of sober fact.

The splash that *Meeting at the Crossroads* is making—well beyond the inbred circles of academic feminism—can be partly credited to the success of Gilligan's earlier (1982) book *In a Different Voice*, which certified her as a feminist icon. There Gilligan challenged a current theory that men make moral decisions at a higher, more abstract plane than women. Leaving intact the dubious notion that the sexes differ morally, she claimed instead that the difference had been wrongly assessed by male standards which devalued feminine morality, and that we should instead say that men adhere to an "ethic of rights," women to an "ethic of caring."

Fire came from all directions. Traditional feminists were alarmed at the boost her theory gave to the stereotypes about women that they had been battling for decades. Some thought her interview sample of 25 Harvard-Radcliffe undergraduates to be too narrow to support such sweeping conclusions. Others said she massaged the data and doubted that what her subjects said about hypothetical situations had much to do with how they would behave in real life.

But the hint that women were not just equal but morally superior to men proved irresistible to most feminists, and so, despite its flaws and controversy, *In a Different Voice* launched Gilligan's career like a rocket. Just as college deans have to scramble to meet affirmative action hiring goals, the keepers of the sparse feminist canon were only too happy to embrace this new work, which is now in its 32nd printing. In 1984 Gloria Steinem's *MS.* magazine anointed Gilligan as "Woman of the Year," complete with a cover photo and five page spread. Today Gilligan is immensely influential and regularly quoted with respect, even reverence, in the mainstream press. Thus the hushed respect with which *Meeting at the Crossroads* has been greeted.

Because of Gilligan's stature, her theory about how girls develop has the potential to become conventional wisdom in education departments and in the practical world of school teachers and counselors. It is simple and pernicious, and goes something like this: mothers, female teachers, and other "good women" of Western Culture (if they are white and middle class) are victims of the patriarchy which forces them to cover up their own feelings, and then victimize the next generation of girls by imposing the "injunction to be 'nice' as a way to control their expression of feelings and thoughts" and to "keep them from saying too much or speaking too loudly." This often causes girls, at adolescence, to lose their resilience, vitality, their immunity to depression, and their sense of self. (Biology is virtually absent from the Gilligan/Brown world view. Down with nature, up with nurture!)

Meeting at the Crossroads, which the authors call "a journey of discovery," is based on a five-year study at the Laurel School in Cleveland, a private day-school for girls. "At the heart of our narrative are the voices of nearly one hundred girls between the ages of seven and eighteen." Most are middle or upper-middle class, but about 20 percent are from working class families and on scholarships. Fourteen percent are "of color."

Gilligan and Brown descended upon the school with an interviewing team to find out why and how little girls (honest, open, rambunctious, "authentic") turn into big girls (conforming, reticent, insecure, believing they have to be "nice" and therefore ripe for abuse by males). They wanted "to understand more about girls' response to a dominant culture that is out of tune with girls' voices and for the most part uninterested in girls' experiences, which objectifies and idealizes young women and at the same time trivializes and denigrates them...." The fact that the authors don't understand that this is a deeply held prejudice on their part, rather than a theory capable of sustaining scientific observation, fatally infects all the work that followed.

Despite all the busy talk about empiricism and putting together a team approach to the problem, after their first year on the job, Gilligan/Brown have managed to put together almost no real research—that is, objective data-gathering. Almost at once the project was bedeviled by its own methodology. The kids (bless their hearts) resisted, compared notes, and clammed up, causing the research team to have doubts about the study design, which initially, at least, had some semblance of established research practice. The authors claim that they worried about the effects they themselves were having on the girls: "We became another reason for girls to feel bad or feel judged [for being unresponsive to the interviewers]." At first they repressed their unease: "We overrode our own feelings. As women we found this easy to do." In other words, they saw themselves in their research. (You can almost hear a catch in their throats.)

Soon they decided that their initial hard-nosed standards for psychological interviewing had to go if they were to get the results they wanted. "Unwittingly we [had] set into motion a method of psychological inquiry appropriated from this very [male centered] system....As Audrey Lorde [martyred saint of radical feminism] warns us, 'The master's tools will never dismantle the master's house.'" To deconstruct the house of maleness, they needed "to create a practice of psychology that was something more like a practice of relationship."

Science, it would seem, is a Guy Thing—which must come as a shock to the countless women who do real research. This insult to women is made worse by special pleading: "We know that women, in particular, often speak in indirect discourse, in voices deeply encoded, deliberately or unwittingly opaque. As white, heterosexual women living in the context of twentieth-century North America—as women whose families in childhood were working class and Jewish, respectively—we know from our own experience about...capitulation—about complicity and accommodation."

If traditional research techniques had to be jettisoned, the shackling language of traditional psychology, in which "androcentricity" is "deeply rooted," was next to go. "We draw on language used by women poets and novelists who write about girls' and women's lives, at times we draw from music a language of voices, counterpoint, and theme." They tout their "Listener's Guide" to the girls' voices which is "responsive to the harmonics of psychic life, the nonlinear, recursive, nontransparent play, interplay, and orchestration of feelings and thoughts, the polyphonic nature of any utterance, and the symbolic nature not only of what is said but also of what is not said." Had the authors spent less time honing this neo-psychobabble and more time in the design of the study, the final result might have been better.

The girls' narratives, selected and annotated to serve the authors' purposes, portray a rogues' gallery of masculine awfulness: bullying neighborhood boys, spoiled, sadistic brothers (one is a voyeur), self-absorbed, drunken and violent fathers, a smothering, possessive boyfriend. It stretches credulity that the authors did not stumble upon even one girl's narrative that portrayed an affectionate, uncomplicated relationship with a dad, uncle, or brother.

Clearly, *Meeting at the Crossroads* cannot be taken seriously as a research study because its "data" are hopelessly biased. But what about Gilligan and Brown's thesis: are they onto something in spite of themselves? To decide, one needs to learn how the authors make their case.

The social climate of the Laurel School should dispel anyone's fantasies about the moral superiority of female society. Snobbery, cliques, telling secrets, conformism, obsession with popularity, the tyranny of the Popular Girl—they all flourish there, impervious to those "silencing voices" of mothers, female teachers, and other "good women" whom Gilligan and Brown accuse of acting as gender fifth columnists admonishing girls to be "nice."

This realistic group picture of the girls of Laurel clashes with the authors' romanticized portraits of them as individuals: the youngest (not yet ground down by Western Culture) are for Gilligan and Brown little Noble Savages who "speak out to those with whom they are in relationship about bad or hurt feelings, anger...as well as feelings of love, fondness, and loyalty." Appreciative of differences, they are willing to "grow to like someone," and (unlike boys) in play will change the rules of the game rather than argue over differences. "And yet," the authors assure us, "this is not to say these girls will back away from open disagreement."

But already (the authors tell us) these seven and eight year-olds are anticipating the reactions of adults, and they begin to monitor each other and report on "nice behavior." Here the careening train of the argument tumbles over a precipice: "The demand for nice and kind can be oppressive, a means of controlling and being controlled. 'Whispering,' 'telling secrets,' 'making fun of,' and 'laughing at' others are ways to prevent girls from risking too much or acting in ways that are too threatening, too different." The authors seem to be telling us that the rotten things girls often do to one another are really the fault of mothers and female teachers urging them not to do rotten things to one another.

To Gilligan and Brown, "nice" means little more than middle-class decorum, hypocrisy, and superficial relationships. They never consider the fact that only adults can teach children civility and humanity—they certainly would not learn it from one another—and that this "niceness" allows human society to function. Someone should lend them a copy of *Lord of the Flies*.

It is hardly news that girls, like boys, can be cruel, tyrannical, and intolerant of differences. But the notion that they would be less so—or emotionally better off—if encouraged by adults to squabble and say whatever pops into their heads, even when angry, carries an eerie echo of one of the more destructive injunctions of the Sixties: "Let it all hang out." Part of growing up is learning not only how but also when to speak one's mind—and discovering how to judge situations and to examine the validity of one's own thoughts and emotions. It is learning to just say no—to one's own worse instincts and psychological barbarities.

Gilligan and Brown's dime store Rousseauism doesn't allow them to consider this possibility. That their thesis is not only simplistic and derivative, but also unsupported and irresponsible, is revealed in their commentary and analyses of the girls' narratives. An example: "Lauren," age 9, tells the following story: "I had this project and I didn't turn it in on time. And I was in trouble because it was on a Sunday and it was due the next day and it was time for my bedtime and... I told my sister and she told my mom and that got me in trouble that my mom wanted to yell and scream at me. So I started to work on it but... I couldn't really, I just didn't want to do it right at that moment, because I was really tired and it was really hard for me to tell her why I didn't do it over the weekend."

Lauren would like to tell her teacher that she thinks it is a "really dumb assignment" and that she is so busy that she might turn in something late. But she knows that meeting the deadline means she "won't get a bad grade," her parents will be proud of her, and she'll get to go somewhere of her own choice, "like to Burger King or Wendy's." Lauren's admirable grasp on reality does not impress the authors: "No one seems to notice that Lauren doesn't say what she wants....Burying her feelings about the 'dumb' assignment and also her growing 'rage' at her sister for telling her mother, Lauren describes a reality in which... selflessness pays." *Selflessness?* Opting for a good grade, pleased parents, and a hamburger with fries sounds more like enlightened self-interest. One has to shudder at the kind of school the authors might design, where legitimate authority—feminine authority at that—can be flouted and assignments can be late—or ignored entirely—because the child doesn't feel like doing them and pronounces them dumb.

The authors repeatedly offer similarly outlandish interpretations but give the nonplussed reader no real argument for them—nor against more obvious and sensible interpretations of the "facts" they present. As if working through divine revelation, Gilligan and Brown simply assert; the reader must take it or leave it. They seem not to know that a genuine study must look at other possible interpretations of its data in order to make the case that its own interpretation is the most compelling. Doubtless Gilligan and Brown would see all this as another "male" requirement, but the fact is that neither men nor women can expect anyone to take seriously their claims to offer new knowledge without this rigorous use of argument.

Note too in these examples the authors' gullibility about the girls' stories. They are skeptical only when they decide that a girl is suppressing her "true feelings." It never occurs to them that the girls might be saying what they believe the interviewers want to hear, or that their accounts are trimmed to present themselves in their best light, or simply that most kids are masters of hyperbole: "dumb" homework, for example, often means "homework I can't be bothered to do."

"Judy," age 13, talks about a friend who "goes out with guys" and "goes further than most people would." This is behavior she finds disturbing: "...I mean, we are like thirteen, but still you want to be romantic... That just made me, if I had done something like that, I would feel like total dirt and totally worthless and she's so proud of it. I just can't know how she did that. No one else would ever do that, because they don't—that's not romantic, that's just plain disgusting."

Judy's prose may not be stylish, but her attitudes are what most parents would like to see in their thirteen year olds. She would like to have a boyfriend but believes she is too young to be sexually active. Reasonable enough. But it's thumbs down from Gilligan and Brown: Judy is "losing her mind" to the voices [of others]" and covering over "bodily desires and sexual feelings with romantic ideals.... Wanting romance without sexuality... Judy feels the pressure of norms and conventions inside her brain, particularly those of feminine goodness, which, taken in, are creating ideas of reality that are at odds with her experience of living as a feeling mind/body."

The authors never speak of the real-life consequences of their Flower Child views, but wading through this psychobabble one has to conclude that sexual activity among thirteen year-olds doesn't bother them. They even frown on Judy for saying that promiscuity at this age bothers her. And they criticize meddling mothers who have the gall to try to pass on some of their adult wisdom and experience—not to speak of values—to their daughters. (Another Sixties slogan can be heard murmuring in the background of this work: "*Never trust anyone over thirty.*") Not to put too fine a point on it: here is a Harvard professor, lionized by feminists, using the prestige of her position to imply to teachers and mothers (and ultimately children) that it is OK for girls to sleep around—at age 13!

"Edie," age 11, tells how her mother sometimes won't let her "go to a party, a sleep-over, maybe...because she doesn't trust the people or something." Initially Edie was angry, she says, but later realizes that her mother does this because she cares about her, doesn't want her "to get hurt." More crepe-hanging from Gilligan and Brown when they come to their version of a Dear Abby gloss on this position: "Edie's struggle to name unfairness and to stay with her feelings and thoughts about being overruled by her mother is overshadowed by her mother's seemingly selfless love and concern." No explanation is offered as to why this mother's love and concern should be doubted, or why, with no knowledge of the details, the authors think they can second-guess her judgment of the actual situation. As usual, the "good woman" is the culprit.

Does any Laurel girl win the Gilligan/Brown seal of approval? "Sonia," who is black, does. (The authors smile upon anyone who is minority or working class.) Had they not told us, we would never guess Sonia's race—her thoughts and complaints sound much like those of the other girls. It is amusing to watch Gilligan and Brown grubbing through Sonia's narrative to find any clue that she is suffering because she is black. The best they can come up with is a story Sonia tells about a teacher who wouldn't let her read a book of her own choice, insisting instead that she read a book that had won an award.

Assuming (as always) that this "good woman's" decision had no validity, the authors' imaginations soar into PC hyperspace. "Though Sonia does not tell her interviewer what book she did not want to read or why, her resistance seems healthy, even admirable given that awards and prizes in this culture are more often handed out by those to those who would reflect and sustain the privileged status quo." Imagine: here are educators recommending that children be encouraged to ignore their teachers' opinions about what they should read because the kids' choices are likely to be better! The authors cannot resist a footnote enlightening the reader about how very few children's books are written by black authors.

Even when a black interviewer is assigned to her, Sonia doesn't speak of race or exclusion. The authors gush anyway about "palpable communication" and "shared knowledge," about how "Sonia and her interviewer are moved by each other, by familiar language and experience." By the way, Sonia is thriving socially and academically, and it never occurs to Gilligan and Brown that perhaps this elite, middle-class school deserves some of the credit.

"Noura," age 11, who is Syrian, sets the authors' hearts aflutter when she hatches a plan to deal with the strife between her treacherous and gossiping gang of friends. She makes the family leave the house so that her friends can make a lot of noise, say "what really bothers" them and what they "don't like about each other." Catch that musky whiff of the Sixties again? Remember encounter groups? The authors lap it up, unperturbed by the emotional damage such a free-for-all might cause girls less outspoken and secure than Noura.

But the coveted In-your-face Award goes to the teenaged "Anna," the authors' favorite at Laurel School. Working class (her father and brothers are prone to "violent outbursts") and on scholarship, she is a top student who says whatever she thinks and feels, knowing she is "disruptive and disturbing." She fantasizes about giving a senior speech that will shock people, and asks pointed questions of her classmates "about God and about violence and about privilege."

Anna wants (in the authors' words) "to get underneath this patina of niceness and piety," and is not sure she wants to join the "normal, elite" world to which her education will give her entry. She speaks instead of getting a Ph.D. and then living at the bottom of a mountain in Montana, being "just one of those weird people," having a chicken farm: "I'll just write books or something." Most good parents of egghead daughters learn to view such whimsies with affectionate skepticism. But Gilligan and Brown, in a swoon of ecstasy, see great significance in Anna's musings, comparing them to Virginia Woolf's suggestion in *Three Guineas*—that women gain a university education, enter the professions, and then form a "Society of Outsiders."

Anna questions the "inconsistencies in her school's position on economic differences—where money is available, for what reasons and for whom, and where it isn't—and the limits of the meritocracy which is espoused." The authors' ill-concealed delight with Anna's tales of sticking it to everyone at Laurel leaves a bad taste, given the five years of hospitality and help this school gave to the team of Harvard "experts."

The authors' conclusions are predictably grim: "Women's psychological development within patriarchal societies and male-voiced cultures is inherently traumatic," and "Girls, we thought, were undergoing a kind of psychological foot-binding." (Carolyn Heilbrun, writing effusively about the book in The New York *Times* Book Review, upped the ante by going beyond foot-binding to genital mutilation for a comparison.)

In the final chapter, Gilligan and Brown allow us a peek at the mischief they can make in real people's lives. A number of Laurel teachers, joined by Gilligan and Brown, attended three retreats. One participant rhapsodizes about the sanctuary of the retreat which "allowed us to understand our knowledge and feelings with a clarity not possible in hierarchical work settings." (A Harvard professor buzzes into town to enlighten these benighted "good women": this is not hierarchy?) The same woman describes the group's "sense of shock and deep, knowing sadness" for having failed so miserably as teachers: "...We listened to the voices of the girls tell us that it was the adult women in their lives that provided the models for silencing themselves and behaving like 'good little girls.' We wept." Embarrassing, isn't it?

One reformed teacher proudly reports that she permitted a loud, personal argument between two girls in her classroom. (No one seems to worry about the precedent this scene will set for future class discussions.) But girlish glasnost can be treacherous. A student announces that she prefers men teachers because "they treat us like people" and "bring themselves into their teaching." Gasps all around. Other girls agree and dismiss one teacher's game explanation of this embarrassing news: girls, she says, are often in conflict with their mothers and project that conflict onto their female teachers. A vintage Gilligan/Brown pronouncement breaks this awkward impasse: "For women to bring themselves into their teaching and be in genuine relationship with girls...is far more disruptive and radical than for men. It means changing their practice as teachers and thus changing education." Why? No justification is offered for this far from obvious claim.

Gilligan and Brown mean to "initiate societal and cultural change." How? Through the sale of their book, of course, in Women's Studies and education courses. And through retreats where teachers can "think and feel with other women"—in other words, academic feminism's favorite cash cow, workshops!

But much as the authors wish it were so, they cannot build Utopia by tearing down the connection between generations, letting kids raise themselves and make their own rules. America's inner cities have become an unintended laboratory demonstrating what happens when children are denied the guidance of parents and adult mentors. Absent fathers, teenage mothers, non-functioning parents, and schools that barely work have produced the despair and virtual social collapse of the underclass. But the minds of Gilligan and Brown are so numbed by radical feminist ideology and Sixties primitivism that they apparently don't see this, or, if they see it, just don't get it. So like vandals they blithely hack away at the trust and respect between "good women" and their daughters and students.

Thanks, ladies.

October, 1993

MacKinnon Lunacy

by David Horowitz

Catharine MacKinnon's *Only Words* is a dishonest, intellectually worthless, malicious book. Masquerading as a legal brief against pornography, trussed up with pedantic footnotes and forensic citations, it is actually an embarrassing display of perversity on the part of a female Savanarola innocent of human nature and in desperate need of public attention. Pages of hyperventilated prose disfigured by wild accusations and zany hypotheses, all advanced with a Mad Hatter logic, leave only one clear and lasting impression: its author's hatred of men, sex and women in that order.

This is how Professor MacKinnon opens her case: "Imagine that for hundreds of years your most formative traumas, your daily suffering and pain, the abuse you live through the terror you live with are unspeakable —the basis of literature. You grow up with your father holding you down and covering your mouth so another man can make a horrible searing pain between your legs. When you are older, your husband ties you to the bed and drips hot wax on your nipples and brings in other men to watch and makes you smile through it. Your doctor will not give you drugs he has addicted you to unless you suck his penis."

Who is the "you" here? The only clue provided by MacKinnon is in a footnote to this paragraph which explains: "Some of these facts are taken from years of confidential consultations with women who have been used in pornography; some are adapted from People v. Burnham, ... and media reports on it; and Norberg v. Wynrib." That is the whole footnote (itself an insult to the intelligence). MacKinnon justifies her contention that for hundreds of years women who make pornography have been horribly abused by interviews with a handful of anonymous women who—need I point this out?—are certainty not hundreds of years old.

Where is an acknowledgment of the thousands of female porn stars who not only do not complain of abuse but seem to positively enjoy their craft, return to it film after film and year after year, attend the annual Adult Film Awards ceremonies to celebrate their achievements, and parade themselves on Geraldo and Oprah to defend and luxuriate in the pleasures and satisfactions of their profession? (There is even at least one politically radical porn film star who has been featured in the left press explaining her work as a mission of sexual liberation.)

The only thing that is clear from MacKinnon's opening dramatics is that she has neither an intention nor the ability to make an argument justifying her blanket indictments of the male gender and pornography, which she sees as a metaphor for male violence against women. What can MacKinnon mean by her central thesis that "pornography is rape," a statement that on the face of it is so obviously meaningless? Such silly provocations actually proliferate throughout this text without explanation, but in this case there is at least an attempt: "In pornography women are gang raped so they can be filmed."

At some time, in some place, a pornographic film may have been made of an actual gang rape. But even if this were true, it would no more justify the implication that all pornographers are rapists than would the murder conviction of Aileen Wuoronos lead to the conclusion that all lesbians are serial killers.

MacKinnon's statement is about as illuminating as a parallel one claiming, say, that "in Hollywood men are killed so they can be filmed." Men have been killed in the course of making some films, mainly stunt men but most recently actor Brandon Lee who, while on location, was shot and killed by what should have been a blank. But if someone advanced the above proposition they would be laughed out of town. Why doesn't somebody laugh MacKinnon out of the privileged place she has fraudulently occupied in the nation's legal-intellectual life?

MacKinnon actually notes that murders in films do not have to take place in reality in order to be filmed. They are "staged." On the other hand, the sex in pornographic films is always "real." Well, yes, although there are degrees of realness, as any connoisseur of "good" porn can testify. In any case, this is hardly the same as saying that the sex in pornographic films is *rape*. (Actually, the "rapes" in pornographic films are not only *not* real, but they also seem much less real than the "rapes" in Hollywood films, because the viewer does not take the characters in porn films as seriously.)

To justify the claim that sex in pornography is rape, MacKinnon argues: "It is for pornography, and not by the ideas in it, that women are hurt and penetrated, tied and gagged, undressed and genitally spread and sprayed with lacquer and water so sex pictures can be made... It is unnecessary to do any of these things to express, as ideas, the ideas pornography expresses. It is essential to do them to make pornography."

This is just nonsense. It is not only possible to make pornographic films that do not hurt or abuse women, but by all the evidence available, the vast majority of pornographic films are just as harmless in their making as Hollywood films. They are made no differently from any other kind of film and the women who make them do so willingly and not only for money, but in some cases because they enjoy having sex on camera. It is obvious to any normally adjusted person that in the vast majority of pornographic films no one is being hurt or coerced or abused in any manner. (Most pornographic films do not even involve *simulated* abuse, although one would never suspect this from reading MacKinnon.) In addition, there are pornographic films written, produced and directed by women; there are "all girl" films in which the sex is just as "nasty" as in heterosexual porn except that the penises "ramming vaginas" (as MacKinnon puts it) are plastic and in the hands of other women. For every actress that MacKinnon has found with complaints about being abused by a filmmaker there are hundreds who would testify to the absence of such abuse.

In an article I once wrote about women who make X-rated films, I asked each of them whether they had ever been abused and never got an affirmative answer. (This, of course, does not mean such abuse doesn't exist; but what people *actually say* ought to count for something.) Among the actresses I interviewed was a reigning star of the industry, Annette Haven, who told me (on tape) that the *only* time she ever felt abused over the course of many years as a porn actress, was when she went for an audition for a legitimate Hollywood production. The casting director asked her if she "partied." She said: "I do sex *in* the part; I don't do sex *for* the part." Annette Haven makes *ten times* the salary per porn film that her male counterparts do. So much for MacKinnon's claim that pornography entails the subordination of women.

Once in awhile, MacKinnon seems to become aware of the insubstantiality of the factual base on which she has been erecting her extravagant web. To hide the gaping hole in her argument, she offers the following aside: "This does not presume that all pornography is made through abuse or rely on the fact that some pornography is made through coercion as a legal basis for restricting all of it."

The rationale by which she justifies outlawing all pornography (including *Playboy* and its genre) in the absence of abuse by the pornographers themselves is the abuse that women experience in society at large: "Empirically, all pornography is made under conditions of inequality based on sex, overwhelmingly by poor, desperate, homeless, pimped women who were sexually abused as children."

The word "empirically" is a hoot given the absence of empirical evidence in this book. But even if MacKinnon's claim were true, so what? Are we to believe that the remedy for homelessness, child abuse and poverty is to outlaw pornography? Not even MacKinnon, in her guise as Victorian harridan, believes this. It is a simple *non sequitur* to argue that because poverty makes someone unequal, their choice to perform a particular job for money is coerced and/or the result of the abuse. Ninety-percent of the violent felons in San Quentin were abused as children. Does this fact absolve them of their responsibility for choosing to abuse others? Do women who make pornographic films, even if they are poor, lack the free will to decide whether or not to act in them? MacKinnon's entire thesis rests on the claim that they do.

If it were true that social inequality forced women to make porn films for money, how could one explain the most booming aspect of the current porn industry—the explosion of "amateur videos," for which the actresses and actors aren't even paid? And even if they were paid, why would the need to be paid compel one to make porn films and not, for example, flip hamburgers at McDonald's? MacKinnon's argument is cognate to the discredited one sometimes advanced by liberal racists who claim that blacks commit crime because of their inferior social status.

Pornography is defined by MacKinnon arbitrarily and indefensibly as "graphic sexually explicit materials that subordinate women through pictures or words." *Playboy*, which is defined by her as pornography, pays women $25,000 to appear as centerfolds. If elected Centerfold of the Year they can earn as much as a million dollars, merely by being photographed with their clothes off. If we accept MacKinnon's metaphysics, we have to regard this woman as a subordinated female, a victim. Has this woman been homeless, abused, pimped and therefore *coerced* into accepting a million dollars merely to take her clothes off in front of a camera? This is where MacKinnon's arguments lead. It is a view so far removed from the reality of actual women as to border on psychosis.

Like all radical elitists, MacKinnon's rhetorical compassion is driven by actual contempt for the victim group she pretends to defend. Otherwise, how could she fail to be embarrassed by her own argument, which assumes that women are poor ninnies who do not have free will? A female like Annette Haven is clearly beyond the impoverished ken of a Catharine MacKinnon. The product of a sexually repressive Mormon family, Haven was not abused or poverty stricken or homeless when she became a porn star. By her own account, she chose this profession out of a missionary desire to show others that sex was not sinful and could even be pleasurable. Haven's rationale for making pornography is, not surprisingly, identical to that of *Playboy* publisher Hugh Hefner. But we need not accept their self-aggrandizing explanations to know that life is complex and people make decisions to create and consume pornography for complex reasons which rarely have anything to do with MacKinnon's demonological system of domination and submission.

MacKinnon's effort to force pornography to fit the radical melodrama of oppression is finally based on a fraudulent presentation of what pornography is. The fraud is made easier by the absence of any discussion of any particular X-rated films. (Even the specific contents of the one she does mention, *Deep Throat*, are ignored.) As anyone who has viewed it knows, pornography is not about domination and submission. The sadomasochistic element is only a small portion of the X-rated film business and—contrary to everything that MacKinnon's argument would lead one to suspect—the sadomasochism primarily features women dominating men.

What pornography is really about is far more innocent and on the surface. It is the psychological element at the heart of all theater:

exhibitionism and voyeurism. Some like to show and some like to watch. This is the basis for a market exchange which is not dissimilar to the exchange involved in any theatrical production. Pornography is not a sexual version of the Marxist melodrama. In explaining away the apparent free choice of women to act in pornographic films, MacKinnon argues that "money is the medium of force." But this is just more Marxist claptrap. Money is not a medium of force anymore than rape is a form of dance.

If MacKinnon has contempt for women, however, it is men that she hates. (Her contempt for women derives from the fact that there are women so enmeshed in false consciousness that they actually like men.) This animus is revealed in innumerable vicious asides in the text (e.g: "the ultimate male bond [is] between pimp and john"). But it is captured best in her passing reference to *Deep Throat*, the only pornographic film even mentioned in a text which pretends to be about pornography. The star of *Deep Throat*, Linda Lovelace, is a special object of MacKinnon's concern, because she is one of the few porn stars ever to make the claim that she was coerced (by her husband) into performing sex acts on camera. Asks MacKinnon: "If a woman had to be coerced to make *Deep Throat*, doesn't that suggest that *Deep Throat* is dangerous to all women anywhere near a man who wants do what he saw in it?"

Other critics have noted MacKinnon's primitive understanding of male psychology. *Monkey see, monkey do* seems to be as elaborate a theory as MacKinnon is able devise to explain the reactions of the opposite sex. But more interesting is what MacKinnon's question reveals about her own attitudes towards sexuality.

What is it, after all, that is done in *Deep Throat*, that will impel men to go out and do what they saw in it, imperilling women in the process? What is done is *fellatio*. Why is the male desire to be fellated dangerous to all women? MacKinnon's perverse interest in fellatio is not confined to this tract. In another book, she asks: "Who listens to a woman with a penis in her mouth?" as though fellatio were a male plot to silence women. It might just as easily—and absurdly—be asked, Who listens to a man with his mouth in a crotch?

Admittedly, this is lunatic stuff. But it is the intellectual currency of a woman whom 33 members of the Harvard Law School recently voted to appoint to their faculty. And this book of lunacies was originally delivered as the prestigious Gauss Lectures at Princeton. If ever there was an index to measure the intellectual debasement of the contemporary university, it must surely lie in these honors accorded to Catharine MacKinnon.

November, 1993

Digging The Grave Of Archaeology

by Anita Sue Grossman

The multiculturalist movement has been widely recognized as a threat to higher education for promoting ethnic quotas in hiring and admissions, and establishing various politicized "victim studies" departments. Far less well publicized is the movement's outright attack on scholarship in the name of minority rights, an attack that has had such success on the state and federal level that it may put an end to some disciplines entirely. One example of this attack is the demand for the "repatriation" of Indian bones and artifacts currently held in museum collections, and the restrictions proposed on future archaeological investigation of such remains.

The idea that museum collections of ancient bones and art objects of Native American peoples should be returned to present-day tribes for reburial is a fairly recent one, which arose over the past two decades concurrently with other militant rights movements, all of them sharing the same general political orientation and multiculturalist agenda. It has flourished in an intellectual climate which idealizes primitive peoples as living in harmony with nature, and downgrades most Western institutions as oppressive, racist, and Eurocentric. According to these historical revisionists, Columbus' arrival in the New World marked a 500-year epoch of tragedy for its native peoples, meriting a day of national mourning rather than the traditional celebration. Similarly, the settling of the Western frontier by pioneers has been described as nothing less that the rape of a continent, a crime for which their modern-day descendants can never sufficiently atone.

Some of the leaders of the Indian rights movements make no secret of their contempt for archaeology, and the data about Native Americans this science provides. A North Dakota attorney for the Three Affiliated Tribes remarked a few years ago in *Harper's* that the current agitation for reburial of the bones "is just the beginning." He went on to say, "It's conceivable that some time in the not-so-distant future there won't be a single Indian skeleton in any museum in the country. We're going to put them [the physical anthropologists] out of business." Another Indian activist, Suzan Shown Harjo, Executive Director of the National Congress of American Indians, has denounced the Smithsonian Institution's collection of Native American skeletons as "one of the last vestiges of colonialism, dehumanization and racism against our people."

Such sentiments are astounding to archaeologists and physical anthropologists, who for over a century have seen themselves as allies of American Indians, unearthing and preserving aspects of their cultures which otherwise would have been unknown. Indeed, their disciplines have provided the basis of what information we have about preliterate peoples. In attempting to shut down future study of Indian remains, these activists (such scholars contend) are working against the long-term interest of their own people, destroying the source of any future knowledge of their history. Activists and their political allies reply that we know enough already. The bones, housed for decades in museum collections, have no further value and ought to be catalogued and then given away as quickly as possible to whatever Indian claimants appear to demand them.

California State Assemblyman Richard Katz, one of the most strident legislative advocates of reburial of Indian remains, chided the University of California at a 1991 Regents' meeting for not divesting itself more speedily of its enormous and unique collection of Indian bones, calling the five-year deadline set by UC policy, in conformity with the new federal law, "unduly lenient." At present the University has more than a million items, including skeletal remains and artifacts, on five of its nine campuses, with the lion's share housed in UC Berkeley's Phoebe Hearst Museum of Anthropology. This museum holds the nation's third largest collection of human remains, representing some 11,000 individuals, most dating from pre-Columbian times. Assemblyman Katz has said that he would "like to see the university take the leadership as one of the most prestigious universities in the world" adding, "You will be watched by everybody." Just how long the University would retain its world-class reputation after destroying its renowned collection, Katz did not say; but it is doubtless true that the rest of the world is watching what the University of California does.

Another vocal opponent of archaeology in California is Rosemary Cambra, of the Ohlone Families Consulting Service in San Jose, who denied in a newspaper interview that anyone benefits from museum collections:

> *If it benefited Indians [for scientists] to keep the bones— if they were utilizing these collections to develop a body of knowledge— it would make me feel very good. But the scientists are just storing them in boxes, or wrapped in some kind of newspaper, and nobody is benefiting. With all the research work the scientists say they have done, they cannot add a single day to the life of an Indian. That bothers me very much. The question should be asked, how often are these collections actually used?*

To this, UC Berkeley anthropology professor Tim White has replied in a newspaper interview, "I study these bones at least biweekly." White notes that graduate and undergraduate students and faculty also use them, as do researchers from across the country. Moreover, he believes that frequency of use should not be the decisive criterion:

> *Just as in a library, there might be a book that is not used all the time but which is necessary to keep as a resource in the event that someone needs it— bones work that way. Scientists need continual access to bones; you can never predict when they'll be needed. No one knows what the scientific landscape will look like in twenty years.*

This opinion has been echoed by other scholars, among them, Douglas Owsley, a forensic anthropologist and associate curator at the Smithsonian Institution, who told a reporter for *Science* in 1989 that because of new techniques for working with bones, he was "involved in projects I never would have dreamed possible eleven years ago when I got my Ph.D." Some of these techniques of analysis include methods of extracting antibodies and genetic material from human remains. According to Owsley, studying the bones will eventually enable researchers to trace the evolution of specific human diseases— and with such knowledge may come, perhaps, the means of eliminating them.

When the Smithsonian announced in 1988 that it was planning to give up many of the Indian bones in its vast collection of remains from about 35,000 individuals, half of whom are Native Americans, dismayed researchers pointed out the enormous value their holdings have had for science. Not only do such bones help reconstruct the social history of ancient peoples, but they provide information about their clinical history—including their predisposition to various diseases—which in turn gives us an insight into present-day medical problems. As Bennett Bronson, chairman of the anthropology department at Chicago's Field Museum of Natural History observed, American Indians are the direct beneficiaries of the studies of diabetes and rheumatoid arthritis conducted with the aid of skeletal remains. Doctors, dentists, and forensic pathologists have all had recourse to museum collections. The Smithsonian alone has been visited annually by anywhere from 75 to 150 medical researchers. Because hip angles, for example, vary between ethnotypes, orthopedists have consulted the Smithsonian collection to obtain the proper angle for the prostheses they design; similarly, a plastic surgeon has used the Indian skulls to create a new model for his non-Caucasian patients requiring reconstructive facial surgery.

Those unfamiliar with techniques of statistical sampling have argued that most of the bones in museum collections could be returned to Indian claimants, leaving a few for researchers to work on. However, scientists require a large number of samples to arrive at meaningful generalizations. Also, more recent bones that can be identified and requested by tribes claiming descent or affiliation are often more useful for scientists for that very reason: from them researchers can study death rates, disease patterns and other conditions specific to given tribes at given times.

These facts did not have much effect on the general public debate of the past few years, when a number of museums reached agreements with Indian activists to return the bones and other objects in their collections for reburial, at the same time that laws were being passed on the state and federal level mandating the return of these items, and more generally placing severe restrictions on the practice of archaeology.

One sign of the times was the Smithsonian's highly publicized decision in 1988 to return its collection of Blackfoot (Montana) Indian bones to the tribe and to return many of the rest of its 18,000 Indian skeletal remains. This was a turnabout from its earlier policy whereby such items would be de-accessioned only to next of kin with proof of blood relationship to the deceased. The Museum has since set up a Repatriation Office and has returned about 260 sets of human remains to Blackfoot, Modoc, Sisseton-Wahpeton Sioux, and Native Hawaiian claimants.

A far more significant loss to the Museum was the return—and subsequent reburial—in Larsen Bay, Alaska, of a collection of artifacts and bones from 756 individuals, some of them dating back 2,000 years. The material had been excavated in the 1930s by Alex Hrdlicka, the founder of the Division of Physical Anthropology at the Smithsonian, over the course of ten expeditions in Alaska. At Larsen Bay, his largest excavation site, Hrdlicka found hundreds of ancient artifacts in addition to skeletons in some 800 unmarked graves.

When the Larsen Bay Tribal Council first asked for the material, the Smithsonian refused. The Museum put up a five year legal battle to retain these materials. Officials claimed (in the summary of one reporter) "that the objects represented the museum's largest and most highly valued collection and the return them would mean a deep loss to the museum." But in the end the Smithsonian gave in, and 370 cardboard boxes were shipped to Larsen Bay, where the contents were reinterred at a public ceremony in 1991 after being blessed, ironically enough, in a Russian Orthodox ceremony.

Stanford University became the first university in the country to agree to give up its collection, when it sent some 550 skeletons to the Muskewma group. It was quickly followed by similar actions on the part of the Universities of Minnesota, South Dakota, and Nebraska.

Stanford's decision was by no means greeted with universal acclaim, even among Native Americans. Andrew Galvan, a cousin of activist

Rosemary Cambra, publicly deplored the University's haste to rebury his people's bones, thereby destroying any chance to learn more about his Ohlone heritage. Others have denied that the specimens, 400 to 3,000 years old, have any ties at all to contemporary tribes at all, and denounced Stanford's action for its disservice to science. San Jose State University anthropologist Robert Jermain, who has used the Stanford collection, called the agreement "scientifically indefensible" and a "dangerous precedent."

Particularly upset was Emeritus Professor of Anthropology Bert Gerow, former curator of the museum housing the bones, many of which he and his students had collected for the University during his forty-year tenure at Stanford. He contended that the University had reneged on its previous guarantee of lifetime access to the bones for his research. In the ensuing struggle over the custody of the archaeological specimens, the University obtained a court order keeping Professor Gerow away from the collection and changed the locks on the doors leading to them, whereupon the Stanford chapter of the American Association of University Professors passed a resolution condemning the University for denying Gerow's academic freedom by confiscating his research material. In the end, the bones were reburied, reportedly in such a manner that they will soon by destroyed by decomposition.

In 1990 President Bush signed into law the Native American Graves Protection and Repatriation Act. This bill requires all federally funded institutions, especially universities and historical associations, to inventory all Indian skeletal remains and other associated objects preparatory to returning them to their tribes of origin, at the latter's request. Depending upon the size and type of the collection, such institutions will have five years to compile their inventory; under extraordinary circumstances, they can appeal for an extension of time. Grants are provided to museums and Native American groups to assist them in the inventory and repatriation process. No funds have been allocated, however, for any additional study of the bones before they are returned. As a result, scholars across the country are hastening to gather what data they can from the remains on their limited budgets before the specimens disappear forever.

Perhaps the single greatest loss to North American archaeology caused by reburial legislation occurred in Idaho last year when a skeleton approximately 10,700 years old was reinterred only two years after it had been discovered in a gravel pit in 1989 along with three artifacts—a stone knife, a bone needle, and a badger penis bone. The specimen may have been the oldest yet found in the New World, but the media largely ignored the story of its discovery. (In contrast, when a 5,300 year old mummified body was discovered in the Italian Alps shortly afterward, it was the subject of much publicity, including a *Newsweek* cover story on the "Iceman.")

Todd Fenton, a physical anthropologist at the University of Arizona, managed to determine that the skeleton was that of female 18 to 20 years old, and about 5'2" tall. But other crucial studies employing DNA and chemical analysis were not done, and now never will be. The antiquity of this specimen was such that it makes it impossible to establish any relationship to living Indians of any tribe. Conceivably, it might have been ancestral to Indians now residing as far away as South America. Nevertheless, Idaho officials decided to return the bones to the Shoshone-Bannock tribes on the Fort Hall Reservation, where they were reburied. Idaho State Archaeologist and Deputy State Historic Preservation Officer Thomas J. Green justified the decision to discard this ancient specimen by observing that Idaho state law does not require the groups claiming them to establish any degree of cultural affiliation; neither does the age of the remains influence the decision.

A sense of the research opportunity lost is suggested by an account of the affair given in the April 1992 *ACPAC Newsletter* (the publication of the American Committee for Preservation of Archaeological Specimens). One archaeologist commented:

> *Are we going to know all we need to know from the people who did the studies of the Idaho burial? There are no second chances here...[I]t appears to me that the story of the discovery, excavation, analysis, and disposition of this highly significant Paleo skeleton and artifacts was deliberately held up until the remains could be safely re-interred.*

Other recent archaeological horror stories can be found in just about every state. In West Virginia, the State Department of Transportation signed an agreement in 1991 with a group of Indian rights activists giving them unprecedented control over a federally-funded excavation (costing $1.8 million) of a 2,000 year old Adena mound unearthed by a highway project. According to this agreement, *everything* dug up in the course of the project—not just remains and artifacts but soil and pollen samples, good debris, chipping waste, animal bones—had to be reburied within a year. Moreover, during the year when archaeologists were allowed to examine the material, the bones and artifacts could not be touched by menstruating women, and when not in use had to be kept covered in red flannel (a material unknown, of course, to the builders of the mound.) An educational video was authorized, but it could not show the human remains, and was in any case subject to the censorship of the West Virginia Committee on Native American Archaeological and Burial Policies. None of the Indians on this Committee could demonstrate any relationship to the mound builders; for that matter, some were from tribes outside West Virginia.

In 1992, political correctness struck again when the State of Illinois closed off and covered with a concrete slab a display of ancient bones dating from about 900 to 1300 A.D. at the Dickson Mounds site. This unique display *in situ* of 234 open graves had been unearthed on Dickson family property in 1927. Over the years, in addition to being a resource for archaeologists, it had been a well-known tourist attraction with a state museum built around it. Indian activists over the years have protested the museum, on a few recent occasions jumping into the graves with a blanket to cover the skeletons, or marching with shovels to cover the bones with earth. In April 1992, Governor Jim Edgar closed the display, allowing scholars to make one final rushed study of the bones before the concrete entombment.

California's policies on native bones and artifacts is a case study in itself. In 1977, California created a Native American Heritage Commission charged with supervising archaeology in the state. According to current laws, any human remains discovered in an excavation must be reported to a coroner, who in turn must notify the NAHC. A political rather than a scientific body, the Commission determines the most likely tribal descendants to be notified, with the latter given authority to determine the ultimate fate of the archaeological finds. This legislation has been extended to include not only human bones but nearby objects on ancient sites which might be considered sacred.

The attitude of the NAHC towards archaeologists can be gauged by a recent remark of their executive director, Larry Myers: " . . . They know about the diet. They know enough about right-handed and left-handed. They know that everyone suffered from arthritis. Do they really need to know more? "

Referring to the return of a collection of 3,000-year-old bones and artifacts housed at California State University, Long Beach, Myers said, "It's not a question of scientific value, but of religious rights. It's important to get archaeologists out of the graveyards of Indians."

California's "cultural resource" law conflicts with other statutes which require archaeologists to remove bones and artifacts for analysis in order to mitigate the destructive effect on sites of potential historic or prehistoric significance. Archaeologists are thus caught between two sets of laws, one of which orders them to analyze and report their finds, the other requiring them to leave them in place.

Archaeologist David Van Horn was caught between these two imperatives and charged with a felony by the State Attorney General's Office in 1990 for having conducted an investigation at a site near Indio, California. Hired to survey the site for possible North American Indian artifacts, Dr. Van Horn had found some tiny bits of burned bone, which he sent to a University of California laboratory for identification. After 3% of the total fragments were shown to be part of a human cremation, he delivered them to the property owner with instructions to contact the Native American Heritage Commission. The Riverside County deputy district attorney argued that Dr. Van Horn should not have removed or studied these bones, even though it took a specialist to identify some of the fragments as human, and even though such a study was mandated by one set of laws.

After a three-day hearing attended by many archaeologists testifying for the defense, a judge threw out the case. Had Van Horn been found guilty of desecrating Indian gravesites as charged, he could have faced three years in prison. As it is, he was left with substantial legal costs to pay, the prosecution having been underwritten with state tax dollars.

Van Horn had fallen afoul of the anti-archaeology brigade a few years earlier, when in 1986 he fought a demand by the Native American Heritage Commission for custody of a pair of grinding stones (used to cover shallow graves) which he had found in the course of an excavation. Indian activists contended that the stones were "sacred offerings" and demanded their reburial. After a legal battle costing taxpayers as much as an estimated $150,000, the two stones were put in the ground.

In response to pending federal legislation as well as growing sentiment in favor of returning native bones, former University of California President David P. Gardner appointed a committee in April 1990 to review University policies regarding its collection and to recommend any changes to be made. The Committee report, issued the following August, surveyed the arguments for and against repatriation, and concluded by recommending that human remains be returned only to those descendants able to demonstrate biological or cultural ties. The report noted that about 95% of the skeletal remains and associated objects housed at the University are from the period preceding contact with Europeans, dating from between 5,000 BC and 1,500 AD; thus the overwhelming majority of these items are at least 500 years old. In addition to the Native American remains from the Northern California coast and the Sacramento River Valley (representing about 8,000 individuals), the Hearst collection contains bones from over 1,200 individuals from Peru, over 600 from Egypt, with other remains from Asia, Europe, Australia, and North America. The second largest collection of bones is at the University of California Los Angeles Fowler Museum of Cultural History, with remains of some 2,300 individuals, mostly form California.

On April 1, 1991, President Gardner issued a policy statement describing how the University would inventory its collection on a campus-by-campus basis, contact Native American tribes, and return bones and artifacts on request. It states that those branches of the University with collections are establishing committees to assist the chancellors in conducting the required processes and reviewing repatriation requests. In accord with federal law, the campuses will have five years to complete their inventory and notification.

Since 1991, archaeology in California has suffered other major setbacks. That year, Representative Richard Katz sponsored a bill which was passed and signed into law by Governor Pete Wilson which flatly announced, "It is the policy of the state that Native American remains and associated grave artifacts shall be repatriated."

In keeping with this directive, a collection of ancient Indian skeletons and artifacts housed for nearly two decades at California State University, Long Beach, was removed in May 1992 to the custody of the U.S. Army Corps of Engineers preparatory to reburial by Native American tribes. The remains of 60 prehistoric Indians and their artifacts, dating from about 3,000 years ago, had been excavated by CSULB Professor of Anthropology Franklin Fenenga and some 400 of his students during a series of expeditions from 1971 to 1978 in the San Joaquin Valley. The excavations had been commissioned by the Army Corps of Engineers, which had been constructing Hensley Dam and had discovered the sites of dozens of prehistoric villages by the Madera River. Professor Fenenga, emeritus since 1987, told the Los Angeles *Times* that the loss of the collection would be a "great tragedy" and "a loss to science." Nevertheless, the University handed over all the materials on May 27. The Army Corps of Engineers, short of funds with which to perform required studies on these materials before giving them away to tribal claimants, has put the specimens in storage at their Hensley Lake facility— not very far from where they were originally dug up.

California's Department of Parks and Recreation also got on the anti-archaeology bandwagon several years ago. In 1983 it agreed to give away for reburial the 850 skeletons and 10,000 associated artifacts housed in the State Indian Museum, a publicly owned and tax-supported institution. When archaeologists sued, the Department was ordered by the State Superior Court to issue an environmental impact report on repatriation policy. The final version, released in September 1992, was titled "Repatriation of Human Skeletal Remains and Burial-Related Artifacts in Custody of the California Department of Parks and Recreation." The lengthy document admits that the reburial of archaeological materials will be an incalculable loss to scholarship. Nonetheless, it concludes that "the rights of Native Americans to determine the fate of Native American Grave Protection and Repatriation Act (NAGPRA) to be of greater public interest than the scientific knowledge to be gained by studying the burials." Accordingly, the report "assumes that most, if not all, of the burial collections will be reinterred."

Although issued by a presumably impartial state agency, the report makes no secret of its sympathy with the agenda of Indian Rights advocates or of its bias against modern technological society. We are told, for example, that:

> *"Man's use of the environment in California today is progressively expansive, destructive and unsustainable. By contrast, the cultures of the California Indians were highly adapted to the*

> *region's environment. In favorable locations, large numbers of people were sustained in relative abundance for thousands of years. Perhaps a greater understanding of those early Californians could steer modern Californians toward a more environmentally-aware way of life.*

Even if this notion of an ecological Eden were true— and its fallaciousness has long been pointed out by serious scholars such as Bernard Powell and Jared Diamond—we will be unable to gain a "greater understanding" of these early Californians' "more environmentally-aware way of life" if such material evidence of it as we have is lost to future study, as the California Department of Parks and Recreation evidently intends it to be. At the present time all the human remains and grave artifacts formerly in the State Indian Museum and other museums of the Department of Parks and Recreation have been removed to their West Sacramento facility in anticipation of their being given away to tribal claimants.

The question naturally arises why there has been so little opposition to the growing movement to disband museum collections of Indian bones and artifacts. Apart from the general cultural climate of white guilt, there are several reasons for this movement's success. In contrast to the forceful and well publicized group of political activists agitating for reburial legislation, for instance, there has no correspondingly unified pressure group willing to oppose them. Few citizens have any direct financial interest in maintaining museum collections.

Moreover, the past few decades have seen a breakdown in the tacit public consensus that the research involved in such collections was inherently worthwhile and should be supported. Until recently, people understood that with few exceptions—chiefly in medicine and engineering—basic research does not "pay for itself" in terms of immediate short-term gain but they supported such research anyway as valuable in its own right. Prior to the political assault on the academy of the past two decades, scholars did not see the need to form pressure groups to fend off attacks on their disciplines, something that they were at any rate not particularly well equipped to do, by temperament or training.

Other circumstances made physical anthropologists and archaeologists uniquely vulnerable when Indian activists began to make their demands. Museums housing the Indian bones and artifacts are generally tax-supported institutions. As such they are dependent on public goodwill, and would naturally seek to avoid any controversy that might, however indirectly, endanger their funding. These museums are often umbrella organizations housing many different kinds of collections, and their administrators are more likely to have backgrounds in art history or museum administration than in archaeology or any of the physical sciences. It should hardly be surprising, then, that professional organizations of museum administrators have, by and large, capitulated to demands for "repatriation" of their holdings in the interest of public relations. The Council of the American Association of Museums announced in 1988 that it was generally supportive of Indian demands, and even suggested releasing pre-Columbian human remains "unless there are compelling and overriding reasons to retain them."

The January-February 1991 issue of *Museum News*, the organ of the American Museum Association, devoted several articles to an upbeat portrayal of the repatriation movement without a dissenting opinion. More recently, the October-November 1992 issue featured an article titled "Three Voices for Repatriation." (No voices were raised against it.)

Physical anthropologists were at another disadvantage in their own university departments, where they are almost always outnumbered by cultural anthropologists. The latter group of scholars have little interest in osteological collections. Their first concern is maintaining good relations with the living tribes with whom they work—even if it means acceding to demands for the return of grave materials excavated by their own colleagues. By profession, such anthropologists are guided in their work by respect for native tradition and the wish to accommodate them to the fullest extent possible. One might go further to note that as a group, cultural anthropologists are accustomed to immersing themselves sympathetically in cultures alien to their own, and conversely, to viewing their own society with the cold, clinical gaze of cultural relativism.

If academics as a rule tend to be further to the political left of the average American, cultural anthropologists may be well to the left of the average college professor. Symptomatic of the deep inroads made into the field by the "adversary culture" was a 1990 Ph.D. dissertation titled, "My Momma the State: A Socio-Cultural Study of the Criminalization of Chicanos." Directed by a former chairman of Berkeley's anthropology department, with its then-current chairman as its second reader, the thesis took as its underlying premise that American society is racist and the criminal justice system biased against minorities. As the author states, "The intent here then is not to prove that institutionalized racism exists in the criminal justice system; that it exists is manifest." Her particular focus, according to the abstract, is "the use of law and legal-judicial institutions to establish and enforce systems of social inequality based on racial and class distinctions."

Given the ascendancy of left-wing ideology among some members of the profession, and their propensity to view American minority groups as victims of a malevolent white Eurocentric majority, their support for the Indian activists on the issue of returning the bones was a foregone conclusion.

Archaeologists, the other major group of academics involved in the dispute, have tried to strike a more reasonable balance between the claims of the Indians and of scholarship. Initially opposed to any reburial of human remains, the executive group of the Society for American Archaeology announced in 1985 that it would negotiate with proven next of kin or these individuals who could demonstrate a genetic tie to remains in museum collections. They remained opposed to federal legislation, preferring that cases be settled on an individual basis. However, a dissident group led by Professor Larry Zimmerman of the University of South Dakota, and calling itself the World Archaeological Congress, split off from the International Union of Prehistoric and Protohistoric Scientists because it was "dominated by white American and European interests." Unlike most other archaeologists, the group generally favors reburial of Indian remains.

The single most active organization of scholars devoted to maintaining museum holdings is the American Committee for the Preservation of Archaeological Collections (ACPAC), founded in 1981 by UCLA anthropology professor Clement W. Meighan, now emeritus. With members in 49 states, it is devoted to preserving and safeguarding archaeological collections as "part of the historical and cultural heritage of the nation and the property of all citizens," according to its statement of purpose.

One irony is that the reburial issue, like the ethnic studies movement with which it is allied, often functions as a noisy sideshow, deflecting attention from the genuine problems of Native Americans, such as poverty, unemployment, and rampant alcoholism. Instead of addressing any of these, reburial is used to advance the political careers of those claiming special victim status in the larger society and group entitlements as compensations for past wrongs. In both cases, the activists chose a soft target, the scholarly community, whose members collectively represent one of the least racist institutions in the country. Moreover, neither movement seems ultimately concerned with true knowledge of the groups in whose interest they purport to act, but rather with political control of such knowledge.

The Chronicle of Higher Education reported that some Indian groups are opposed to "having the history of their people written by "outsiders." This is nothing new to those who have listened to the separatist rhetoric of ethnic studies departments over the years. Once again, the claim is made that knowledge is the special preserve of a particular ethnic or racial group. To put it another way, they are denying that objective knowledge is possible, since what we call "truth" they believe to be merely successful propaganda that has drowned out competing claims. History is useful, but only as a club with which to bludgeon one's political opponents.

In this view, science likewise becomes a tool of ideology. If that is so, we had not only better divest museums of their collections, but shut down the universities themselves, which are founded on quite other premises— that objective knowledge is possible, if often difficult to arrive at; that it should be treasured for its own sake; and that it should be made available to all.

May – June, 1993

The Death of Criticism

by Steve Kogan

To read modern literary theory and criticism for any length of time is like going into a linguistic twilight zone, where tangible realities are questioned beyond all limits of reason and sense, turned into their opposites, equated with anything and everything, or made to disappear entirely. As for prose style and specific expressions of thought, the effect is like wandering through an airless world of unnatural growths or listening to a schizophrenic talking uncontrollably to a compulsive presence in his head.

Upon entering this new criticism, we find ourselves in a world of strange verbal creatures where weird phrases continually rise up from the texts, phrases such as "the amorphous cognition of the endocept" (Silvano Arieti), "the absence of the transcendental signified" (Jacques Derrida), "I is nothing other than the instance saying I" (Roland Barthes). There is also, of course, "the still, dark center of the heart of the gynocosmos," in which women "stalk the void and dance the dervish of significance that is born through our parted lips and legs" (Paula Gunn Allen).

Is this writing believable? A "dervish of significance?" A "transcendental signified?" An "instance" that can speak? Derrida, in particular, often seems incapable of writing a single sentence of intelligible prose.

> *Like every history, the history of a culture no doubt presupposes an identifiable heading, a telos toward which the movement, the memory and the promise, the identity—even if it be as different to itself—dreams of gathering itself: by taking the initiative, by going on ahead, in anticipation (anticipatio, anticipare, antecapere). . . I believe that if there is any event today, it is taking place here [in Europe], in this act of memory that consists in betraying a certain order of capital in order to be faithful to the other heading and to the other of the heading.*

For those benighted readers who still value sense and clarity, we have Gerald Graff come from the etheric borderlands to tell them that they "have things exactly backward." According to Graff, what looks like "narcissistic specialization" is in reality on the cutting edge of new frontiers; for what frustrated readers "mistake for specialization are in fact new languages of generalization, languages that have so far resisted popularization but are not intrinsically incapable of it."

Does Graff hear what he's saying? Does he seriously believe that the Euro-babble of Luce Iragary's "topo-(logy) of *jouissance*" and Jacques Derrida's "overabundance of the signifier" might one day enter the mainstream of American thought and idiom? Is it even possible to translate "the amorphous cognition of the endocept" or "the dervish of significance into common modes of thought? Graff argues that current academic discourse looks more "remote from the general goals of society than it actually is, enabling its journalistic detractors to present it as absurdly esoteric," to which one might respond that 1) there are scholars and other writers who feel the same thing, 2) journalists are sometimes right, and 3) if "intradiegetic vignettes," "trans-cliches," and "gender-critical metadiscourses" are not "absurdly esoteric," what absurdities does he reserve this phrase for? If he's interested in "the general goals of society," as he says he is, why doesn't it disturb him that this language is being promoted in graduate education at the very moment when reading and writing levels in schools across the country are in precipitous decline, as witness the remedial writing programs that have been instituted throughout two and four year colleges?

Graff's hedging defense that this overblown language is not "intrinsically incapable" of "popularization" flies in the face of our natural perception, which tells us that it is, in fact, resistant to popular speech and understanding, while such favorite terms as "problematized," "univocal," and "valorized" are used in place of common words and phrases that would express the same meaning but without that air of bureaucracy and dogmatic authority which these terms are intended to convey. What is most disturbing, however, is that the interpretations and conclusions that are drawn from this inflated language are often slipshod and self-contradictory and in actual practice lead to grotesque results.

There *is* a whirling dervish out there, not of meaning, however, but of misrepresentation and intellectual absurdity, in which "theorists" generate contradictions at dizzying rates of speed. If one examines the field of literature, one finds critics proclaiming, for example, that there are no fixed truths, although they themselves talk in absolutes; that earlier criticism projected its own "hegemonic" assumptions onto literature, although they promote overtly politicized research; that traditional criticism did not recognize the prime function of the reader, although their own writing is often turgid, ugly, and self-absorbed; and that Western literature from Homer to Hemingway is narrow and oppressive, while they defend biological and racial definitions of culture and discredited economic views of history, which they claim are open and liberating.

For those who object to the abstruse and self-enclosed world of theoretical studies, there is Paul de Man to put us in our place by proclaiming that "resistance to theory is in fact resistance to reading." And for those who still think in terms of traditional discourse at all, there is Iragary insisting that logic is an oppressive, masculine trait, a linguistic tyranny from which women writers should immediately liberate themselves:

> *Turn everything upside down, inside out, back to front...Insist also upon those blanks in discourse which recall the places of her [woman's] exclusion...Reinscribe them...as divergences, in ellipses and eclipses...that deconstruct the logical grid of the reader-writer, drive him out of his mind. Overthrow syntax...*

There you have it. A battle cry on behalf of confusion, all in the name of women's liberation from the tyrannical rule of sanity.

I could fill a volume with examples taken from "influential" critics who engage in raving pedantry and dogmatic claims, with cult-like followers repeating arcane formulas and interpreting all language and literature in the name of liberation from oppressive "hegemonies" of one kind or another. What seems at times particularly frightening to me are the echoes of the corrosive intellectual scene in Germany in the 1920s, in which, as Robert Musil writes in his essay "Surrounded by Poets and Thinkers":

> *thousands of little groups each peddle their own set notion of life, so that it ought not to surprise us if soon a genuine paranoiac will hardly still be able to resist competing with the amateurs.*

One finds a similar overheated atmosphere surrounding current literary criticism (often hyped as "Theory"), in which paranoia, disguised as "the hermenuetics of suspicion," fills the pages of this material, and "resistance to theory" is seen as giving "aid and comfort to the enemy" (G. Douglas Atkins). If one reads these works carefully, one finds that the "enemy" is common sense, intelligibility in critical prose, a love of Western literature, respect for the text, and objectivity itself, which is considered a main source of oppression. The idea that earlier scholars and teachers might have actually known something is disparaged as "the transmission of ready-made knowledge" through a "master-slave relationship" (Atkins).

Apart from giving "the appearance of solidity to pure wind," as George Orwell would have said, a good deal of current critical writing is therefore driven by destructive impulses (always in the name of freedom) and suffers from shoddy and erroneous ideas, particularly the idea that nothing has its own identity and that language and literature are significant for what they do not say.

According to modern studies, language is arbitrary, indeterminate, and "decentered," having no "reference to a *center*, to a *subject*, to a privileged *reference*, to an origin or to an absolute *archia* [beginning]" (Derrida), not even to an author, depicted in several disparaging ways as the "numinous authority" (Stephen Greenblatt) and the "Author-God" (Barthes). Ever since Nietzsche wrote that God is dead, the task of "Theory," according to Michel Foucault, has been to "locate the space left empty by the author's disappearance, and follow the distribution of gaps and breaches, and watch for the openings that disappearance uncovers." For critics who follow the general premises of this neurotic-sounding plan, reading becomes a confused combination of argumentativeness and anxiety, obtuseness and vigilance, as scholars go about exposing the hidden issues of race, class, and gender and the "hegemonic" preconception of objectivity.

However erroneous the conclusions may be, "Theory" insists that the concept of individual authors and texts is a tyranny based on "the old model" of interpretation, which assumed that writers "were in the business of handing over ready-made or prefabricated meanings" (Fish) to the reader. In the new dispensation, however,

> *We know now that a text is not a line of words releasing a single "theological" meaning (the 'message' of the Author-God) but a multi-dimensional space inwhich a variety of writings, none of them original, blend and clash. (Barthes)*

Note how common words become hyped and overblown: meaning becomes "theological" a writer becomes an "Author-God," and a text "a multi-dimensional space," absolute pronouncements that sound as if they came from the very same "Author-God" which Barthes claims does not exist. His criticism of traditional teaching and scholarship is nothing more than a projection of his own drive toward dogmatic pronouncements.

It is a curious fact that earlier poet-critics such as Eliot, Pound and Frost and scholars such as Bradley, Williamson, and Goddard had superbly individual styles and points of view, whereas recent and supposedly liberated studies parrot the same ideas and the same absurdities, like a weird mantra of ideological cliches:

> *... canon formation as a concept has lost whatever innocence it might ever in reality have possessed.(Joe Weixlmann)*

> *There are no innocent, objective accounts of Melville family history. (Michael Rogin)*

> *...no language is innocent... (Claire J. Kramsch)*

A rhetoric can never be innocent ... (James Berlin)

Once upon a time, history was an innocent word in an innocent world. (John W. Kronik)

Cheerfully surrendering their questioning faculties, critics not only engage in the group-think of mindless repetition but also practice double-think by believing contradictory assertions simultaneously; for example, that there are no unique texts and that marginal voices must be respected for their "Otherness" and that the old hegemony which was "innocent" was also tyrannical.

And everyone is hip. Everyone sees absences. Nothing is whole:

> *"one's own language is never a single language" (Mikhail Bakhtin); "we can only picture things which are not there" (Wolfgang Iser); "... the semantic force of what is not said" (Michael Johnson); "no story is complete without its absences" (Kronik).*

Each statement is seriously flawed, but the last is particularly absurd, since no one can know how many absences it would take to complete a narrative. (Kronik apparently forgot that there is no "closure" in literature.)

Nevertheless, despite the irrationality of the project (or perhaps because of it), critics today repeat ad nauseam that the thing to look for in a text is "what is not said," which removes the burden of reading what it *does* say. Every reader now becomes a "rereader/rewriter" (Johnson), with complete license to "reinscribe" the "blanks" (Irigary) and look for "ideological and figurational shortcomings" among the "so-called masterpieces of literature," in Weixlmann's astonishingly cynical phrase. In other words, critics can attack a work for being restrictive and oppressive because it excludes anything they happen to think is important, i.e., women (or women's "otherness"), oppressed workers, "cultures of color," the lower classes, etc. The critic thus displaces the author and becomes the center of attention in what is sometimes referred to as "reader response theory." Conjuring up an academic Twilight of the Gods, Barthes makes the grandiose pronouncement that "The birth of the reader must be at the cost of the death of the Author."

Since the oppressive "Author-God" is dead and readers have been liberated, they are free to find "gaps and breaches" and proclaim dire warning about the tyranny they have just escaped, such as "Shakespeare's hegemony" over English literature and the absences he did not fill. In the critic's wisdom over the author, "We can understand what Shakespeare did not only if we understand what he didn't do and understand too that what he didn't do was worth doing" (Gary Taylor). Shakespeare, you see, did not dramatize Elizabethan "unemployment and economic exploitation, inflation and dislocation," to which one might add that he did not write about Elizabethan shipbuilding either, or the development of Dutch landscape painting and the state of England's public health, all of which would have been "worth doing."

The consequences of Theory, in true Kafkaesque fashion, are both absurd and controlling, for instead of beginning with a predisposition to study literature on its own terms, critics believe that it has no separate reality and no boundaries of its own, and constantly look for faults according to their own "set notion of life." Weixlmann, for example, provides a checklist of ideological flaws, including sexism in Chaucer and Milton, Twain's "apparent (if unintended) racism, Hemingway's homophobia, and the like." Taylor actually subjects Shakespeare's plays to a democratic voting list and finds that "Like women, the lower and middle classes are systematically underrepresented" in his works. It is as though art were a matter of quotas rather than imaginative power—as though Juliet, Gertrude, Ophelia, Rosalind, Viola, Kate, Miranda, Cordelia, Mistress Quickly, Desdemona, Lady Macbeth, and Cleopatra (for openers) meant nothing; and as though Shakespeare should have had an imagination that agreed with Taylor's.

In contrast to this radical devaluation of Shakespeare's humanity, my students are surprised to discover that mental illness, homelessness, and profound social injustice, which they think of as contemporary problems, are right there in Shakespeare's *King Lear*, powerfully and compassionately expressed. What would Taylor want me to tell them? That they were seduced by "Shakespeare's hegemony" into a state of false consciousness?

To understand the new learning, one has to remember that old values have been reversed, so that objectivity is now seen as a ploy to maintain a "logocentric perspective" that "privileges presence" (Danny Anderson), whereas that hunt for absences frees us from repressive thinking and opens us to the *"jouissance"* of intellectual play. For Atkins, who sounds as if he's selling trampolines, "theory can be fun."

There is a kind of comic value to Derrida's being "faithful to the other heading and to the other of that heading," but Atkins means *serious* fun, the kind that comes from turning things upside down and back to front . In the hands of modern critics, "Theory can *become* literature." Even more delightful, it can simply replace it. Ezra Pound, for example, foolishly thought that "literature gives us eyes to see with," whereas we now know that "it is actually theory that does so." Traditional literature, in other words, is based on ideologies that have huge blind spots, whereas dogmatic and unreadable theory is really literature and permits us to see the world as it is. Thanks to Atkins we can now see that Pound (that "notorious Hellene") didn't champion Old English, medieval Italian,

Provencal, modern French, and Chinese poetry, along with Greek, even though he did.

Once politicized theory replaces literature, anything can be said about an author or a text, no matter how erroneous. Stephen Greenblatt, for example, asserts that Shakespeare's plays are "a fetish of Western civilization," an instrument of social control that "Caliban curiously anticipates" in *The Tempest*, because he recognizes the power of Prospero's magic books. By the same reasoning, of course, Faustus' cry for redemption at the end of Marlowe's tragedy—"I'll burn my books"—could be taken as a foreshadowing of the Nazi bookburnings in the 1930s.

Beyond all evidence, judicious analogy, and poetic insight, Shakespeare must be depicted as the great "fetish" of Western literature, the arch-hegemonist who blinds us by his "privileged presence" from seeing repressed humanity. Greenblatt's idea that Prospero is a colonialist who believes in "the dream of power" and that Caliban is a Third-World victim has by now achieved the status of dogma. This interpretation, however, is as false to the text as his other pronouncements on the play. In *Shakespearean Negotiations*, for example, he characterizes Prospero as a power-hungry narcissist, even though Prospero 1) uses his magic powers for the purpose of arousing the conscience of his enemies and reconciling everyone, 2) gives up this power just before the reconciliations are completed, 3) says that when he returns as the rightful duke of Milan, "Every third thought shall be my grave," 4) acts throughout the play in keeping with the motive that he gave Miranda when he created the tempest, "I have done nothing but in care of thee,/ Of thee my dear one, thee, my daughter," and 5) frees Caliban at the end, who recognizes his folly in having blindly accepted the drunken Stephano and Trinculo as his liberators.

How could someone possibly acknowledge these facts, however, if he believes that pardoning people, as Prospero pardons his enemies, is actually "a demonstration of supreme force"? Greenblatt not only turns pardoning into coercion but also transforms evil into good, in which he idealizes Antonio as a kind of rebel sibling for having "escaped subordination to his older brother Prospero." This interpretation of the play makes sense, however, only if one believes that rulers are inherently wicked, since Antonio betrays his brother's trust in him, usurps his power, and attempts to kill him and his three year old daughter Miranda by casting them out to sea without sails or provisions in the dead of night. Moreover, he extends his malice to people who are trying to aid him when he curses and slanders the crew during the storm, and he plots to kill the compassionate counselor Gonzalo and take over the island later in the play.

Greenblatt is not alone in these distortions. Peter Hulme, for example, thinks that Caliban may not have tried to rape Miranda, as Prospero says he did, since Prospero could have taken any attempt at courtship as a violation of his daughter. The fact that Caliban agrees with him and reveals his true character when he replies "O ho, O ho! would't had been done!" is simply ignored, no doubt because Miranda is the daughter of a ruler and therefore unfit to be believed as a victim of attempted rape.

The new learning does not make judgments on texts but invades them; and the ideologue's ability to gloss over wickedness in the name of freedom from oppression is aptly suggested in these perverse interpretations of the play.

Under the new critical world order, discussions of great critics are often as invasive and dismissive as interpretations of great literature. Just as Atkins makes an ignorant accusation against Pound and Graff criticizes traditional scholarship for not putting "knowledge into larger contexts," Taylor insinuatingly disparages the eminent nineteenth-century Shakespearean critic A.C. Bradley by attacking his methodical style. In fact, nothing seems to please him, not even unmethodical, exciting criticism, such as the insights of Kean, Keats, and Coleridge, whose dazzling phrases "attach themselves like lint to our memories." Bradley, on the other hand, is faulted for turning Shakespeare studies into "a routine." As the master over his student slaves (Prospero and Caliban all over again), "He imposes a relentless clarity on his material; he defines by a steady aggregation of phrases, of examples, of arguments. Meaning piles up." Yes, that is Taylor's accusation: Bradley argues from reason and evidence and commits the cardinal sin of providing significant insights into Shakespeare. Note that reason and meaning for Taylor are completely negative. Bradley's clarity is "relentless," as though he should have been mercifully vague from time to time (and perhaps thrown in a few "transcendental signifieds" and "dervishes of significance.") As for meaning, Keats and Coleridge only offered lint, whereas in Bradley's lectures, "Meaning piles up," like garbage or boxes in a factory. One might ask what Taylor thinks he's doing if not piling up meanings of his own, but the image suits his purpose of depicting 19th-century Shakespeare studies as an extension of English industrialism and Bradley as its arch scholar-capitalist.

The truth, as is often the case in modern Theory and politicized interpretation, is precisely the opposite. Bradley was something of a radical. In his introduction to the published lectures, he states that he will not consider Shakespeare's place in English literature, discuss his life or the development of his art, examine source materials and textual history, or deal with technical questions of poetry, all of which exemplify the major areas of Victorian Shakespeare scholarship.

Taylor cannot accept the existence of a text even when it stares him in the face:

What happened when Shakespeare finished King Lear? Accord-

> *ing to traditional story [standard Shakespeare scholarship], he never revised his work, and so after he had written the last page of* King Lear *he closed the book—and that was that. But fewer and fewer critics believe in closure. Shakespeare may at some point have closed the book; but he could reopen it again whenever he wanted. There is no Last Judgment anymore. You can appeal yourconviction; you can remarry your ex-wife. Even death is no longer final; we resuscitate the dead, we put them on life-support systems, we distinguish between heart death and brain death,*

and on and on. What outrageous nonsense! It is really true that for all the advances in modern medicine "death is no longer final"? Does it make any sense to say that a work is never complete, since the creator can always revise it, even though he doesn't?

Concerning this issue of indeterminacy, Foucalt has long, complicated discussions on the authoritativeness of texts, in which he sometimes sounds completely perverse:

> *When undertaking the publication of Nietzsche's works, for example, where should one stop? Surely everything must be published, but what is "everything"? Everything that Nietzsche himself published, certainly. And what about the rough drafts for his works? Obviously. . . What if, within a workbook filled with aphorisms, one finds a reference, the notation of a meeting, or of an address, or a laundry list: is it a work, or not? Why not? And so on, ad infinitum. How can one define a work amid the millions of traces left by someone after his death?*

How, indeed? Let's suppose that someone turned up the complete shopping lists of Herman Melville and published them with scholarly annotations and suggested references to his works. Would anyone in his right mind have trouble understanding that they have a separate reality in form, motive, and significance from *Moby-Dick?*

Foucault's argument on definition leads to the kind of sophomoric politicized thinking that one finds, among other places, in the new *Columbia History of the American Novel*, in which the title of the first chapter ("The Early American Novel") is deconstructed to the point where it no longer means anything. At the outset, the author declares that,

> *in fact, there is no such thing as the "early American novel." To prove my point, I carefully examine each term in the phrase to show that its intended meaning necessarily evaporates under critical scrutiny.*

By the end of the chapter, we come to the startling revelation that the American novel "did not truly become 'American' until the politically disenfranchised and culturally dispossessed of American society were finally heard in the pages of our literature." As a result of new works and revised anthologies, we may therefore have to accept the possibility that the early American novel did not "truly" begin until the 1960s.

These are some of the results of "demystifiying" literature, in which Western culture is revised according to current radical beliefs and books are rewritten to the point where they no longer resemble themselves. Better perhaps if they had not been written at all. This is in fact the conclusion to which the narrator arrives in Malcolm Bradbury's recent novel *Doctor Criminale* after having studied during the 1980s at the University of Sussex, where he learned to dehegemonize, decanonize, and dephallicize history and literature. Before graduating, he tells his neo-Marxist tutor that all he wants to do now is spend the rest of his life "sitting drinking beer in Bavaria," since "He had proved to me conclusively that all literature was written by the wrong people, of the wrong class, race and gender, for entirely the wrong reasons."

If traditional teaching should happen to improve reading skills and foster a love of great literature, we have Annette Kolodny telling us that "We read well, and with pleasure, what we already know how to read." According to her, the classics fit into an elitist ideology, so that one is automatically predisposed to favor them and read them well. In other words, nothing is learned, no one grows, and there is really nothing to learn. If *War and Peace* "is a more valued text than *Peanuts*," writes Lori Hope Lefkowitz, it is not because of its merits but "because powerful communities of readers have agreed to prefer epic novels to comic strips." In this conspiracy theory by the new theorists of literature, humanist values were laid down in some capitalist backroom, where, to this day, "powerful communities of readers" enforce the idea that *Les Miserables* and *The Magic Mountain* have more to say than *Little Lulu* or *Donald Duck*.

In the bizarre atmosphere of modern literary-pedagogical ideas, everything one might normally think of as worthwhile in education has become suspect and vilified. This attack is not confined to the higher reaches of "Theory," but takes place at the workaday level as well. In a publication of the National Council of Teachers of English, for example, *Teaching English in the Two-Year College*, (December, 1992), Lynda Haas refers to the teaching of English skills as "Imperial Literacy," a system of oppression in which students "become the instruments of language of those in power." According to Haas, traditional English teaching is "characterized by a strict emphasis on rules," a method that trains students to be "future blue collar workers," proletarian wage slaves who will "docilely accept rules handed down from above" and fit into "hegemonic society." (As if functionally illiterate workers would be more independent.) It's strange to think that teachers could be against teaching the very skills that they possess, yet Haas insists that this is an "imperialistic education," derived from "the current, ruling power," namely, "those who are white, male," and "propertied." As for teachers who are more modern and "progresssive," they use "process" teaching (which is an instrument of "Colonial Literacy") to arrive at the same goal of perpetuating "a hierarchical class system."

In this pedagogy of paranoia, the good is particularly bad. For Haas, the liberal emphasis on the student's own thinking process is a subterfuge to inculcate a "rational heuristics," a belief in "the ability of cognitive methods to solve problems." This wicked goal of rational problem solving does not teach students to question "how the oppressive features of schooling were created in the first place by political, economic, and social conditions of the dominant culture." You would think that she was talking about indoctrination sessions in Nazi Germany, but no. Haas is talking about American education, an institution so lax that many of my Caribbean, South American, and West-African students tell me of being depressed by what they feel is a general lack of respect for education in America compared to what they experienced in their English, Spanish, and French-model schools back home.

What then are we left with under the regime envisioned by Haas and her ilk? Independence without skills, cultural relativism without impartiality, and intellectual play without pleasure or delight. Look through the pages of Derrida, Rogin, Greenblatt, Taylor, and other influential critics and ask yourself if they actually care about literature, as earlier scholars and writers demonstrably did, such as Bradley, Lucas, Wedgwood, Nicolson, Eliot, Frost, and Pound. They have nothing to say about the artistic imagination, their judgments of texts are invariably shallow and skewed, and there is always a sour note in their politicized interpretations, an unpleasant carping that makes me wonder why they bother with it in the first place if it is such a negative experience. My own view is that negativity is precisely the driving force behind their work and that a major source of their intellectual pleasure is to attack the culture in which the works were created; as Ronald Takaki, for example, considers Captain Ahab "the embodiment" of nineteenth-century America's "demonic 'iron cage,'" and as Jonathan Arac, agreeing with Foucault, concludes that Dickens and Twain supported "the growth of the repressive state apparatus." At the beginning of the same article, Arac states that "The debates over Proletarian Culture and Socialist Realism in the Soviet Union counted heavily for the mediation and production of literature throughout the western world." The murder of Russian writers such as Nikolai Gumilev, Isaac Babel, and Osip Mandelstam means nothing to him because he is working from a formula: Dickens and Twain evil/Stalin good.

Projecting their destructive ideologies onto Western literature and history, radical critics bear out the truth of Nietzsche's aphorism that "He who would fight monsters should be careful lest he become a monster himself." In this respect, it is interesting to note that for all their proclaimed indebtedness to Nietzsche, critics such as Derrida and Foucault do not seem to have learned some obvious lessons from the author of *The Genealogy of Morals, Ecce Homo*, and *Beyond Good and Evil*, such as Nietzsche's intense disgust with theorists and systematizers, his radical skepticism and insights into the psychology of dogmatists, and the clarity, freshness and intimacy of his style.

Modern literary studies have in far less common with Nietzsche than with the deadly Marxist sophistries that Nadezda Mandelstam describes in *Hope Against Hope* and *Hope Abandoned*, together making up one of the greatest intellectual autobiographies of the 20th century, which feminists, incidentally, seem to know nothing about.

Then again there is so much that radical critics seem to know nothing about. I would not feel as strongly as I do about such gross ignorance, however, were it were not linked to the politicizing of literary studies, whose distortions, intellectual absurdities, and outright falsehoods deserve to be exposed for the shams they are.

May – June, 1993

WAR STORIES

Hand To Hand Combat

BODIES OF EVIDENCE
by Scott Kerr

As campus protests go, the SASH bake sale here last April was almost surrealistically sedate. Outside a lecture hall in the prestigious, avant-garde Center for Twentieth Century Studies at the University of Wisconsin-Milwaukee, a group calling itself Students Against Sexual Harassment set about selling cookies, muffins and day-glow bumper stickers which read, "Distinguished Professors do it Pedagogically."

The message was aimed at Jane Gallop, UWM distinguished Professor of English and Comparative Literature, who had organized the national conference then in progress: Pedagogy: The Question of the Personal. A feminist theoretician renowned and controversial both nationally and at UWM, Gallop has been under investigation by UWM's affirmative action office on two complaints by female graduate students that the professor made unwanted sexual overtures. Thus the bumper stickers and the bake sale.

"A conference on pedagogy needs to address this issue," said bake sale organizer Eileen Schell. Sexual harassment issues have been "traditionally silenced at UWM," Schell said. Indeed, the school has been beset in the past three years by increasing complaints. Schell and other English Department students decided to make public the mounting controversy within the department over the implications of the allegations against Gallop.

Ironically, student and faculty sources believe that Gallop's conference was intended to respond to well-publicized sexual harassment controversies on campus involving two male instructors. In one case, Art Professor Stephen Samerjan was suspended after attempting to deflect allegations he had a sexual relationship with one female grad student by citing a letter from another in which she insisted that her affair with him had been a "positive" experience. And in an incident with a somewhat comic subtext, Ceramics Professor Gary Schlappal had been recently fired after not contesting charges that a kiln overheated and suffered damage while he was engaged in sex with a female student.

In any case, critics of the Pedagogy Conference both at the bake sale and elsewhere claimed that many of the lectures it featured could be seen as sanctioning "eroticization" of the classroom to the point of creating a "hostile environment." Lecture titles included: "I Walk the Line; The Body of the Graduate Student TA [Teaching Assistant] in the University"; "Discipline, Spectacle, and Melancholia in and around the Gay Studies Classroom"; and "On Waking Up One Morning and Discovering We Are Them: Power and Privilege on the Margins."

But the real drama had to do with Jane Gallop. Dana Beckelman, a SASH member, has accused Gallop of harassment. A soft-spoken, articulate Texan and matter-of-fact lesbian who was seeking a Ph.D. in Rhetoric at the time of the controversy, Beckelman maintains that Gallop created a "hostile work environment" with flirtatious comments and physical advances. When Beckelman rejected the overtures, she claims Gallop retaliated by making her graduate student work increasingly odious, ultimately forcing her to change majors from English to Rhetoric. Gallop's attorney, Walter Kelly, emphatically denies that Jane Gallop created a hostile working environment for Dana Beckelman or anyone else.

Beckelman concedes she originally admired Gallop as "a famous theorist," and had wanted a mentor figure. But through 1990 and early 1991, the professor's remarks and flirtations in class and at social occasions puzzled her, Beckelman said, so she asked Gallop how it was all intended.

"She said it was a radical pedagogical strategy. She wanted to seduce her students to learn. And so I thought I was engaging in the latest hip and trendy, cutting-edge theoretical act by flirting..." Gallop, who is married to another UWM professor, will not discuss the allegations and refers all questions to her attorney.

Even a brief survey of Gallop's work makes clear why she is viewed as a time bomb on a campus which prohibits teacher-student sex. In her 1988 book, *Thinking Through the Body* (Columbia University Press), Gallop has a chapter titled "The Student Body" where she describes how while she herself was a grad student she had "a series of affairs with thirty-six year-old men (at the time I was in my mid-twenties) ... all unavailable men, some married, some otherwise unavailable—a certain Oedipal insistence which this paper interprets."

In the same book, Gallop uses the Marquis de Sade's "Philosophy of the Bedroom" to argue: "Pederasty is undoubtedly a useful paradigm for Classic European pedagogy. A greater man penetrates a lesser man with his knowledge. The student is empty, a receptacle for the phallus; the teacher is the phallic fullness of knowledge."

But Beckelman contends her professor's strategy "crossed from a theoretical act to a physical act" at an event titled, "Flaunting It: The First National Graduate Student Conference on Lesbian and Gay Studies," hosted by UWM in April, 1991.

"She stood up and said, 'I'm excited about this conference because it is about graduate students' sexual preferences, and my sexual preference is graduate students.' That night, a group of us went out and she came on to me..." Beckelman said Gallop kissed her and touched her.

While not commenting on Beckelman's harassment charges, Gallop has denied making the statement attributed to her. However, others who attended the conference recall it too. "People chuckled," said one UWM staffer who was there.

The following day, Beckelman delivered a paper to the conference which she considered a strong rejection of the professor's behavior: "I don't have a problem fucking Jane Gallop as long as she practices safe sex. After all, she is merely another woman. But I do have a problem fucking my dissertation adviser." Beckelman said she had hoped the message would get through, and that the problem would be handled "in the family." At issue, in Beckelman's view, was not sex, but the power imbalance between teacher and student. Not until complaining to the school's affirmative action office, Beckelman said, did she become unaware of the university rule which outlaws faculty-student sex,

"The bottom line was even if I had tried to seduce her and she had done it, she would have been in the wrong," Beckelman said. But Beckelman maintains Gallop's flirtations continued and "she told me sexual fantasies...even after I thought I had publicly handled it." Beckelman said she continued her rejection and this was where the problems began.

"Previously, my work had been acceptable. Suddenly my work was unacceptable." Beckelman ended up leaving the program. To bolster her contention that the professor's pedagogy strategy came off as more than theoretical, Beckelman points out that the introduction to Gallop's latest book, *Around l98l* (Routledge, 1992), reads as follows: "To my students— the bright, hot, hip (young) women who fire my thoughts, my loins, my prose. I write this to move, to please, to shake you."

Walter Kelly, Gallop's attorney, has criticized Beckelman for not observing by "the confidentiality of the investigatory process." Kelly argues that Beckelman's going public was an attempt to harm Gallop's reputation. Beckelman insists otherwise.

"I am not trying to get her. I'm trying to point out her behavior to the university, and to have it examine whether or not it condones that behavior and to judge whether it is right or wrong."

There is no word as to how long UWM investigators will take before releasing the findings on the allegations against Gallop. Attorney Kelly indicates there remain numerous "factual errors" in the preliminary findings. For Beckelman's part, while frustrated by the delay, she said she is relieved to be done with school.

"Graduate school is strange enough in terms of the paranoias and anxieties it creates in people about achievement. And then you have this added factor. Here you are, trying to prove yourself as an intellectual and someone says, 'I'm not interested in your intellect, I'm interested in your body.' "

May – June, 1993

BLACKS AND JEWS AND ALL THE NEWS by Alyson Todd

As Nannerl Keohane leaves the presidency of Wellesley College to assume that same position at Duke University, her legacy is comprised of several controversies left ticking at the College like time bombs. Many of them center around Professor of Africana Studies Tony Martin, whom Keohane and the rest of the Wellesley administration have coddled for several years now.

Martin has presented problems on a personal as well as a political level. On the night of October 30, 1991, he was found walking unescorted through a student dormitory. In accordance with college policy which states that all non-Wellesley students must be escorted when walking through a dorm, student resident Michelle Plantec upon seeing Martin alone said, "Excuse me, sir, who are you with?" Professor Martin ignored her. Ms. Plantec repeated the question, "Excuse me, who are you with?" At this point, according to Ms. Plantec and 15 witnesses who later signed letters testifying to what they had seen, Professor Martin responded explosively. He called her a "white fucking bitch," "a racist," and "a bigot," among other things. The young woman fell down as a result of his onslaught and Martin bent over to continue to rage at her. Professor Martin became so violent, in fact, that the Head of House for the dormitory called the campus police.

After the campus police left, Professor Martin returned to the meeting he had been attending in the living room of the dormitory. He announced to the group of students and faculty attending the meeting that Ms. Plantec stopped him while he was on his way to the bathroom only because he is black. Ms. Plantec meanwhile was left stunned by Martin's outburst. She said later on, "I don't know how to express how violent his reaction was...I was left scared and shaking." Some witnesses reported that at the time of the incident they were afraid that Martin was going to strike Ms. Plantec.

Molly Campbell, Dean of Students, was informed of Professor Martin's behavior later that night. She referred Plantec to Owen Bookman, who serves as the assistant to President Nannerl Keohane and the Affirmative Action Officer. Ms. Bookman suggested to Plantec that she meet with Martin to discuss the "misunderstanding." Ms. Plantec agreed to meet with him, but no further action was taken by the administration, either to arrange the meeting or to investigate the incident. "I got consolation calls from Dean Marshall, Dean Campbell and Nannerl Keohane," says Plantec, "basically very superficial gestures."

Frustrated with the administration, Plantec called her father and asked for help. He responded by writing a letter to Professor Martin denying that his daughter was a racist and saying that his behavior in the dorm had been inappropriate. He closed the letter by telling Martin that he could not use the fact that he was black as a shield to hide behind. He requested a public apology to his daughter.

Not only did Martin refuse to apologize (he said, "I have never apologized to a racist and I have no intentions at this point in my life of apologizing to someone who perpetrated a racist attack on me"), but he read Mr. Plantec's letter at a Black Student Association meeting. He defended his action by claiming that he felt an obligation to "make black people on this campus aware of what was happening." According to Ms. Plantec, Professor Martin also told his students that she was "a racist" who was "receiving psychiatric care" and being "paid off by the college."

At this point, it was apparent to Michelle Plantec that the administration was not only refusing to support her but also leaking details from her medical file to Martin. In the weeks ahead, she was treated as a confirmed racist by the black community at Wellesley. Even some women she believed to be her friends denounced her as a bigot. Under immense stress, she suffered a nervous breakdown and left Wellesley. Her family has brought legal action against the college.

More shocking than the behavior of Tony Martin in this matter are the actions taken by the Wellesley College administration to create a cover-up. All student witnesses were informed in strong terms that they were to remain silent. All members of the resident staff and the Head of Work Council were forbidden to speak of the incident.

For eighteen months, while Michelle Plantec was being stigmatized, the code of silence stood unbroken. If you ventured to ask anyone who was involved in the incident as a witness or as a member of student government about what happened, you were met with a denial that the incident even transpired.

The editors of the two major Wellesley College publications received phone calls from a member of the administration. These student journalists were informed by an administration that they were not to publish anything about the "Tony Martin incident" in their newspapers. One student journalist who wishes to remain anonymous reports that she was threatened by the administration. She was told that if she wrote anything about Martin, she would not receive her recommendations for graduate school. It was not until May of this year that the *Galenstone* finally published an interview with Michelle Plantec which was conducted over a year ago, in March of 1992. It took a year and a half for the story to break.

Perhaps the Wellesley administration would have been more successful in suppressing the Michelle Plantec story if Tony Martin had not gotten embroiled in other controversies. But he continued to make himself the center of attention—an embarrassment to most but a cause to some.

The first issue concerned his decision to use the Nation of Islam's *The Secret Relationship Between Blacks and Jews* in one of his classes, a book that is overtly anti-Semetic. Five Jewish students from the campus organization Hillel went to him after a class session to ask him why he had assigned such an offensive work. Martin rudely dismissed them. Later he made it clear that he felt they were part of a conspiracy by Jews on campus to "get" him.

In the letters that were printed in the *Wellesley News* about Martin and *The Secret Relationship* some of those who spoke out were in fact Jews, notably the eminent classics scholar Mary Lefkowitz. But Martin was also attacked by black faculty members like Economist Andrew Marcellus. (Ultimately, Africana Studies Chair Sedgeway Cudgoe would imply, in an interview on "Nightline," that Martin was an anti-Semite.) Yet a number of black students gathered together in an organization called Ethos had adopted Martin as a mentor and they accused all who spoke out against him of being "racist." Martin himself said that blacks who disagreed with him were "handkerchief heads."

Martin devoted time to writing an angry manifesto. He would claim later on that the *Wellesley News* wanted to censor his opinions, but in fact the student paper was willing to print what Martin had to say with the proviso that campus figures he attacked in his screed be given a chance to respond to the ad hominem arguments. Martin decided instead to self-publish his "self defense," a pamphlet with the catchy title *Blacks and Jews and the Wellesley News.*

In this pamphlet, Martin did not simply claim that he had assigned *The Secret Relationship Between the Blacks and the Jews* as collateral reading, one of many views, although even his supporters pointed out that this would have been the "smart" thing to do. Instead he embraced the entire anti-Semetic thesis of the work and elaborated on its major points, notably that Jews not only controlled the African slave trade but also organized "the international prostitution of (mainly) Jewish women, by Jewish entrepreneurs in the nineteenth and early twentieth centuries," and participated in "the extermination of the Native Americans."

Martin reserved special venom for Mary Lefkowitz, whose sins included not only speaking out on his choice of books at Wellesley, but having given a less than enthusiastic review of Martin Bernal's *Black Athena*, which has become central to Martin and other Afrocentrist conspiracy theorists. He also asserted in his pamphlet that the Jewish conspiracy against blacks can be documented by studying "the conservative Jewish owned The New Republic" and "Ted Koppel and the other

Jews on ABC's Nightline program."

The Wellesley community is largely disgusted by Martin's ravings and by the fact that he has caused such bitter divisions at the college. Students and staff also have trouble understanding why President Nan Keohane has not done something about Professor Martin's violent behavior and anti-Semitic rhetoric and put a stop to his campus terrorism. That she has chosen to look the other way while still issuing platitudes about diversity is taken by many to be proof of the hypocrisy at the heart of multiculturalism and by all to be an act of irresponsibility on her part. As one Wellesley dorm master said, "The fish rots from the head down."

May – June, 1993

THE SMELL OF NAPALM IN THE MORNING by Bill Cerveny

Spring has come to the college campuses of America, bringing with it final exams, graduation parties, and long afternoons in the sun. This year, however, the usual fragrances wafting out of the groves of academe have been replaced by the smell of burning books. As the cultural warfare within the university intensifies, debate has been replaced by confrontation. In a series of disturbing scenes reminiscent of the literary bonfires that lit up Germany a generation ago, opponents of free speech have tried to eradicate dissent by taking a match to what they find objectionable.

It is ironic that the book burners should be active at Dartmouth College since it was here, in 1953, that President Dwight Eisenhower made a speech decrying the evils of McCarthyism and the suppression of free print as well as free speech.. In front of the graduating senior class, he took the podium saying "Don't join the book burners. Don't think you're going to conceal faults by concealing evidence that they ever existed."

Eisenhower's lecture seemed at the time to have canonized free speech at Dartmouth. But today that canon, like others, has been called into question. Naturally, the controversy in Hanover centers around Dartmouth's conservative student newspaper, *The Dartmouth Review*. Embroiled in fiery debates with campus leftists since its inception in 1980, *The Review* has, at one time or another, successfully chafed every liberal organization at the college. It is no surprise, therefore, that members of Dartmouth's Afro-American Society recently became upset over an article titled "Good Times."

The focus of the article was on Malik Hassan-Mustafa Franklin, a black student who was arrested in February for assaulting fellow student Tracy Gainor at an Afro-American Society meeting. Franklin became upset with Gainor when he saw that she was wearing one of his black fraternity's T-shirts, a right traditionally reserved for fraternity members. The argument ended with the girl slapping Franklin. He responded with a closed-fisted punch to her face. Gainor's head smashed against the wall behind her and she crumpled to the ground unconscious.

In covering the episode, *The Review* noted that since Franklin's arrest he had been accepted into the E.E. Just Program, supposedly a competitive scholarship program designed to draw more black students into science-based careers. Because of this, *The Review* questioned the program's prestige, sarcastically saying that "Mr. Franklin's recent arrest adds much to the diversity of this pool of scholars."

When the article appeared, Dartmouth's militant black population went up in arms. They seeded the campus with posters that called *The Review* a "racist organization which has no other goal than slander." The letter was signed by "The Black Freshman Forum," an *ad hoc* organization consisting of members of the Afro-American Society. The black students drew their lines in the sand, saying that they would not tolerate *The Review's* "bigotry" any longer.

On April 9, the publishers of *The Review* went through their weekly ritual of dropping their latest issue at the threshold of every student's dorm room. As they did, four members of the Black Freshman Forum trailed behind them, stealing every issue that was laid out. Seeing what was happening, *The Review* confronted the black students, who refused to leave the issues of the paper alone. The campus police were called, but they simply stood by and watched as the black students continued to steal copies of the *The Review*.

The following week, *The Review* staff again tried to distribute their magazines and the same thing happened. In a battle of wills, *The Review* reprinted their issues three days later. They were again stolen and destroyed by the black students. Erica Greenwood, a white female student, approached Amiri Barksdale, incoming President of the Afro-American Society and spokesperson for The Black Freshman Forum, as he was taking her copy of *The Review*. Barksdale refused to give the paper back and shoved Greenwood out of his way, calling her a "white bimbo" and a "fucking whore."

Amiri Barksdale denies that the Black Freshman Forum's actions are a violation of *The Review's* First Amendment Rights. He feels that "this isn't an issue about freedom of speech, because in the Constitution's application here at Dartmouth...it's not censorship. Censorship would entail us stopping them from printing or distributing..." Barksdale goes on to say that nowhere in the Constitution does it mention someone's right to read something like *The Review*. "People seem to believe the Constitution says that," he says incredulously.

"With Dartmouth's long history as a free speech proponent," says *Review* editor Orron Strause, "this would be a perfect time for the college to take a strong stance, but they haven't lifted a finger to do anything about this situation." Dartmouth's administration refused to take any disciplinary action against members of The Black Freshman Forum beyond a verbal reprimand. In a unique take on freedom of the press, the college has said that it views *The Review* in the same way that it does "unsolicited restaurant menus, free samples of soap and other 'litter' found in dormitory halls." It chooses to view *The Review* as junk mail because it has never agreed with the paper's contents. Strause is not alone in believing that if publications by a black group were being stolen and destroyed, school administrators would have quite a different attitude.

Yet students agree that this incident has had a perverse educational value. The attack by black radicals on free speech so galvanized student concern at the college (the New Hampshire ACLU even took a stand against the Black Freshman Forum) that political pressure has forced Amiri Barksdale to resign as the President-elect of the Afro-American Society. As one student said, "The book burners got burned themselves on this one."

The Lionhearted, Penn State's conservative paper, was not as fortunate as *The Dartmouth Review*. Engaged in a year long feud with campus feminists, *The Lionhearted* has published a number of articles that criticize Penn State's Women's Studies Department and what they see as its persistent "male bashing." Apparently believing that the sword is mightier than the pen, the women and their supporters have fought back. In mid-April, Mike De Thomas and Matt Snavely, sales managers for the paper, received a call. The voice was male and he said, "We've had it, we're going to deal with you directly and we're going to kill you."

Then, in late April 6,000 issues of *The Lionhearted*, along with hundreds of other conservative publications, were stolen from their distribution bins. No one claimed responsibility for the theft. Later that evening, Ben Novak, faculty adviser to *The Lionhearted* and a university trustee, was working late in his office. He heard something on his front lawn and looked out to witness a scene from a time warp connecting his campus to 1933 Berlin. In front of his office was a blazing bonfire. Novak and his partner ran out to douse the flames. There they found the stolen papers and magazines, now a smouldering pile of ash.

The *Centre Daily Times*, a local newspaper in State College, Pennsylvania, was so horrified by the incident that it reprinted 6,000 issues of the *Lionhearted* free of charge. *Times* publisher Jim Moss asserted that "agreement with the content of *The Lionhearted* is not the issue in making this offer, freedom of speech is."

These magazines were to be handed out the following weekend at a football scrimmage staged for school alumni. When the alumni arrived, however, they were greeted by a group of women protesting *The Lionhearted's* "hate propaganda." The women chanted mantras about misogyny and intolerance and carried signs that called for Ben Novak's resignation from the Board of Trustees.

Donna M. Hughes, a lecturer in the Women's Studies Program, read a statement from the "Womyn" of Penn State denouncing *The Lionhearted* and saying that feminists had stolen the issues in an act of protest and self defense. "The issue is NOT free speech," Hughes continued, "it is hate speech," and this justified the women in taking the newspapers.

Many of Penn State's alumni were so put off by these protesters that they covertly slipped substantial contributions to the editor of *The Lionhearted*. Though the women involved in the magazine theft have openly confessed their guilt, no action has been taken by the university or the local police. The death threats against De Thomas and Snavely have not received more than a cursory investigation.

The University of Pennsylvania has been making headlines because of the appointment of its President Sheldon Hackney to head the National Endowment of the Humanities and because of the administration's pusillanimous handling of the racial harassment trial of Eden Jacobowitz, which seemed to call Hackney's qualifications into question.

The story of Jacobowitz, a university freshman, is by now well known. He was studying in his dorm room after midnight and five members of Delta Sigma Theta, an all black sorority, were singing and chanting underneath his window. Jacobowitz's patience was exhausted and he yelled "Shut up, you water buffalo!". He told the girls that if they wanted a party they should go to the local zoo. For this, Jacobowitz was dragged before the school's Judicial Inquiry Office and charged with racial harassment. He was told that it didn't matter how he had *intended* his comments. He was threatened with possible expulsion.

Ultimately, the five women who had accused Jacobowitz agreed not to press their complaint and he, in turn, agreed not to sue the University for suppression of free speech. But at the same time that this matter was slouching toward resolution, another one involving weighty free speech issues continued to simmer at Penn.

The dispute focused on Greg Pavlik, one of the few conservative student columnists writing for the *Daily Pennsylvanian*. Pavlik has written a number of controversial columns in which he has criticized the University's affirmative action policies. He has also taken on the school's Judicial Inquiry Office and what he sees as their preferential treatment of black students. In one of his recent columns, Pavlik quoted another journalist as saying that "in U.S. history, there were 4,743 lynchings, 3,446 of them of blacks. Ironically, more than 3,500 whites are now shot, stabbed, or otherwise 'lynched' by black criminals every year." This pulled the pin on a sensitivity grenade.

In early March, Pavlik received a call from Catherine Schifter, an officer in the U. Penn Judicial Inquiry Office. Schifter told him that 34 charges of racial harassment had been filed against him. These accusations stemmed solely from what he had written in his biweekly column. Schifter went on to tell Pavlik that he could settle this disagreement if he would agree to a faculty monitored "discussion" between him and the 34 complainants. Not wanting to be a designated whipping-boy, Pavlik turned down Schifter's offer.

Because of a preexisting agreement that prohibits the university from prosecuting any student for views expressed in *The Daily Pennsylvanian*, the Judicial Inquiry Office could not continue to pursue the case. Alan Kors, a Professor of History at Penn and a champion of student First Amendment rights, commented about the case: "The fact that Greg Pavlik would receive such a phone call [from the J.I.O.] is chilling of free speech. It says something about the climate [of the university]." As it worked out, however, this was a chill that merely preceded the winter storm.

Shortly after Pavlik's name was cleared, *The Daily Pennsylvanian* received a letter that was signed by 202 of Penn's black students. Angry with the newspaper's ongoing "insensitivity" toward racial issues, they said, "We have grown up in your social system, read your English, and learned your history. Have any of you ever experienced our many cultures?" They added that they had given *The Daily Pennsylvanian* the "benefit of the doubt," but could not put up with the continued publication of Pavlik's column.

Coincidental with this letter, on April 15, 14,000 issues of *The Daily Pennsylvanian* were stolen from their newsstands. In each of the 52 empty racks were left notes saying that "the Black Community has come together to make a statement...protesting the blatant and voluntary perpetuation of institutional racism against the Black Community by the D[aily] P[ennsylvanian], the administration, and/or any independent entities affiliated with the University." The newspapers were later found heaped in dumpsters around the campus.

President Sheldon Hackney responded to the newspaper theft with words befitting one who has been a political figure (Hackney not only supported Bill Clinton, but his wife gave $1,000 to Hillary's favorite charity, the Children's Defense Fund). He said that the destruction of the papers was "an instance in which...two important university values, diversity and open expression, seem to be in conflict." Yet instead of condemning the assault on free speech, Hackney proceeded to apologize for a security guard who had tried to stop one of the black student who was stealing a stack of *Daily Pennsylvanians.* He said that the guard was unaware that the student was involved in a "protest activity." The Campus Police Commissioner has since "addressed the community's understandable concerns" by placing the security guard in question on indefinite probation. Hackney concluded by saying that though free speech is important, "there can be no ignoring the pain that expression may cause."

Even First Person Hillary Rodham Clinton, during a recent commencement address at the University of Pennsylvania, called for the protection of free speech. Hillary said, "We have to believe that in the free-exchange of ideas, justice will prevail over injustice, tolerance over intolerance and progress over reaction." If the college administrators will sign on to this statement, maybe the book burners will put their matches away.

May – June, 1993

CRYING RAPE IN A CROWDED THEATRE
by Neil Patel

Nine of the women in associate art professor Josephine Withers' class at the University of Maryland decided they were fed up with what they termed "the prevalence of phenomena which devalue women and encourage the belief that sexual violence against women is acceptable." They felt the media depicted women as passive sex objects. They were tired of verbal abuse of a sexual nature and uninvited sexual advances. They were angry about sexual assault taking place on their campus. They decided to do something about it.

The nine women from Withers' Contemporary Issues in Feminist Art class formed an ad hoc group called the Women's Coalition for Change. They decided to use the university's annual Art Attack festival—a time of harmless agitprop—as a vehicle for their message. The women spent hours preparing for the April 30 event. They went through the campus directory picking out male names at random and placing them on fliers below the heading "Notice: These men are potential rapists". Each flier listed a different group of men and invited people concerned by the existence of potential rapists to visit the Women's Coalition for Change at McKeldin Mall at 3:30 on the afternoon of the Art Attack. They posted the fliers all over campus on the day before the Art Attack.

The next day students began noticing the "potential rapists" fliers around campus. At first there was shock. Then came anger as groups of students searched for the fliers and tore down an estimated 400 of them. Many went to McKeldin Mall to find the people responsible.

Members of the WCC were there with giant six foot tall billboards that stated "Many of these men have the potential to be rapists" and then listed the name of every male student on campus. Four masked women, dressed in black, stood around the billboards painting each other with the names of individuals and institutions which they claimed perpetuate the "rape culture." They also painted each other with slogans such as "stop rape" and "fight back." In the background someone read the names of random women chosen from the campus directory. This was done "to personalize the issue of rape and to make individual women aware that they, and all women, are at risk."

This was meant to be performance art as well as accusation. But the audience was soon performing and accusing along with the members of the Women's Coalition for Change as outraged students, both male and female, began crossing names off the billboards and writing statements on them deploring the event. They shouted at the masked women and complained to school authorities. As the actual event came to a close, the saga for Professor Josephine Withers and her students had just begun.

At first, Professor Withers was very happy with the outcome of her pet project. "I think it was wildly successful. I'm very satisfied. It was intended to open up dialogue. Sometimes that dialogue can be painful. That's okay. It's okay for people to be mad." But then the adverse reviews of the art project started accumulating and Withers' reactions made it clear that she meant it was okay for other people to be mad.

On May 4, Mara Stanley, a reporter for *The Diamondback*, Maryland's campus newspaper, wrote the first of many articles on the "potential rapists" controversy. The article mentioned that many students were outraged by the lists. By the following day, the focus started to shift from the male victims of the action to the female perpetrators. People on campus wanted the know the names of the masked women of the WCC. But these women refused to come forward and defend their actions. They wanted to remain anonymous, a privilege they had already taken away from their victims. Over the next several days, as the controversy continued to simmer, students kept demanding answers. Davar Azarbeygui, a senior graphics design major, waited outside the Contemporary Issues in Feminist Art class. "I want to know who (they are). If they have the guts to release the names of 'potential rapists', they should have the guts to come out," he told *The Diamondback*. Others voiced similar appeals. Chris Hoffman, a freshman, said, "If they published our names, then they should publish theirs. Stand up for what you believe in." Marcy Markowitz, a sophomore, added, "I think they should come out and say who they are. It's unwarranted harassment. You can't post people's names like that. They knew they were going to provoke controversy."

By May 7, the national media caught on to the story. Meanwhile, tensions on the campus continued to soar. Another anonymous group, dubbing itself The Politically Incorrect Coalition Against Feminazis, began posting their own fliers saying that Ms. Withers "may be a whore." And asking, "Are you angry yet, Jo?" in response to the professor's earlier smug comment that anger can be useful. Predictably, Ms. Withers was not happy with the turn of events. She stopped speaking with the press, announcing that she and her students had "gotten not very good cooperation from the press," and that the issue had "been hopelessly distorted."

On May 9, University President William E. Kirwan released the institution's first official statement on the controversy. He said that although the school understood the intentions of the WCC, it does not approve of its actions which "had the effect of impugning innocent individuals." He reaffirmed the University's defense of free speech, but noted "we cannot condone actions that cause anguish and potential harm to innocent people." The words were textbook adminstrationspeak, but sentiment on campus was for action, not just words.

If the University was unwilling to act, some students were not so as reticent. Many of those randomly named on the fliers were seriously investigating the possibility of filing libel suits. One undergraduate student said he was exploring the possibility of three different lawsuits: one against the students involved; one against Professor Withers, since he believes that the lists were directly related to her course; and yet another one against the University itself, since it hadn't taken any action against either the teacher or the nine individuals responsible. "The only reason I would even consider suing the University is because it has yet to do anything about this and something really needs to be done," he said. "This isn't even a thing about making money. It's about getting someone to do something about it. Nobody has done anything about it yet."

By mid-May, the Washington, D.C.-based Center for Individual Rights was also investigating the possibility of taking on a libel case for at least one University of Maryland student under their Academic Freedom Defense Fund. Michael McDonald, the center's President, said it is more difficult than a libel case against a newspaper or magazine because the physical evidence is hard to come by. Most of the posters and fliers had been torn down and destroyed. An additional question was who exactly was responsible. Depending on facts yet to be revealed, the lawsuit might focus on the University, the students, the professor, or all three together.

One student named on the fliers said that he was surprised to find the people who are most encouraging him to file suit are his professors. One faculty member he spoke with said, "Every member of the faculty, except for the radical feminists, is extremely upset with her [Professor Withers]." According to his account, even some of the very liberal faculty members are angered over this issue.

Another professor said that this was the sort of action that might be expected of someone whose scholarly record is less than stellar. "She has been kind a 'cause' person and has made her presence felt on committees and campus forums," said this colleague. "The fact that she is still an associate professor at the age of 55 or so means that she has not been productive in a scholarly sense." One of Withers' few works is an anthology she edited in 1989 as part of a "Project to Mainstream Scholarship by and about Women into the Curriculum." This work includes chapters such as "Attic Mythology: Barren Goddesses, Male Wombs and the Cult of Rape," from books with titles like *The Reign of the Phallus*.

Some of the women in the WCC are also well known on campus. One student said he knows one of the members and that she "is well known on the University of Maryland campus as 'the vagina girl'." This is because "she dressed up in a vagina costume last semester and sat outside of fraternity row for the whole day, protesting the evils that the Greek system does to women."

If Withers meant the incident to be educational, she achieved her intention. The trouble is that students at Maryland have learned something she probably wishes they hadn't, and this is that false accusations of rape or "potential rape" have been potent realities on campuses across the country.

At Oberlin College, a small liberal arts school in Ohio, an unsigned poster distributed around the campus last April read, "Take Back the Night is proud to introduce itself to Oberlin College and disgusted to introduce its first rapist of the month." (There followed the name of a freshman student.) The posters went on to state that "a female student came to us in anguish," afraid of pressing charges "because undertaking such an action in a paternalistic, anti-womyn society would involve a great deal more undeserved hardship to her." Furthermore, the victim did not "have the responsibility to endure more pain at the hands of a misogynistic administration, student body and judicial system."

The only problem was that the accused freshman denied the charges. He said he hadn't "gotten into any situation close to sex" at Oberlin. He went on to say "I haven't even dated anybody at Oberlin. I don't do drugs. I don't drink, so it's not like I went to a party and forgot. The only explanation is that it's a weird hoax. It can't be a joke, because it's not funny." Now, according to the Cleveland *Plain Dealer*, "Rumors have circulated around campus that the writers confused the student with someone else with the same first name."

Last year at Princeton University's annual Take Back the Night march, a rape "survivor" got up to tell her horrifying story. She spoke of being dragged back to a drunken undergrad's room and being raped. While he was raping her the man growled degrading and obscene comments in her ear, saying "My father buys me cheap girls like you to use up and throw away." She said that after he raped her the man repeatedly smashed her head against a metal bed frame until she lost consciousness. He then dropped her off, leaving her lying at the entryway to her dorm. She said she approached the Dean of Students Office, but was told "not to press the issue" and to "let bygones be bygones." She said the man was given a year's suspension, but was already back on campus.

The woman repeated her story in an op-ed column for the *Princetonian* published three days later. Three days after that, however, the Dean of Students wrote a letter to the campus paper refuting many parts of the woman's story. The Dean specifically noted that no complaint or mention of the incident had ever been filed. After this letter the purported victim began to circulate the name of a particular student in conjunction with her rape story. The name spread around the campus and soon was made public.

The accused student filed a formal complaint with the Dean. After a lengthy investigation, the woman who told the rape story wrote a second article for the *Princetonian.* This piece was titled, "Apologizing for False Accusation of Rape." In it the woman admitted she had fabricated the whole story and that, in fact, she had never even met, or spoken with, the person whom she falsely accused.

The sad irony in such events is that the women leveling these false accusations are undermining the very objectives they claim to be striving for. Accusing the entire male student body of being "potential rapists" didn't promote discussion of the issue of rape at the University of Maryland. It promoted discussion of whether the zealots in the Women's Coalition for Change had libeled the men whose names they printed in their fliers. It promoted discussion and editorials commenting on radical feminism and whether it had "gone too far." Lost in the shuffle is the fact that women do face legitimate dangers of rape, on campus and off. Josephine Withers and her followers may have thought that they were engaging in performance art, but actually it turned out to be a Punch and Judy show in which they beat themselves over the head.

May – June, 1993

Growing up Absurd at Wellesley

by Alyson Todd

My father wanted me to attend the United States Military Academy at West Point, as my older brother had. But I had known since I was thirteen that I would one day be an alumnae of Wellesley College. In Kenya at the age of thirteen, I met a radiant sixty year old Wellesley graduate who was working in the Amboseli Game Park. This woman could fly planes, speak five languages, and was an expert on lion behavior. She highly praised this small women's college, Wellesley. This vital woman was very impressive to a young girl like myself with dreams of a life filled with travel, adventure and romance.

Five years later I was still dedicated to Wellesley, applying to no other schools. I envisioned Wellesley to be the epitome of grace and excellence. It was a beautiful lakeside campus situated in a picturesque New England town with Gothic architecture, a splendid arboretum, and learned schools. I felt I could not ask for anything more. I had spent the first fifteen years of my life overseas in India, Kenya, Cameroon, and Western Europe. Coming back to the U.S. and attending a small, conservative southern prep school had been difficult: the other students there considered me a liberal, feminist weirdo. I believed that at Wellesley people would be more open minded, tolerant and interesting and that I would be free to be myself.

Arriving at Wellesley in the fall of 1989, I confronted the first of many disappointments. I was housed in an ugly brick box with an appalling distasteful modern sculpture in front. I was shocked; I had been expecting to live in one of the beautiful Gothic towers profiled in the brochure.

After meeting my roommate, I examined my "first-year" orientation itinerary. After lunch we were to attend a mandatory Inter-Cultural Awareness Now (ICAN) workshop, to which each of us was to bring an item which expressed our "cultural identities." I was baffled: what cultural identity did I have? Like many Americans, my heritage is a mix of many different nationalities, including Irish, English, Dutch, German, French and a dash of Italian. I did not really have any possessions which expressed the essence of any of those cultures. (I did have a Norwegian wool sweater, but I could not claim Norwegian descent.) So I decided that

I am an American, and that I would bring to the workshop something that expressed American culture; the American dollar bill. I would discuss the meaning of the Great Seal; I thought that other students might be interested in learning why the Masonic pyramid is on the dollar bill. I was wrong.

We, the first-years, were divided into small groups led by a facilitator. Everyone went around the room showing proudly their items of cultural significance. I saw African jewelry, Native American art, East Asian tea ware, and Greek food. When it came my turn I identified myself as an American. I proudly took out my dollar bill and declared that the symbolism of the Great Seal expressed my cultural identity. As I gave what I thought to be an insightful talk about reason, liberty, equality, and the birth of American democracy, the "women" in the room (I put the term in quotes because I could see it was an assumed identity) were giving me icy stares and stony silence. At this point, I realized I had committed a *faux-pas.* I silently wished that I had worn the Norwegian sweater.

The next exercise was directed at rooting out one's unconscious racism in order to make one more "sensitive to the pain of others." The event degenerated into a tearful encounter group with women crying as they described the various ways they had been oppressed by sexism, racism, homophobia, etc. One woman even shed tears recalling the fact that no one head asked her to her senior prom the previous spring. I, on the other hand, did not begin to cry until I got back to my dorm room and had begun to relate the incident to my mother over the telephone.

It is difficult to express how that afternoon distressed me. The ICAN workshop may have seemed relatively innocuous, but I saw that the group had a fundamentally sinister aspect to it. The psychological conditioning, clumsy though it was, reminded me of something out of Orwell. I felt that I should have spent my first eight hours on campus getting to know my roommate, exploring the town, maybe even throwing a Frisbee around. Instead, I had been trapped for four hours in a room feeling stigmatized and alienated because I was an American with blonde hair. I had learned only one thing from the session: you have to be a victim to fit in at Wellesley.

It began to feel a little better a few days later when classes began. I was enrolled in four classes I was really excited about. But as the term progressed my enthusiasm evaporated as I saw that everything we learned had to be forced into a template of feminism. At first it was an interesting change of pace, but after a while it became tiresome, especially because I felt there were so many other interesting things to talk about. Also, I started to notice that the academic atmosphere was constantly undermined by the injection of student emotions, something the instructors encouraged. I kept hearing in my classrooms sentences that began with "I feel...", "When I was young...", "I had a friend once...". Most students felt compelled to evaluate texts written thousands of years ago by their own values. Dead White European Males like Plato and Aristotle were simply targets. Wellesley students were encouraged to dismiss them out of hand and to regard the greatest works of Western culture as little more than receptacles of sexism, elitism, racism, class struggle, or whatever.

A class in which this revisionism was particularly marked was called "Classic Texts in Contemporary Perspective." I did not realize at the time just what "Contemporary Perspective" would entail, but I was hopeful. Unfortunately, however, the lectures were centered around histrionics regarding sexism. Most interesting was the day we discussed Homer's *Odyssey.* I was excited as I walked to class that day, for I felt I had found an interesting irony in the Sirens' singing a song which represents complete knowledge yet kills whomever hears it. Judging from Homer's lyrics, along with the Oedipus trilogy and the *Myth of Sisyphus,* I thought that perhaps the Greeks felt that knowledge was ultimately destructive to mankind. (Later, in my junior year, I would read *The Birth of Tragedy* and feel smugly validated by Nietzsche's discussion of this idea.) Yet when I shared my thoughts with the class, I was met by silence. Not a single person responded to me — even critically. Eventually, a student infamous for her annoying whine complained that Odysseus was "very elitist" when he ordered the men to tie him up and put wax in their ears so that they could not hear the song and be lured to their death. This woman felt that it was unfair that Odysseus got to listen to the song; if everyone could not have listened to the song, then no one should have. This occasioned a debate that lasted for the entire hour on how Odysseus should have managed the situation in a more democratic way. Some students advocated a random lottery to determine who would listen to the song; others felt that Odysseus should hear the song but so should as many of the others as possible. Some raised objections that some men on the ship had to work while the others didn't. Someone else pointed out how insensitively Homer portrayed all of Odysseus' working class sailors as morons. On and on it went with the professors looking amazingly interested. I had discovered the Wellesley mantra: "It's Not Fair."

The next class was dominated by a hysterical student decrying the offensiveness and sexism of Aristophanes' *Lysistrata.* The bawdy jokes and sexual innuendo were incompatible with feminist sentiments. I found this very amusing, since *Lysistrata* is often considered the first feminist play. The professors were obviously moved by the student's tirade, although they attempted to justify why they had chosen the play. They defended themselves by pointing out how they deliberately selected works written by or about females — instead of *Oedipus Rex, Antigone*; instead of *The Clouds, Lysistrata*; and so on.

After that I found myself very sleepy in class; shamefully, I admit that I nodded off during many of the later debates.

Another aspect of Wellesley for which I was unprepared in my first months there was the active and militant lesbianism. Many of the most powerful and outspoken students are lesbians and the community as a whole is very vocal. They spearheaded an intense public relations campaign to make all members of the community "sensitive" to their choice. Posters were plastered everywhere asking, "Are you gay? Are you sure? Is your mother gay? Are you sure?" This sort of thing has increased during my time at Wellesley. The campus walkways are always getting chalked with slogans like "Silence=Death" and "Come Out!" Last year a Protestant minister gave a sermon at the campus-wide "Flower Sunday" event in which she praised the lesbian lifestyle and asked everyone to stand up and show their support for their "lesbian sisters." I came to feel that the sensitivity campaign often shaded over into a recruitment effort.

Strangely enough, however, only once in the past four years have I had a confrontation with a professor. Generally, I have found that most faculty members are decent people with a sincere interest in teaching; they are simply at the mercy of the administration and student evaluation questionnaires and therefore they often have no choice but to conform to the politically correct pieties. Even some of the radical deconstructionists for the most part treat dissenting students with respect. But history professor Alfredo Robbles was an exception.

I am something of a history buff especially interested in twentieth century military history. I was astonished when Robbles announced to the class that the Cold War was merely a social construct of the American military-industrial complex that was used to justify the imperialistic nature of American policy so industrialists could make a lot of money at the expense of the "periphery." Furthermore, he asserted, "The Soviet Union was never a military threat to the U.S. and Europe at all." Finally, I became enraged when he implied that the U.S.S.R. was morally superior to the United States.

I challenged him, confident that I knew enough to prove him wrong. We argued for an entire hour. At first, I was very restrained. I described how intercontinental ballistic missiles pointed at specific American targets could be construed as a military threat. I cited studies of the quantity, range, and sophistication of Soviet conventional forces. "The Soviets never were a threat to Europe," he retorted with a straight face. He remained adamant even after I brought up such episodes as the suppression of Poland, Prague Spring, the Greek Civil War, and the Berlin Airlift.

At one point, he smiled the knowing smile of a chess champion about to mate an opponent. "Have you ever heard of the Yalta Conference?" I felt like screaming, "Of course I have!" but I simply nodded. He then asked the class if anyone "could talk about the Yalta Conference in the context of this conversation?" No one responded. So he proceeded to tell us about spheres of influence. I countered with examples of Soviet expansionism. Frustrated, he turned to the class and pleaded, "Will someone respond to her?" One woman finally did respond, contributing to the discussion in classic Wellesley fashion: "I don't know that much about history and all, but, um, what you were saying, Professor, like, sounds right to me."

Another woman suggested that because I was an American, my "patriotic prejudices" tainted my academic judgment. Another woman declared that my account of the Cold War was simply my "belief." At this point, I lost control and raised my voice. I promised to bring in a list of books which people could read if they want the historical facts. Class ended and I left. Not surprisingly, my grade dropped from a solid B to a C minus.

In truth, I often responded irresponsibly when confronted with a class like this one which I believed to be a waste of my time. Invariably I would fall asleep in lecture, or skip class altogether. My grades, unfortunately, reflect this behavior. I do not quite qualify as an average student at Wellesley, considering that the average grade awarded in the humanities and social sciences is an A minus.

One of the cornerstones of my classical liberal philosophy is self-responsibility; I believe that where there is a will, there is a way. Therefore, if my educational experience has been less than stellar, I have only myself to blame. I think that there is a decent education to be had at Wellesley. One simply has to understand what to seek and how to find it. Four years and $90,000 later, I am only just starting to figure things out.

I was regarded as a liberal feminist renegade in high school. At Wellesley I am infamous for my conservatism.

I did not enter college as an activist — far from it. I became politically active my junior year, joining the staff of a new but short-lived conservative newspaper, *The Analyst.* I wrote a few articles decrying deconstructionism and multiculturalism. I started attending the Student Senate and attending various little meetings on campus "issues."

In retrospect, I was very much like a bull in a china shop. One time at a meeting of students and faculty discussing the curriculum I stood up, attempting to quote Nietzsche, and told the Dean of the College that multicultural education would create "walking encyclopedias of external culture for inner barbarians." The Dean became very angry with me.

Another time, I was asked to participate in a panel discussion on political correctness. I decided to do it, although I knew it was a stacked deck, considering the fact that three professors and a student represented the "liberal" view, while myself and another student represented the other side. My opening statements were very passionate; I suggested that Western civilization might fall if things continued as they were going. I thereby attracted the majority of the audience's questions. Intense grilling continued for about thirty minutes. When asked about the validity of "African-American support groups," I acknowledged the presence of racism in the United States and the need for a sense of community, but maintained that racially exclusive groups, such as the all-black student group Ethos, violated the basic principles we share as a nation. M. Ahadi Bugg, the black activist on the panel, shot back, "You will never understand!" The audience erupted into applause, hoots, and phrases like "Go on, girl!" I realized then it is sometimes pointless to attempt to have a real conversation with some people.

The spring of my junior year was probably the worst time of my entire life. Janet Jones, the coordinator of the Committee for Political and Legislative Action, announced in the Student Senate that her organization had invited the Reverend Al Sharpton to speak at Wellesley. The CPLA passed out his press releases and clippings from the racist *Amsterdam News* in order to "educate the community" about the illustrious "civil rights leader" from New York. The invitation to Sharpton, a man not known for his love of Jews, was all the more questionable because Wellesley had witnessed seven incidents of Nazi and anti-Semitic vandalism that year.

Senators were invited to comment upon the invitation; I decided to speak first: "I cannot support the invitation to Sharpton because he is an anti-Semite, a hate monger, and a second-rate con man who exploits the suffering of his own people for personal aggrandizement." I concluded by saying that he was the moral equivalent of David Duke. (Some time after this, angry letters to the *Wellesley News* falsely claimed that I threatened to bring David Duke to campus.) Another student, Debbie Shapiro, joined me in criticism of the invitation, charging that Sharpton "advocates murder" of Jews.

After I spoke my mind, I was subjected to a steady stream of personal attacks. Many of the students assumed I was Jewish, as if a non-Jew could not be worried about anti-Semitism. They would ask derisively, "What are you, Jewish?" Ahadi Bugg accosted me after the Senate meeting and, with her friends surrounding me, called me "the biggest racist on campus." "I do not know what religion you are," she added curiously, "but you are obviously not living according to God." Then they threatened me: "We'll find out where you live and drag you to Sharpton's speech."

Meanwhile, Avik Roy, publisher of the MIT-Wellesley magazine *Counterpoint*, with which I was associated, wrote a column blasting the activists and talking about how "the usual troop of thugs led by Ahadi Bugg" had intimidated anyone attempting to discuss what Sharpton really believed or who compared Sharpton with someone like Duke: "'Al Sharpton is coming to empower some people on this campus,' [Bugg] explained. Perhaps she might also venture to explain exactly who Rev. Sharpton is trying to empower when he asserts that 'Hitler was right.' Hypocrisy is clearly one of Ms. Bugg's strong suits."

I went home for the vacation, and when I returned, nobody would talk to me. People were giving me strange looks. Finally I bumped into the Student Government Vice President Jen Mosely, who told me that everyone was very distressed by the *Counterpoint* column. Apparently, because I was the News Editor there, many students assumed I had written the column. Roy's use of the word "thugs" was, according to Bugg, an "exploitation of black stereotypes." I was falsely accused of perpetrating racial slurs. The President of Wellesley, Nannerl O. Keohane, called the column a "hate crime."

Things got even worse. Someone smashed the windows of a 1992 white Honda Civic with Maryland plates (my car is of the same year, model, and state). Roy received death threats. Bugg and her colleagues hung posters around campus urging students to call me and express their "anger." Some students even put my phone number on their answering machine message. Others spread rumors that I was the leader of an underground neo-Nazi group. I began to get really nervous. I started to wish I had gone to West Point. I figured that Beast Barracks at Camp Buckner could not have been as bad as this.

At about this time came the Rodney King verdict. Campus emotions reached a hysterical level. The *Wellesley News* was attacked for printing a letter, also classified as a "hate crime," supporting my side of the Al Sharpton incident. Needless to say, I kept a very low profile. I was seriously tempted to wear Groucho Marx glasses with a fake nose and mustache around campus, but I decided not to be so provocative. I finished my exams (the time was extended due to "stress" about the King verdict), and went home.

I returned this past September for my senior year quite apprehensive. Many other students expressed amazement that I actually came back rather than transferring. Now that I am about to graduate I can look back over the previous four years. I see that I could have ignored all the lunacy at Wellesley, tried to salvage a good education, and at least had a lot of fun. For some mysterious reason, I decided to take the hard way. I suspect, though, that my politically incorrect path will lead to its own rewards, and I keep thinking about Mark Twain's famous quip: Never let your education interfere with your learning.

March, 1993

My Days and Nights in the Academic Wilderness

by David John Ayers

In the summer of 1991, as I drove with my family from New York to a new job in Dallas, my academic career seemed and on track. After getting my master's in sociology from Amerincan University in 1986, I had taught for five years at a small, struggling evangelical liberal arts college in New York while completing my doctoral work at NYU. My resume was respectable; I had, in fact, just published a piece in a respected collection that critically examined "evangelical feminist" theories. As a conservative in the leftist world of sociology, I had come to expect difficulty from my peers, and my defense of traditional sex roles produced predictable attacks. But, since I had been honest about my positions on gender and was hired anyway by a mid-sized, growing Baptist university in Dallas, I could not foresee that my doubts about radical feminism would be a barrier to success in my new position. I looked forward to the promise of building the fledgling Social Science program there, and eventually teaching graduate students.

One year later, my life was dramatically changed. My offense was giving a twenty minute talk at a faculty luncheon, where I presented a precis of the anthologized article in which I dared to question the empirical validity of major tenets of the feminist faith. On May 22, 1992, after enduring a two-month hate campaign, I was discharged from my appointment as Assistant Professor of Sociology at Dallas Baptist University, having been judged guilty of transgressing feminist orthodoxy in print and lecture. I was dazed by the experience, having assumed that a religious institution would protect opinions that took exception to the left wing orthodoxy which has triumphed at "mainstream" academic institutions. But the infidels, as it worked out, had taken over even this temple.

In the months since my firing (it had the feeling of something worse — an excommunication, even a public burning) I have thought about my sins. What exactly had I done to call down the wrath of the politically righteous on my head? I had simply pointed out that the best sociological evidence available shows that in every documented society male and female roles seem to be divided along the same basic lines, and this strongly suggests the universality of patriarchy. Further, a growing body of scientific evidence is confirming that some of the differences between men and women have an irreducible basis in biology and genetics. The preponderance of studies suggests, I pointed out, that most mothers of young children, when given the choice, do not opt to work full-time outside their homes, even in developed societies that are pervaded by feminist ideology. One can only conclude, therefore, that the feminist demand for a gender-neutral or unisexual world is contrary to the natural impulses of all human beings as well as the historical practice of all known societies, and hence destructive. Finally, I pointed to some of the aggressive censorship that is impeding sociologists in the area of sex-role studies.

While obviously controversial, this was hardly an unscientific or professionally irresponsible presentation, particularly since it was based on voluminous research material, which I cited. But it was totally unacceptable to the feminists at Dallas Baptist U. and triggered a smear campaign sanctioned by the president of the college, Dr. Gary Cook. I was reviled by name in Algebra, English and physical education classes, hardly appropriate settings for intellectual critiques of my views, let alone personal attacks by professional colleagues. One English professor warned her students not to "write like Ayers" when completing their term papers, since I was "inflammatory," and "relied on outdated sources." Unfounded accusations were circulated accusing me of wanting to end equal opportunity for women working at the school. Some even suggested that my ideas should be censored to preserve the college's "gender equity." I was labeled "intolerant," "rigid" and "narrow-minded" by my anonymous detractors.

The offending views in my paper were heavily referenced, and had been published in an award-winning book (*Recovering Biblical Manhood and Womanhood: A Response to Evangelical Feminism*, Crossway Books, Wheaton, Illinois 1991). Yet I was accused of lacking scholarly integrity and ability. My "Study of the Family" course, which was crowded with female students who said they enjoyed hearing my politically incorrect ponderings on sex roles, received the highest student ratings in our college. Yet I was publicly castigated as a mean-spirited "misogynist," accused of "stirring up campus strife" between the sexes, and maligned for discouraging females from pursuing their "life choices."

The Administration was not satisfied by this informal sniping, however. The Academic Dean, therefore, commissioned English Professor Deborah McCollister to respond to my paper at a lavishly catered public luncheon, sponsored by the university. In the talk, attended by over 100 students, faculty, and staff, McCollister tried to discredit me professionally by directing her attention exclusively to my methodology. McCollister accused me of "extremism," bias and poor scholarship, alleging, for example, that I had deliberately misrepresented sources to "deceive" readers. (Her evidence? I had referred to a 1981 article as "recent.") Another of her criticisms involved my citation of a lengthy, December 1989 *Time* article about the "women's movement" as an example of pro-feminist media bias. McCollister said that the *Time* article was so obviously fair and balanced that I had to have intentionally distorted it in my account. (In fact, the article in question had not quoted a single critic of feminism, had described lesbian rights as a "noble cause," and was written by a feminist.)

So I had been publicly humiliated, exposed as an ideological heretic with ideas that were now suitably tainted and proscribed. I could console myself with the fact that I still had my classroom. But the Christian radicals were not appeased. They wanted me, to use an apt phrase from writer Michael Jones, "swept from the arena of discourse into the outer silence."

A feminist staff-member soon reported a new thought crime of mine: I had allowed students to read or hear "on their own" McCollister's speech (which was, after all, a public text). I had done so during the discussions of sex role theories scheduled for my Family course. But my truly capital offense was to have imprudently referred to her paper in class as the "razor sharp sword of the assassin."

The President of the College had stood behind the feminists' public attacks on my character, and had turned a blind eye to the *sub rosa* campaign of vilification that accompanied these attacks. But now he claimed that my isolated classroom remark about the assassin's sword was "shocking" and "unprofessional" conduct, and convened a special "Ad Hoc Committee" to examine my transgression. I was ordered to appear in 24 hours before four Vice Presidents, the Faculty Senate president and vice president, President Cook and two outspoken feminist staff directors to answer charges based on my alleged sin, which no one on the committee was able to specify. Not one actual breach of policy was ever identified, and in the aftermath of this inquisition, no grievance processes, formal disciplinary hearings, or findings of guilt occurred. But within ten days, I was fired. In a notice sent by messenger to my home, I was given a year's pay, and one working day to clear out my office.

In the entire college only one Dean, Dr. John Jeffrey, had the integrity to suggest that academic freedom and procedure be honored in my case. With a swiftness unknown even in the academic witch-hunts of the Fifties, Jeffrey was fired the very same day and was replaced as Dean by a member of the President's Ad Hoc Committee. We helped each other pack.

Being persecuted for opposing feminist dogmas may no longer be unusual in today's "deconstructed" universities. But to have this grotesque scenario unfold at a Southern Baptist school which — according to its catalog — emphasizes biblical inerrancy, evangelism, traditional morals, and preparation for the ministry, is worthy of some note.

I need to "state an interest" to make this account complete. And I also need to tell those of you who might think that Christian colleges (however ambivalently you may regard them) are breakwaters against the tides of political correctness that you should drop your illusions. *They are everywhere!*

I am one of those people you have read about — not because of my political firing but because I am a "born again." My transformation occurred in the late 70s, after a life of Sixties-style drug abuse and political Leftism. I embraced Christianity as a relationship with a real, living God. I had of course read about liberation theology. But this was largely a Catholic phenomenon, developing out of a symbiosis between left wing Latin Americans and their sympathizers here in this country. Prior to entering the evangelical academy, I would have found it hard to believe that Bible-based colleges could nurture radical tendencies. This is because the Scriptures — which born-agains rigorously observe — propose epistemological and ethical tenets that are diametrically opposed to the theories and tactics of the Left which has taken over secular campuses.

Shortly after accepting my first faculty position at The King's College in New York, however, I found that radical feminists and other leftists had made considerable progress there. In fact, at the time I was hired, they controlled the Dean's office and several departments, had strong alumni support, and had secured considerable discretionary funding for "women's studies" — projects that were, in essence, little different from the radical feminist curricula at secular institutions.

These "evangelical feminists" could also be just as totalitarian as their non-evangelical counterparts. One woman at King's introduced a resolution to force all reports and proposals submitted to faculty to be written in "gender sensitive" language, and regularly harangued speakers who used the old, "male-centered" language forms. Her commitment to feminism was carried to extremes — she proposed, for example, that the college raise rent on subsidized faculty apartments, to "encourage" male faculty to put their wives (many of whom were full-time mothers at home) to work. Another feminist asked the Dean to prevent the discussion of an article opposing women's ordination at a seminar in a private home.

One radical feminist chairwoman at King's refused to call God "Father" or "Son," even during corporate prayer. The head of the faculty committee for promotion and tenure bragged about bringing in an evangelical feminist to speak in chapel who openly advocated rewriting the Bible for "gender neutrality." (She turned out to be a strong advocate of "Christian lesbianism," defending it in the pages of the *Gay Advocate*). Another professor labeled certain Bible texts offensive to women, questioned their appropriateness in public worship, and suggested the need to alter them to accommodate feminist sensitivities. A theologian there even proclaimed, in print, that two noted evangelical feminists who accepted abortion and "Christian" homosexuality had a "high view of Biblical authority;" and declared the officially pro-lesbian Evangelical Women's Caucus to be a legitimate voice within the conservative Protestant world.

Few parents who sent their children to this college, run for years by a well-known radio preacher, imagined that such "broad" interpretations of the Faith were being promoted there. The pious platitudes in the catalog certainly gave no hint of this. I was definitely not prepared for it. I saw at King's what I have since seen expressed in evangelical scholarly conferences, journals, and books, even in their grant applications. These influential people wear many of the trappings of the old evangelicalism, but they embrace most of the tenets and heavy-handed tactics of the New Left.

Usually, proponents of this evangelical "PC" don't smoke, drink or dance. But they do espouse extreme cultural relativism, encouraging students to see ethics and truth as arbitrary and shifting. They support multiculturalism, even where this involves rewriting history and launching crude attacks upon a civilization that has been shaped by a Christianity that has produced more religious freedom than any other. They push affirmative action policies, even if they undermine excellence and personal responsibility, and deny charity to poor whites in order to enroll wealthy blacks on scholarship. Many professors send their pregnant students to abortion clinics. Others propose interpretations claiming a Scriptural basis for "monogamous homosexual unions," attempting to fuse gay rights with the Biblical injunction that only the marital bed is undefiled.

In short, reality at evangelical colleges increasingly mimics the secular scene. There are hidden ethnic quotas and "diversity" curricula; evangelical leftists soft-peddle divorce and sex differences, demonstrate a passion for "self-esteem" psychology, and oppose "outdated" notions of authority, absolutes, and in-dwelling sin.

As in the secular world, a massive influx of Sixties' generation professors fueled the spread of political correctness on evangelical faculties. Liberal evangelical professors continually complain about their "apathetic" pupils, who (they erroneously claim) "only" care about pro-life activism, or the economy; or who demonstrate their "selfishness" and "latent fascism" by supporting Republicans and the Persian Gulf War. Students are invidiously compared to the "compassionate" students of their own college years, who "cared" about minorities, the poor, and "social justice."

As with secular colleges, evangelical traditionalists tend to go with the flow. As long as parents don't see funny stuff when they visit, and as long as radicals don't demand alterations in the school catalog's platitudes about Christian learning, administrators are prepared to turn the other cheek. The Left instinctively knows this, and hypocritically avoids threatening the Bible college's sacred cows. I have rarely seen even the most virulent "evangelical" Marxists or feminists question the rigid campus rules which forbid card-playing, smoking or alcohol.

There may be differences in degree between evangelical and secular colleges, but not in kind. And the gap is closing. In fact, as my experience at Dallas Baptist University has demonstrated, those who have been born again into political correctness may, given the right conditions, even exceed their worldly cousins in meanness and intolerance.

One reason why political correctness has had so much success in the Bible schools is because the initiatives of its passionate Left are not challenged by equal fervor from academic conservatives and other traditionalists. Too often, conservatives would "rather switch than fight;" sometimes, they are just forced out.

Into this situation have come "second thoughters" like myself. In the evangelical world, a second thoughter is a person who was not necessarily born to the faith but who comes to it after spiritual wandering. Such a person is less likely to embrace religion out of habit, and is more inclined to love Christianity for its spiritual realities than its evangelical symbols. I know many who will play cards, smoke or drink in moderation because these are not specifically forbidden in Scripture, but would sooner lose their job than yield a jot of basic doctrine. In my experience, such a one fights theological compromise with an intensity that usually exceeds the opposition's, and cannot be easily bought off with written creeds and codes that are not taken seriously.

This type exists in the secular realm as well among those who have embraced conservative principles after roaming in the socialist wilderness. Having come by these convictions thoughtfully, often after inner struggle, they are not so ready to compromise them. The outcome will be determined by whether such second thoughters have the opportunity to inform concerned publics and to work closely with "old-line" academic traditionalists, perhaps providing them with the energy and will they now lack. In fact, a new President of The King's College, Dr. Friedhelm Radandt, has been doing this with measurable success. He has hired several outspoken second thoughters and protected their right, with all faculty, to speak freely, gain promotion on merit rather than politics, and work cooperatively with the old-liners. Consequently, most of the worst ideologues have now left after realizing they would no longer be allowed to trample the curriculum, pervert doctrine and stifle dissent unchallenged. Political correctness is not a disease without a cure. Especially when treatment begins early, its progress can be reversed.

Such efforts will not be without complications; clashes of personality and style will likely abound. But the stakes are high, and I have become convinced in the last few years that the situation will only be remedied by men and women who are willing to risk personal setbacks and to fight pitched battles with the academic barbarians. I hope I will not seem parochial if I say that in the Christian academy, more perhaps than in the secular one, this is a moral battle with high stakes and it will only be won with patience, principle and courage. I feel that I am a better Christian for my experience at Dallas Baptist U. I know that I value the preciousness of academic freedom and intellectual integrity more than ever before.

January, 1993

Counter Coup

by Bill Cerveny

When members of the Phi Kappa Sigma fraternity kicked off their fall rush a few weeks ago at the University of California at Riverside, they advertised their South of the Border Fiesta with T-shirts featuring a figure in a serape and sombrero sitting on a beach drinking tequila. These symbols were a red flag for the members of the campus Hispanic organization Movimiento Estudiantil Chicano de Aztlan (MEChA), which immediately filed charges against the fraternity brothers with the university administration. After a campaign of intimidation which the fraternity was ill-equipped to withstand and a series of star chamber hearings it was unable legally to contest, the fraternity was stigmatized, stripped of its charter, and kicked off campus.

If this little drama did not cause much comment, it was because it happens all the time. Because of their image as beer-swilling joyriders, the village idiots of the campus community, fraternity members are the most vulnerable of all students to sanctions against free speech and expression. Because they are by their very nature *not serious*, it is generally not seen as a serious matter when they are muzzled and disciplined. Nor, often, do they themselves recognize that what is happening to them is not a sanction that they halfway deserve, but rather a suppression of free speech rights with serious consequences for the entire university.

The Phi Kappa Sigma brothers at the University of California at Riverside were cut adrift by their national chapter and ready to take their punishment. What they faced, after all, was merely a repetition of what had happened to other chapters of other fraternities on other campuses. But this case had a slightly different outcome. The Individual Rights Foundation, a Southern California-based organization fighting against the suppression of free speech on campus heard about the Phi Kappas' problem and came to their defense. After lengthy negotiations with administrators at UCR, Foundation attorneys not only got the fraternity chapter reinstated but also, in a settlement with potentially far reaching consequences, forced the University to agree to force its administrators to undergo several hours of sensitivity training—not in racism, sexism, homophobia or any of the other sins against multiculturalism, but in the First Amendment and the assaults against free speech in the multicultural campus.

This odd (and, from the perspective of Riverside administrators, cautionary) tale began early in the fall semester, when members of Phi Kappa Sigma were geared up for their first fraternity rush of the year.

As tradition demands, the fraternity had scheduled two separate parties to woo perspective members into joining their group. To kick off their rush, the members of Phi Kappa Sigma decided to throw a pair of parties, a South of the Border Fiesta and then, the next night, a Jamaican Island party. In advertising their events, Phi Kappa Sigma ordered some T-shirts featuring a man in a serape and sombrero, sitting on the beach and drinking a bottle of tequila. Next to this figure was a set of steel drums and a wooden Tiki head, in which was carved the word "Jamaica." The lower half of the shirt shows a Rastafarian standing in the doorway of a Mexican cantina donning an ear to ear grin and a six pack of beer. This graphic was wrapped with a lyric from a Bob Marley song: "It doesn't matter where you come from long as you know where you are going."

The members of Phi Kappa Sigma hadn't even considered that the shirts might be considered controversial, since the Marley lyrics were intended to show the inclusiveness of good booze and the universality of partying down. But on the Friday before their Mexican Fiesta party Rick Carrez, the fraternity's president, was approached by a member of the school's campus activities office, telling him that there had been a complaint about the "offensive racial stereotypes" depicted on their rush T-shirts. This caught Carrez by surprise. As he struggled to finish setting up for the evening's party, he said that he would be more than happy to meet with anyone who was offended by their shirts and didn't expect to hear anything more about it.

Later that same day another member of Phi Kappa Sigma was wearing one of the T-shirts while walking across the Riverside campus. He was approached by a Hispanic student who stopped him and, somewhat aggressively, asked to see his T-shirt. After the fraternity member showed him the shirt and turned to leave, the Hispanic student grabbed him by the shoulder and twirled him around, saying "I'm not done looking at it yet." It was clear to the fraternity member that this student was trying to instigate some sort of conflict. To avoid the run-in, the Phi Kappa Sigma brother continued on his way.

The weekend's festivities went off without a hitch. Friday evening's South of the Border party was a success with its disc jockey and margarita bar. Saturday evening was much of the same, the tropical island atmosphere created by reggae music and shish kebabs. A substantial number of freshman showed interest in the fraternity, coming out in large numbers to meet the Phi Kappa Sigma members and talk about joining.

By the following Monday, however, it was clear that the party was over for Phi Kappa Sigma. That morning the fraternity members walked onto campus to find graffiti scrawled across the walls of university buildings. On the concrete walkway in front of the student activities office a spray painted message spread out over 20 square feet reading: "Phi Kappa Sigma Racist Fraternity." They were bothered by what they regarded as slander and tried to cover the words with large sheets of paper. Though no one claimed responsibility for the graffiti, it was clear that someone had declared war against them.

Later that same day, Carrez was approached by Kevin Ferguson, the Director of Campus Activities and the Inter-Fraternity Council Advisor. It seemed that the UCR chapters of MEChA and UER (the Hispanic fraternity on campus) had written a formal letter of complaint to the Chancellor of the university protesting the Phi Kappa Sigma rush T-shirts. In their letter, the Hispanic students charged that Phi Kappa Sigma's sombrero-clad party mascot "promotes negative stereotypes of the Chicana/o community which are offensive and of bad taste" and that they "find it unacceptable and totally misrepresentative of [their] beautiful culture and people." The letter closed by saying that MEChA would make sure that "this matter is handled and given the proper attention it deserves," demanding that they be allowed to play an active role in reprimanding Phi Kappa Sigma.

After telling Carrez that he had better get in contact with the Phi Kappa Sigma National office to arrange some sort of defense for his fraternity, Ferguson followed MEChA's correspondence with a letter of his own to the Chancellor. In it he accused the members of Phi Kappa Sigma of promoting "negative stereotypes" and said that he would have them brought before the Inter Fraternity Council Judiciary Board within the week. Ferguson was hopeful that he could contain the matter by offering to enroll the fraternity brothers in one of the school's sensitivity seminars, saying that "the actions now being taken by the IFC Judiciary Board as well as the students of UCR will be sufficient to educate this chapter on the issues of sensitivity as well as the damage that is caused through the use of negative stereotypes."

Meanwhile, although he felt that they had done nothing wrong, Carrez set up an appointment with MEChA's officers, in which he expressed his regret that the Phi Kappa Sigma T-shirts and party theme had offended them. He told them that in the future his fraternity would steer clear of any theme that might be viewed as inappropriate. Despite Carrez's apologies, however, the members of MEChA rejected any compromise or retraction, saying that they would take further action.

Carrez still couldn't understand why the Chicano students were so upset. They were accusing Phi Kappa Sigma of being racist, yet his was the most racially diverse fraternity on campus. Carrez himself is part Native American, while the fraternity's Vice President is Latino, and the Second Vice President is Chinese-American. Even the student who designed the T-shirt in question is Hispanic. When Carrez pointed this out, MEChA representatives merely said that because of the fraternity's diversity, "they should have known better."

Phi Kappa Sigma's hearing in front of the IFC Judicial Review Board was scheduled for the Friday after the party had taken place. By the time it arrived, tension on the campus was high, some members of the fraternity having had personal possessions stolen and others having had their car tires slashed. Fliers had appeared all over campus reading:

> *Stereotypes: The Phi Kappa Way Of Life.*
>
> *The members of Phi Kappa Sigma have repeatedly committed rude and offensive acts of Stereotyping Women and Minorities. Now they have finally been brought up on charges. Help fight against their Stereotyping.*

Just before the meeting on Friday, Carrez received a letter from the National Office of Phi Kappa Sigma indicating that without further inquiry it was placing a series of sanctions on the fraternity in response to the T-shirt incident. These included 16 hours of community service, two sensitivity seminars on multiculturalism and a formal letter of apology to the offended groups.

Although these penalties were stiff (and indicative of the fact that Phi Kappa Sigma had been left by its elders to twist slowly in the wind) they did not compare to what the fraternity's members felt was coming next when they arrived at the Inter Fraternity Council Judicial Hearing and found that it was open season on them. The room was packed with students from MEChA, who immediately presented the Board with a letter co-signed by the UER, the Union of Gay Lesbian and Bisexuals and the Women's Resource Center, listing their grievances against the fraternity. MEChA was first to take the floor, accusing Phi Kappa Sigma of using their T-shirts to purposefully launch a racist attack on the Latino community. They proceeded by demanding that the fraternity be stripped of its charter and expelled from the UCR campus.

When it was their turn to speak, members of Phi Kappa Sigma apologized for anything that they may have done to offend the Hispanic students. They informed the Board of the punishment that had been meted out by their National, hoping that this in some way might appease the Chicano students. But it didn't, and the IFC's decision came down hard against Phi Kappa Sigma, ordering them to destroy the offending shirts, banning them from intramural sports as well as barring them from any rush activities for the following year. Although the punishments were stringent, the MEChA students were not satisfied, walking out before the Board could finish the sentencing.

The members of Phi Kappa Sigma were devastated by the IFC's decision, but they felt some relief in the fact that their ordeal was over they were still a recognized fraternity by the school. The following Monday, however, Carrez went to his campus mail box to find a letter marked "confidential" addressed to him from Vincent Del Pizzo, the Assistant Vice Chancellor of UCR. Del Pizzo informed that fraternity that he was revoking the decision of the IFC, seeing it as a weak response to a heinous crime. Citing violations of numerous campus conduct codes, Del Pizzo revoked the charter of the fraternity because of its continued "insensitivity to UCR's campus environment." He then proceeded to lay out a laundry list of past offenses as though it were a rap sheet which justified the sentence: singing bawdy drinking songs, throwing a "Doggie Style" party, and writing their fraternity letters on a bus stop. Among the trespasses listed was Phi Kappa Sigma's viewing of "Debbie Does Dallas" in a campus classroom, an act which "incensed women's groups on campus," although this happened in 1984, when the current members of the fraternity were about 12.

At this point, the situation seemed hopeless to Carrez and the rest of the Phi Kappa Sigma members. Del Pizzo's sentiment seemed to be uniformly expressed throughout the college administration. Carrez felt stigmatized and abandoned. He was ready to throw in the towel. It was at this point that he received a call from John Howard of The Individual Rights Foundation.

The Individual Rights Foundation was founded by Southern California attorney John Howard earlier this year. A well known litigator with a successful corporate practice, Howard had become concerned about the advent of speech codes and other threats to free speech on college campuses across the country. What most concerned him was that groups like the ACLU merely made sympathetic noises but really hadn't stepped in to help students who were seeing their rights to free expression assaulted in the name of a "higher morality" involving multiculturalism and diversity.

After talking to some of his colleagues, Howard formed the Individual Rights Foundation and set about gathering a network of attorneys around the country who would function as a sort of First Amendment equivalent of 911 for beleaguered students like Rick Carrez who are unable to defend themselves against the juggernauts which form on campuses like the University of California Riverside. His sales pitch to them was simple:

"'The Greater Good' has replaced individual liberties as the virtue of the day," he says. "The Individual Rights Foundation is trying to reverse this tendency. Once freedom of speech is firmly established on college campuses, then you are going to see a true diversity of discourse and debate. One that you have never seen before...The left will then lose its teeth, because it will no longer be able to completely monopolize debate on college campuses. Their ideas will have to be measured against the ideas of others and will be found as wanting as I believe they are."

Howard had some early successes in rolling back abuses against free speech at Occidental College. When one fraternity was brought up on charges of sexual harassment for a lewd poem published in a private newsletter, Howard filed suit against the school, forcing them to withdraw all of their charges. Receiving dozens of calls a weeks from campuses all over the country—the callers include professors as well as students—he has begun to establish his organization as a sort of court of last resort for people sentenced to political reeducation and even expulsion, usually without due process, for transgressions against good taste and political correctness.

Howard had heard of Phi Kappa Sigma's problems by way of a UCR graduate student. When Howard spoke to Carrez, he found the fraternity president in a defeated mood, ready to accept the punishment about to be meted out to his organization. Howard told Carrez that the school was in violation of the First Amendment of the Constitution and of California's newly ratified Leonard Law, which simply states that whatever is considered protected speech off a college campus is protected speech on campus as well.

Within days Howard travelled to Riverside to meet with the Phi Kappa Sigma alumni board. It did not take much convincing for them to agree to file suit against the University of California at Riverside. Howard's only stipulation was that, once the proceedings began, they had to agree to follow them through to the end.

Working with Moss Gropen, a local area attorney and Phi Kappa Sigma alumnus, Howard filed his action against UCR on October 20. He personally served the court papers to Vice Chancellor Lou Leo and Assistant Vice Chancellor Vincent Del Pizzo.

The University was at first surprised and then alarmed by the suit. Within days, Howard and Gropen had been invited to sit down for negotiations with UCR administrators and their lawyers. Howard listed his demands, saying that he would not settle for anything less than the university's full capitulation. Though the general council for UCR offered a counter-proposal that was riddled with technicalities and compromise, it was clear to the university that they did not have a leg to stand on. After two hours of discussion the university caved in on all accounts.

All charges against the Phi Kappa Sigma fraternity were dropped and immunity from prosecution for any previous misdeeds was granted. It was agreed that the only disciplinary action that could be taken against the fraternity was that which was handed down by their own national office.

Howard had gotten similar results in other cases he had taken. ("Almost always university administrators suppress free speech with the assumption that students will be too intimidated or too strapped financially to make a fight of it," he says.) But because this case was so blatant, he decided to pursue an idea which had been incubating since he began the Individual Rights Foundation. One of the ways that advocates of multiculturalism had succeeded in their drive to close down discourse on campus, Howard had realized, was by sentencing students to sensitivity training sessions, which were both punishment and reeducation for their thought crimes.

Turning this malicious idea on its head, Howard made a final demand on the Riverside authorities. In order for him to withdraw his suit and not press for damages, they would have to agree to send their high-level administrators to sensitivity training—not in racism, sexism and homophobia, but in respect for the First Amendment. In this case, the sensitivity trainer would be a constitutional lawyer and the sessions would be for five hours.

When asked his opinion of the settlement, Del Pizzo, somewhat closed-lipped, said that "If that's what I need to do for the university to resolve [this situation] then that's what I will do." None of the other administrators, however, would comment directly on the university's capitulation.

The brothers of Phi Kappa Sigma are pleased by the fact, perhaps an ironic one, that they are part of a momentous event which may mark the beginning of a counter-offensive against the forces that have succeeded in putting free speech on the defensive on American campuses during the last few years. But for the time being there are more important things to celebrate. Next week marks the beginning of UC Riverside's Greek Games. These particular fraternity boys will be easy to find. Printed across their backs will be a new slogan celebrating their recent victory: "Back By Popular Demand!"

November, 1993

SENSITIVITY ÜBER ALLES

Frat Attack

by Bill Cerveny

Alpha Tau Omega's poet in residence thought the Occidental College fraternity's monthly newsletter was a harmless joke. In announcing the fraternity's homecoming party late in September of last year, he told the ATO members to "start telling your buddies and slutties to make sure they go." He ended the invitation with some smutty doggerel about a man named "Buffalo Pete" and his "thousand pounds of hanging meat." The rhyme told of Pete's affections for a woman named Sally Brown and how, during a brief posterior interlude, Sally emitted a flatus that sent Pete home with "a thousand pounds of shredded meat." Although the poem was mailed to each member's private P.O. box, a copy of the letter was stolen and reprinted in the campus newspaper and that is when the meat, so to speak, hit the fan.

Members of ATO suddenly found themselves the target of campus-wide criticism at the small, Southern California college. Unprepared for the onslaught, they hoped that an admission that they were guilty of poor taste and that their sin was perhaps mitigated by the fact that the newsletter was intended for members only would remove some of the pressure. But campus feminists pumped up the volume of their attack on the fraternity. The newsletter rapidly became a symbol of the sexism feminists alleged infected the college. They made it clear that they would settle for only one verdict regarding ATO: off with their heads!

Upon returning from their Thanksgiving vacation, nine brothers of Alpha Tau Omega sorted through their mail to find plain white envelopes addressed to "An ATO Member." Inside of each envelope was a note written in clipped magazine letters, crookedly arranged to read: OUR BLOOD IS ON YOUR HANDS! At the bottom sat a cruel signature in the form of a bloody tampon taped to each page. These missives characterized the radical feminists' campaign against the Alpha Tau Omega fraternity. They charged that the newsletter showed there was a "rapist mentality" evident in the fraternity. In acts of anonymous solidarity, covert feminist organizations began to sprout up on the Occidental campus to carry the fight. A group calling themselves Random Pissed Off Women (RPOW), blanketed the university with fliers and banners with a clenched fist serving as a crest, urging Occidental students to "make your voices heard." RPOW flew banners accusing ATO members of promoting rape in their poems and "female genital mutilation" in their fraternity songs. (A Bloomian misreading of the verse in question.) This type of behavior, they held, "IS NOT freedom of speech", but rather sexual harassment and as such must be banned. Another feminist group that has still remained unidentified left an indelible message on the campus as they spray painted in large red letters the words "ATO" –circled and slashed through — and "FIGHT RAPE" on walls and stairways all over the campus.

From the time that the newsletter's contents were first reprinted in the campus newspaper, *The Occidental*, it was three weeks until university administrators yielded to the feminists' pressure and began an investigation of Alpha Tau Omega. The issue was handed to a group called The Advocates Against Sexual Harassment, a panel of 24 members, both students and faculty, who have graduated from sensitivity training sessions. It is the role of The Advocates to aid victims of sexual harassment, assist in the resolution of their problems, and to make them aware of their options in confronting and dealing with their antagonists.

The Advocates was established in 1991 after the rape of an Occidental student, but had yet to handle a major case until the ATO incident. Spearheaded by a left-leaning English Professor named John Swift, the Advocates saw a chance to actively seek out and deal with sex offenders. It was a subtle alteration in mission, and it caused controversy in the group. One student member of The Advocates comments: "It was my understanding that the Advocates were founded as a support group for people who have been sexually harassed. Instead they are actively going out and seeking instances of sexual harassment...It alarms me and it sets a dangerous precedent." This student also felt that while it was objectionable, the poem, particularly because of its private circulation, was protected speech.

But such qualms were not shared by everyone. One female faculty member serving on The Advocates cited the ATO newsletter as yet one more example of why the university should get rid of fraternities. When a student asked her, "What do you want to get rid of next, sports teams?" the professor responded, "In good time."

Sixteen of the 24 members of the Advocates Against Sexual Harassment decided that it was their duty to bring charges against ATO. Because of heavy dissent within the group, they could not file a complaint under the banner of The Advocates committee. Instead, they formed their own committee, excluding the eight dissenters who regarded their action as a witch-hunt. Daily memos were sent to one another as this cabal plotted its assault on Alpha Tau Omega.

Ultimately, Professor Swift and his fifteen allies filed a joint complaint against ATO. Although they signed as individuals, in an effort to gain credibility, all of the underwriters identified themselves as Advocate members. To gain credibility for their charges, Swift's crusaders compiled a list of other ATO infractions against good taste. Among these complaints, they dredged up another newsletter in which there was a reference to kicking a girl in the "kitty." This lit the gasoline that had already been poured on troubled waters. The members of the Feminist Consciousness Coalition marched across campus and held a candlelight vigil in front of the ATO house. There they huddled together crying, reading letters to the members of Alpha Tau Omega that told of how deeply they had been hurt.

With the charges now filed against the fraternity, the university began to bow under the pressure of the 16 Advocates and the campus radicals. A hearing date was set. It was there that the fate of ATO would be decided. From the fraternity's point of view, this was the worst possible scenario. Occidental's private hearing committee was sure to find them guilty. ATO faced suspension.

Fraternities are the last group that might be expected to stand on the front lines of the PC battles. Until recently, the rap on them has been that they were primitives who came to college for fun and were filled with beery childishness. They were Animal House, spring vacation at Fort Lauderdale, hazing their pledges, and cheating on exams. They were, in a word, irrelevant. While other students were trying to change the world, fraternity boys were drunk and disorderly.

But then, in the 80s, the universities were conquered by a political correctness offensive, and fraternities found themselves one of the few remaining conservative campus institutions. It was a conservatism of social outlook rather than politics, but that made them all the more inviting a target. Their institutionalized bad taste was a pure expression of the sin in the heart of all white males.

Fraternities are no longer viewed as just a bunch of campus yahoos, but a potential fifth column whose odd position on the edges of the American campus put them beyond the reach of the righteous. Thus the commissars of political correctness, having conquered the admissions policies, curriculum and faculty hiring process, turned its attention to this last stubborn redoubt of opposition. The persecution of Alpha Tau Omega at Occidental was not an isolated incident, therefore, but rather emblematic of the purges that are taking place on college campuses.

At Cal State Northridge, for instance, the Zeta Beta Tau fraternity is no longer recognized by the university. It was banished as the result of a flier that advertised a Mexican Fiesta Party with the following dedication: "This party is in honor of Lupe, Cheech and Chong and Richie Valens." Though the flier was approved for distribution by the student activities department, a number of Chicano students were offended by the reference to Lupe. Lupe is the subject of a UCLA fraternity song that was written about a "fat Mexican whore," and which earned the offending frat a suspension.

At Georgia State University, the Sigma Nu fraternity has come under fire from black student activists as well as the school administration. At a late night fraternity party, one Sigma Nu member scratched the word

'Niger' into the lid of a trash can. Even though he was drunk — and the word was spelled like the country, not the racial slur — the campus exploded. Black student activists staged protests. They closed down the school by taking over the student center as well as the president's office. They presented a list of demands including amnesty for all participants of the sit-in, the immediate formation of an African American Studies Department, a new computer for a minority professor, and the revocation of Sigma Nu's charter. Even though the black students ripped telephones out of the walls of the president's office and stole office equipment, most of their demands were immediately met. The fate of Sigma Nu is still undetermined, but its days at Georgia State seem numbered.

At George Mason's annual "Derby Day," the Sigma Chi fraternity staged a mock beauty pageant, in which sorority members dressed up Sigma Chi brothers as women in trying to raise money for charity. One fraternity brother took the stage dressed in black face, a black curly wig and a pillow stuffed in the back of his skirt. A number of people complained that the Sigma Chi contest perpetuated racial and sexual stereotypes. Although the event was pre-approved by the school activities department, Sigma Chi was placed on probation for two years and is currently embroiled in a protracted legal action.

At Texas A & M, the Sigma Alpha Epsilon fraternity held a "Jungle Party." Keeping with the theme, the initiated SAE members dressed themselves in safari gear. Their pledges painted their entire upper bodies black and wore grass skirts, Afros and fake bone jewelry. As the evening progressed, the brothers chased the pledges through the party with spears. The following day, the band hired for the evening wrote a letter to the student newspaper claiming that the party was offensive and that the members were racially insensitive. The fraternity was fined $1,000 by the Inter-fraternity council, placed on social probation by the school, and forced to sponsor a multicultural sensitivity seminar. Another part of their penance was being forced to listen to the Nation of Islam's Kwata X, brought to campus by a black state legislator to lecture on racism.

For the most part, the assault against fraternities has been spearheaded not by administrations, inured to displays of bad taste, but by radical campus groups for whom bad taste is a political crime. For the most part these groups have been able to outgun the fraternities in the conflicts over speech and behavior that arise. At Occidental, however, there was a different outcome.

The college's proceedings against ATO had the feel of a political move to Anthony Lebrija, President of the fraternity. Lebrija was embarrassed by the offensive newsletter, but he was also disturbed by the fact that charges against his organization were based on mail theft and by the way campus feminists were manipulating the administrators. But he felt helpless and decided to call Occidental President John Slaughter and arrange for a meeting at which he would plea for mercy. It seemed to be the only chance for ATO's survival on campus, the only way to end the harassment and hate mail. An hour after making the appointment, however, Lebrija received a phone call from John Howard, legal counsel for The Individual Rights Project, which protects the constitutional rights of students victimized by political correctness. Howard told Lebrija that the ATO newsletter was protected under the First Amendment and by California state law, and offered his services — pro bono.

Howard explained the reasons he had formed The Individual Rights Foundation. "The First Amendment starts with an assumption: whatever you say or express is protected. These people in the universities want to start from the other end and say that there are a number of things that you are not free to say and everything else is free speech."

Howard refused to read the offending poem. Since not even the critics were claiming libel, whatever it said, however objectionable, was protected speech. Howard told Lebrija that the matter did not rest there. He was willing to move against the individual faculty members and administrators that were involved in the harassment of the fraternity. "They cannot, with impunity, attack other people on campus in the name of their ideology...These people live in a world where their actions have no consequences. We need to make them have consequences." Lebrija decided to take a chance and let Howard defend ATO.

When Lebrija walked into his scheduled meeting with Slaughter, he was armed with two letters from his new attorney. The first letter, Howard told him, was to be given to Slaughter at the beginning of the meeting. This informed the Occidental President about California State Senator William Leonard's recent bill that made speech which is protected under the Constitution off campus protected on campus as well. The law secures students' First Amendment rights, shielding them from any administrative action as a result of having offended against campus speech codes.

Howard spelled out the implications. A private newsletter "irrespective of the insensitivity or bad taste of those materials" is protected free speech. "If this were not the case, *Playboy* and *Penthouse* would long ago have been sued for sexual harassment." Howard informed Slaughter that he was in clear violation of California law and informed him that if he did not abandon the idea of disciplining ATO the college would face a lawsuit.

After Lebrija's initial meeting with President Slaughter, it was not necessary to use Howard's second letter, which stated that if the college failed to stop all proceedings against Alpha Tau Omega, a lawsuit would be filed against Occidental, the administrators, John Swift and all faculty members involved in the assault, as well as all of the trustees of the college as individuals.

After numerous consultations with his lawyers and the Alpha Tau Omega national headquarters, Slaughter realized that Occidental was on shaky legal ground. The college had no choice but to stop its drive against ATO. The school indefinitely postponed any hearings against the fraternity. "President Slaughter seemed almost relieved," Anthony Lebrija said later on. "He didn't approve of what we had done, but he didn't seem to think it was a capital offense either. It was almost as if his heart wasn't in persecuting us and he was looking for a legal reason not to do it."

When asked his opinion of the new California statute, Professor John Swift expressed frustration that a lawsuit stood in the way of determining the right "to be free of sexual harassment." Campus feminist Rebecca Montgomery was also upset. "Everyone is taking up the free speech issue...I think that people are forgetting the larger issue and getting caught up with details...The larger issue is sexism and people are getting caught up with 'Well, is this free speech or isn't this free speech?'" But the day had been carried by attorney Howard, who, in the matter of ATO at Occidental and other cases he has taken against university administrations acceding to pressure from radical groups, has established a precedent that may have consequences for the future. "If universities have no particular interest in protecting the Constitutional rights of its students," he says, "I think the courts certainly will have an interest in protecting them from the universities."

February, 1993

Stranger Than Fact

High Court Backs Hearing Impaired

by Judith Schumann Weizner

In a landmark decision today, the Supreme Court reinforced the principle of affirmative action for the hearing-impaired in a ruling that may transform the nation's symphony orchestras forever.

The Court held 7-2 that the Newark Philharmonia must hire Jane Taubhorner, a hearing-impaired French horn player. It further directed that the symphony immediately implement the Employment Guidelines of the American League of Hearing-Impaired Musicians, of which Ms. Taubhorner is president.

According to these Guidelines, all orchestras that receive funding from the National Council on Art and Music must be comprised of no fewer than nine percent hearing-impaired players by 1997. The Court also directed that the cost of any technical adjustments that must be made in orchestral procedures, in the instruments, or in the players, shall be borne equally by the orchestras and their subscribers.

Although nine percent is far in excess of the percentage of hearing-impaired Americans at present, this figure was set as a means of making reparation to past generations of hearing-impaired people who might have played in symphony orchestras had the opportunity been available to them. The Court left open the question of whether the figures may be revised upward at some future date.

The salient points of the Employment Guidelines of the American League of Hearing-Impaired Musicians were revealed today following the announcement of the decision.

1. Conductors will be required to communicate with the orchestra in American Sign Language (ASL). Translators must be provided for conductors who do not speak English.

2. Hearing-impaired players will occupy the front chairs in the orchestra so that their sight-lines to the conductor can be kept free from obstruction. (Formerly, these places were awarded on the basis of competitive auditions to players who received bonuses for serving as leaders of their sections. These bonuses will not be affected when they relinquish their places.)

3. Music stands must be equipped with oscilloscopes to aid the hearing-impaired players in adjusting their intonation to that of the other musicians.

4. A hearing player who becomes hearing-impaired in the course

of his employment cannot be dismissed on that account.

5. The U.S. Symphony Orchestra Association must establish a fund to be used in the immediate training of sixteen percussionists. (Since there are at present few identified hearing-impaired students of orchestral instruments in the country, immediate action must be taken to fill the needs of the future. It is generally thought by professional musicians that the percussion instruments can be learned more quickly than either strings or winds. They have the added feature of being highly noticeable, thus providing hearing-impaired persons with the inspiration to study music.)

6. As of June 30 of the fifth year after the implementation of the Guidelines, string and wind players must be hired until the nine percent goal is reached.

7. The hiring of hearing-impaired musicians will begin immediately with Ms. Taubhorner.

In an exclusive interview following today's announcement Ms. Taubhorner emphasized a unique attribute that makes hearing-impaired players highly suitable for employment in the modern symphony orchestra: they are unlikely to suffer from the emotional problems that plague many hearing players who are frequently required to perform contemporary music. Ms. Taubhorner expressed confidence that the decision would have the additional effect of creating a warmer climate within the professional music world for young composers.

Jane Taubhorner's interest in music began while she was a student at the N.Y.C.U. School of Social Work. Research for a paper led her to the discovery that there were no known instances of hearing-impaired orchestral players or conductors since 1827. Immediately upon graduation from N.Y.C.U. she undertook the mastery of the French horn, at the same time founding the A.L.H.M. of which she has been re-elected president every year. Now sixty-seven years of age, Ms. Taubhorner will be eligible for retirement from the Newark Philharmonia in five years—just as the first of the newly trained string and wind players provided for in the Supreme Court decision begin to take their places in the nation's orchestras. "It is the fulfillment of a life-long dream," she said.

Outside the Supreme Court building, as Ms. Taubhorner and her supporters celebrated their victory with a wild cacophony of triumphant chants, a spokesperson for the Confederation for the Sight-Impaired indicated that the Confederation plans to institute legal proceedings tomorrow as there are no sight-impaired players in any symphony orchestra in the country. Noting that they have just won a suit against the Amalgamated Bus Drivers' Association, he seemed confident of victory.

November, 1992

Economics Of Panhandling

by Steven Plant

In direct contrast with the popular view that panhandling is a symptom of the failures of capitalism, it is in fact a clear illustration of the vitality of capitalism, where enterprise, innovation and initiative are rewarded. This would be the view of the discipline of Economics, which would argue that panhandling—like absolutely everything in life—should be viewed as a market. In this market there are producers and consumers of services. The producers are the panhandlers themselves, "panhandling entrepreneurs" who supply "homelessness services." The consumers of these services are of course those willing to pay for them, those who contribute their "spare change" to the panhandling entrepreneurs.

Now at first glance the reader might find it upsetting that panhandling should be represented here as entrepreneurial activity, rather than a nuisance or form of charity. But anyone watching behavior on the streets of San Francisco or New York would have to acknowledge that a sizeable portion of the American public is interested in consuming "homelessness services" from our panhandling industry, and so demand creates supply.

Panhandling is clearly a contestable market in the Baumol sense, with low barriers to entry. Indeed homeless rights advocates constantly confirm this when they argue that anyone could become homeless. The size of the market must therefore be demand determined, not supply determined.

As in all forms of consumption it is impossible to really know "why" the service itself is being demanded. It may be that American consumers simply enjoy the charitable posturing involved in purchasing panhandling services. In some cases they may enjoy seeing streets filled with panhandlers and are willing to subsidize their activities. For example, in Berkeley, where I taught as a Visiting Professor of Business Administration, the city council did everything in its powers to fill city streets with panhandlers in order to prove to the world the failure and the heartlessness of Reagan-Bush economic policies. In other cases, the panhandling industry provides supporters with a cheap outlet for recreational compassion.

That the American public derives consumer utility from purchasing panhandling services should be obvious. Why else would they insist on forcing so many people out of comfortable institutions in order to work the streets selling panhandling services? Apparently many American consumers like to see misfortune firsthand, to wring their hands over it, smell it, and feel they are exhibiting "caring." They are willing to pay for this recreation. For a while they hoped that impoverished immigrants to America from the underdeveloped countries would supply them with these services, but the immigrants have apparently preferred to get jobs and so it has been necessary to develop a domestic homeless "work force."

Contrary to the opinion of some, Americans are really quite savvy people. They clearly understand that when a panhandler asks you for money in order to buy food, the money will not be spent on food. After all if buyers of panhandling services cared the least whether or not the panhandlers were eating they would buy them pastrami sandwiches or fajita pitas, rather than handing them spare change. Or perhaps they would express their compassion by donating money to one of the countless soup kitchens operating in the country. The problem is that there is no functioning secondary market to speak of for converting salads or sandwiches into drugs and booze (in the latter case one might say there is illiquidity in the liquidity exchange), and so most panhandlers deal only on a cash basis.

Americans are also wise enough to realize that a panhandler with a sign asking you for either a handout or a job generally does not want you to offer him a job. Hence consumers of panhandling do not give the panhandler the classified ad section of the local newspaper, nor inform him that there is a help-wanted sign near his panhandling station.

Now while it is always dangerous to tamper with successful growth industries, nevertheless I would like to make a proposal for improving the operations of the panhandling market. This important industry should be reorganized by launching a national Pushups-for-Panhandlers campaign, or PFP for short. Its operations would be quite simple.

Any panhandler asking for spare change would be instructed to drop down on all fours and do pushups, to be compensated at the reasonable rate of, say, three cents per pushup. No pushups, no change. Those over 60 or pregnant could do them from the knees. Such a national campaign would do wonders for America.

First it would work for the benefit of the panhandling entrepreneurs themselves. Many of these might actually choose to spend their business revenues on nutrition rather than drugs and drink in order to improve their future revenue generating capabilities. Indeed they would have financial incentives to avoid these unwholesome addictions altogether in order to preserve their pushup capacity. Panhandlers would have the satisfaction of engaging in physical production and contributing to the GNP. Our cities would be so much more pleasant, as a panhandler doing pushups is no more annoying for passersby than a street musician. A fit panhandler could earn more than the minimum wage. It could be the biggest national physical fitness campaign since President Kennedy. Pushup panhandling might even prove more profitable than prostitution, and besides it presents no public health danger when performed without a condom.

Most importantly, pushup panhandling would remove the stigma of getting something for nothing from producers in this valuable industry. Citizens concerned with homelessness should put on their red, white and blue PFP buttons and answer every request for spare change with an invitation to finance pushups.

February, 1993

High Court Upholds Justice Concept

by Judith Schumann Weizner

In a major decision one year after the sweeping reform of the legal system mandated by the Clinton Administration's Judicial Reform Act of 1994, the Supreme Court today upheld the manslaughter conviction of a middle-aged piano teacher who killed a homeless woman in a street fight in New York City.

The case received much publicity when the jury in the original trial rendered an acquittal which was overturned on appeal due to an incorrect calculation of Justice Points.

The facts in the case were never in dispute. Stephanie West had been on her way home from giving a piano lesson on the evening of December 15 when she was accosted on the street by Laticia Riggs, who demanded a dollar. Ms. West ignored Ms. Riggs and continued to walk along West End Avenue where both women resided. When Ms. Riggs grabbed Ms. West by the arm, spun her around and punched her in the face, Ms. West reacted. Falling to the ground, Ms. West saw a beer bottle lying by the curb. She picked it up by the neck, smashed it on the sidewalk and held it in front of herself as she got to her feet. When Ms. Riggs charged her again, Ms. West swiped at her with the broken bottle, severing Ms. Riggs' jugular.

Ms. West was charged with manslaughter and subsequently acquitted by the jury. The Appeals Court pointed out, however, that a serious error had been made in calculating the Justice Points that led to its verdict.

The Essential Points were correctly assessed. Ms. Riggs had precipitated the attack, making Ms. West a victim and thus eligible for one hundred points. Both principals were women, meriting fifty points each. But since Ms. West is white and Ms. Riggs was black, Ms. West was penalized twenty points.

The error in the decision was in the calculation of the Circumstantial Points. Since both women reside on lower middle class West End Avenue, each received ten points. But because Ms. West lived indoors at an address in the low four hundreds, she forfeited her ten points and Ms. Riggs received a grant of ten percent of Ms. West's street address. Additionally, Ms. West had armed herself against someone poorer than she, costing her five percent of her total adjusted points. It was further pointed out that the reason Ms. West had chosen that particular weapon was that she had seen it on television. Since Ms. Riggs had no television, she was awarded an additional ten points.

When the Circumstantials were computed, Ms. West earned four more Justice Points than Ms. Riggs, and so the decision went to Ms. West. However, the Appeals Court pointed out that Ms. West had been on the way home after giving a classical piano lesson and so Ms. Riggs had been entitled to an additional Circumstantial Award of ten percent of her total.

The case went to the Supreme Court because Ms. West's lawyers argued that the piano is also used to play blues, jazz and rock, and that although Ms. West had indeed just given a lesson in classical music she is also able to play music of the underclass. One of the telling arguments was that one week prior to the incident Ms. West's classical student had asked to learn "The Entertainer" by black composer Scott Joplin and had been given this music immediately.

It was a surprise, therefore, when the High Court upheld Ms. West's conviction. Justice Lamont Tripe spoke for the minority of Justices when he wrote, "The killing of a homeless woman cannot be excused on the grounds that the killer could also play jazz. That excuse is akin to the disclaimer 'Some of my best friends are Jews' that is often used by anti-Semites to explain away their behavior. But more important than this in arriving at the decision was the fact that the proportion of white females in the penal system is not yet commensurate with the proportion of white females in the population. The conviction must stand."

With this decision the Judicial Reform Act of 1994 has demonstrated its validity. Enacted to eliminate both the subjectivity and bias that had become evident in verdicts and the legal congestion resulting from an overwhelming number of hung juries, it provides a means of assuring impartiality in the justice system. The proviso that in odd-numbered years the minority opinion on the Supreme Court shall prevail has been hailed by legal scholars as the final embodiment of judicial equity.

December, 1992

Homeless Man To Get Law Doctorate

by Judith Schumann Weizner

Dr. Maximilian Shellout, dean of the National Law School, announced yesterday that National would grant an honorary Doctor of Laws degree to Lucien Sacrevache of New York City, a 43-year-old homeless undocumented alien, because of the remarkably broad knowledge of the law he has exhibited.

Dr. Shellout said that since arriving in the United States in 1983 Mr. Sacrevache, appearing pro se in at least ten cases, some of which he has argued before the Supreme Court, has compiled a winning record that would be the envy of any member of any blue ribbon law firm.

In his latest stunning victory, Sacrevache vs. Pan-Global International Insurance Company, Inc., Mr. Sacrevache won an appeal that will effectively extend to the homeless the same right to buy homeowner's insurance that homeowners and renters have long enjoyed.

Last March the Court of Appeals held that Pan-Global must pay the claim of Mr. Sacrevache, whose lean-to was destroyed when fire swept the rubbish-strewn area under the West Side Highway where he and twelve other homeless persons lived.

Following the fire a year and a half ago Mr. Sacrevache submitted a claim to Pan-Global for twenty-thousand dollars which the company refused on the grounds that Mr. Sacrevache had not only never purchased one of its policies, but had never even applied for coverage either on his abode or on its contents.

Citing the precedent set in Sacrevache vs. Burger Queen, Mr. Sacrevache stated that although he had not actually purchased insurance, he had intended to do so, therefore entitling himself to coverage. (In Sacrevache vs. Burger Queen, the restaurant was compelled to retain Mr. Sacrevache, then a beggar, as its doorman because Sacrevache had sought conventional employment by the Burger Queen on many occasions, thereby demonstrating a willingness to work. The court ruled that Sacrevache's impressive lack of hygiene could not be held against him in the presence of such an obvious and ardent desire for employment.)

In his original action against Pan-Global in State Supreme Court, Mr.

Sacrevache was unable to produce any concrete proof of his desire to be insured and case was dismissed for lack of evidence. However, subsequent questioning of fire department officials elicited possible recollections of a pile of soggy insurance company brochures seen amid the rubble of melted VCR's and twisted TV's and computers after the fire. The case was thus brought forward once again on grounds of newly-discovered evidence.

Pan-Global insisted that if indeed there were brochures, said brochures must be produced in court so that their authenticity could be determined. Mr. Sacrevache was unable to produce them but instead introduced testimony from the captain on duty at the fire who swore that one of his men had told him he had seen "a lot of papers in the corner."

Mr. Sacrevache swore that these papers included brochures from several insurance companies regarding their homeowner policies. He said he had been comparing coverage on electronic equipment on the evening of the fire, that he had decided on the Pan-Global policy as most comprehensive, and had been on the point of going to a nearby pay phone to call Pan-Global's 800 number when his washing machine overflowed, pouring water onto the cord connecting his microwave to the traffic light at the corner of Fifty-eighth Street and Twelfth Avenue, starting the fire.

The fire captain's testimony as to the existence of the brochures was dismissed as hearsay and the verdict went once again to Pan-Global. But as soon as he settled into a new non-home, Mr. Sacrevache filed an appeal. Citing Sacrevache vs. City of New York, Mr. Sacrevache held that the testimony of the fire fighter had been inappropriately rejected as hearsay because Sacrevache vs. City of New York renders it improper to doubt the word of a homeless person in the presence of any corroborating testimony, however tenuous.

(Several years prior to the fire, Mr. Sacrevache had sued the city when the refrigerator crate in which he was then living was run over by a garbage truck. The sanitation department argued that Mr. Sacrevache's home had protruded into the street and that instead of receiving an award he should have been charged with obstructing traffic. Mr. Sacrevache maintained that his crate had been precisely where it had always been and that the city had never asked him to move it. A spokesman for the police department testified that Mr. Sacrevache had been told to move the crate, but that no citation had been issued. However, another homeless man swore that he had often seen police smiling and joking with Mr. Sacrevache in front of his abode, but that he had never heard anyone tell him to move the crate, nor had Mr. Sacrevache ever spoken of having been given such an order. After a lengthy court battle, the Supreme Court held that, as with deathbed statements, testimony given either by the homeless or corroborating that of a homeless person must receive special weight due to the desperate nature of their circumstances.)

On appeal, therefore, the recollection of the fire captain concerning the existence of the brochures was held to be such corroborative testimony and the decision was reversed. The Court directed Pan-Global to pay the twenty-thousand-dollar claim.

During the time he was proceeding with his appeal, Mr. Sacrevache also handily won a product liability suit against the Swirlpool Washing Machine Company and a settlement of undisclosed magnitude from Bronze Star Microwave. (He argued successfully that the homeless, having no address, can not subscribe to consumer magazines and are not in a position to know about possible defects in products. Furthermore, since the homeless nearly always acquire their electronic equipment unboxed, without instructions and without warranties, the manufacturer must assume responsibility for damage stemming from use of its products.) A suit against City Signal Co., which provides New York's traffic lights, is still pending.

This afternoon, following Dr. Shellout's announcement, Mr. Sacrevache, embracing once again his identity as an undocumented alien, expressed his thanks to the National Law School and to the United States. "I am especially grateful to this country for the many opportunities it has given me. Long before I came here I heard a saying — 'Only in America' — whose true meaning escaped me until today. Now I too can say, Only in America."

March, 1993

Inmates Settle With Authorities At Rolling Hills

by Judith Schumann Weizner

An uprising at the Rolling Hills Correctional Facility in which residents threatened the life of the lieutenant governor was aborted yesterday when the institution's director, Ward Clinton, successfully negotiated an end to the unrest that has plagued the facility for the past four months.

Anonymous sources report that one Allan Greenberg, who is serving ten to fifteen years for a hate crime, provided crucial assistance in the negotiations that ended the stand-off.

Yesterday's mutiny was the latest in a series of uprisings at Rolling Hills that began four months ago with a demonstration over the serving of pork in the non-vegetarian dining hall. Amid shouts of "Jihad!" Muslim residents refused to eat the pork chops they had been given, insisting that officials of the institution knew that their religion forbids the consumption of pork. When Greenberg, the only Jewish resident in the institution, did not join in their demands, saying instead that he was not religious and had always liked to eat pork, the Muslim residents threatened to dismember him, but before they could carry out their threat, Greenberg persuaded Clinton to order the dietitian to substitute beef for the pork. The jihad was revoked and Greenberg was not harmed.

However, the matter did not end there. The non-Muslim residents who were served pork called for a hunger strike to dramatize their contention that they were being discriminated against because pork, since it cannot be eaten rare, is inferior to beef. Director Clinton finally issued an order forbidding pork at the institution. Greenberg than filed suit in Federal Court, alleging that his Eighth Amendment rights were being violated because forbidding him to eat pork constituted cruel and unusual punishment. Judge Belle Clinton (no close relation to the Rolling Hills Director) dismissed the suit with the observation that if Greenberg had been religious he probably wouldn't have been at Rolling Hills in the first place.

An uneasy calm prevailed for several weeks until residents in the fragrance-free module demanded the replacement of a corrections counselor who had come to work wearing after-shave. Director Clinton explained that the corrections counselor, whose name has not been revealed, had indeed reported for duty wearing after-shave, expecting to be assigned to the smokers' module, but that his assignment had been changed subsequent to his arrival at work. He had showered but it was impossible for him to remove the last traces of Aramis from his skin. Residents demanded a replacement for the corrections counselor, but the other possible replacements had also come to work wearing cologne or after-shave. When Clinton explained to the residents that he could not allow the fragrance-free module to be undermanned, the residents jammed the governor's switchboard with calls of complaint from their cellular phones.

At Greenberg's suggestion the dispute was resolved with an order forbidding the corrections counselors to wear scents of any kind while on duty or in the twenty-four hours prior to their reporting for duty.

But by far the most serious incident occurred yesterday when the lieutenant governor, during an inspection of Rolling Hills, stepped on a cockroach while touring the animist module and was immediately taken hostage by animist residents, who explained that they would have no compunction about killing him since their beliefs did not compel them to respect the lives of creatures that showed no respect for weaker life forms. Since the lieutenant governor's action demonstrated that he regarded the cockroach as a "mere" insect, the animists did not consider that he fell under the protection of their belief system.

The hostage situation appeared grave and it seemed like a complete impasse had been reached until Greenberg made an impassioned speech to residents explaining that if they persisted with their threat, Clinton would undoubtedly call in the National Guard and that in the violence that was sure to follow every rat and cockroach in the institution would be killed. "The blood of these creatures will be on your hands," he said. The animists reluctantly released the lieutenant governor.

These recent demonstrations have taken corrections department officials completely be surprise. The advanced concepts underlying the design and management of Rolling Hills were considered practically a guarantee of an atmosphere conducive to cooperative behavior among inmates and speedy rehabilitation.

Rolling Hills is a prize-winning, state-of-the-art maximum-security institution nestled in the foothills of the Ozark Mountains. It houses eight hundred convicted felons in a bucolic setting. Residents live in cottages, grouped according to common interest. All rooms are equipped with color television, a VCR, a small microwave oven for cooking late-night snacks, a mini-bar and a cellular phone. Computers may be requisitioned, although faxes are limited. The health club is open daily from 7 a.m. to l0 p.m. The VCR tape library receives first-run films at the same time they become available to the general public. Conjugal visits are allowed on a daily basis. Just last year Greenberg won the governor's permission for each resident to have one pet whose upkeep is funded by the environmental check-off option on the state income tax form.

Innovations in the design of the Rolling Hills have been hailed as next-century improvements over the typical prison design of older institutions. Instead of the traditional concrete walls and wire fences, there are plexiglass walls topped with electric wires painted to match the scenery, enabling residents to enjoy the marvelous vistas that bring them into closer contact with nature without the unpleasant distraction of the rows of razor wire characteristic of older institutions. Current research shows that appreciation of nature results in a less hostile attitude toward the larger society and encourages a more spiritual outlook. Indeed, that appears to be the case, since, in the six years that Rolling Hills has been operational, four residents who previously had no religious inclination have sought an affiliation.

Following the resolution of yesterday's crisis the governor promised to reconvene the Horton Commission before month's end to determine what changes are necessary at Rolling Hills. Greenberg, who was sentenced to Rolling Hills for having scribbled an obscenity on the top of his income tax form three years ago, has reportedly turned down the offer of a transfer to Allenwood.

May – June, 1993

President Of SMACT-UP Protests Discrimination

by Turk Richards

"It's time discrimination against 'people of pain' came to an end!" In the opening words of his recent press conference, Will B'Hert, President of SMACT-UP (Sado-Masochists Action Committee), whipped himself into a frenzy over what he regards as the continued rampant S&Mophobia permeating the fabric of American society.

"Our lifestyle should be recognized as part of the beautiful rainbow of American culture," B'Hert said. "People of pain are as normal as anyone else." He spoke flanked by other members of the organization who chanted, "We're the news! We're bruised!"

The SMACT-UP leader cited a recent study by sex researchers Masters and Bonds which he claimed indicates that one in ten Americans are either practicing sadomasochists or have engaged in at least one sadomasochistic experience in their lifetime.

"Millions of us live, work and study amongst you," B'Hert asserted, "but we are denied many of the basic civil rights guaranteed to all Americans under the Constitution. What we do in our basements is our business."

Discrimination against people of pain is no figment of the S&M community's collective imagination. There are statutes on the books of every state except Massachusetts prohibiting sadomasochistic families from adopting children. These laws remain despite a number of studies conducted by Ivy League universities which indicate that youngsters reared in S&M households are no more likely to embrace the lifestyle than other children. Prohibiting adoptions "smacks of S&Mophobia," according to B'Hert. "Like any other dedicated parents, we can provide our children with love and stability, and above all, with sorely needed discipline."

B'Hert and his group were particularly incensed by the refusal this spring of Boston's St. Patrick's Day Committee to allow members of S.M.I.T.E (Sado-Masochistic Irish Torment Enhancers) to march in this year's parade. For them, this was another case of exclusion based on prejudice. SMITE and SMACT-UP have hit parade organizers with a Federal lawsuit aimed at reversing the decision, an action which one long-time South Boston resident says threatens to tear apart the local community. "Let 'em do what they wanna in their own basements, but not on our streets," said one city resident, "enough is enough!"

B'Hert, author of the best-sellers *Getting to No* and *What Did I Do To Get So Black And Blue?*, which was optioned recently by Madonna's production company, called such thinking, "An example of a phobic mentality based on prejudice, a mentality which has never read de Sade or von Masoch, has socially constructed an image of what we are, and uses that image to condemn its sadomasochistic sons and daughters to a life of denial and to being in the closet for the wrong reasons."

S&Mophobic attitudes like those in South Boston must be "attacked head on," according to the SMACT-UP President. B'Hert outlined an eight point plan for achieving this goal:

1. Introduction of new pain-sensitive textbooks such as *Heather's Daddy Beats Her Mommy* into the first-grade curriculum at elementary schools throughout the nation.

2. Opening of fully funded S&M Centers on college campuses to provide counseling and technical know-how. "If people can learn the right way to put on a condom they ought to know how to properly use handcuffs."

3. Adding Sadomasochistic Studies to the core course requirements at all state universities and engaging in an active recruitment effort for S&M instructors as role models for students of pain.

4. Gaining a commitment from President Clinton to appoint openly sadomasochistic men or women to key posts his administration, so that the cabinet "not only looks like, but FEELS like America."

5. Ending the practice of banning sadomasochists from the military. "S&M soldiers have been physically attacked by their straight peers, which is all right, but it is also true that once liberated from the constraints of S&M-ophobia they could effectively employ aspects of their culture in combat situations."

6. Boycotting any state that refuses to pass laws banning discrimination against people of pain.

7. Repeated invasion of churches, particularly Catholic churches, until the hierarchy allows sadomasochists into the priesthood. "It's a prejudice from the Dark Ages. Who better to provide examples of how sinners can scourge away past offenses?"

8. Recognizing April 1, the Marquis de Sade's birthday, as "National S&M Pride Day."

Many sociologists and S&M activists predict that even if these efforts are successful, however, long-held values will be difficult to change. But B'Hert is hopeful that others can adopt the high level of tolerance exercised by SMACT-UP: "As people of pain, we embrace diversity without regard to race, class or gender. Our credo, 'If you can do it to us, we can do it to you,' is about as ecumenical as it gets."

B'Hert's determination at this press conference recalled his dramatic appearance at the Democratic National Convention last July as part of a campaign "to put people of pain in the national eye and lead them into bondage." On that occasion, his impassioned words brought Hillary Clinton to her feet in the Presidential box to start a foot-stomping ovation.

"We at SMACT-UP are chained together in our fight for justice and bound to the goal of acceptance by the dominating culture. Next time you see the symbol of our oppression, the black and blue triangle, on a bumper sticker or a pin sticking into our chest, remember, please, do not punish us for our lifestyle, we'd rather do that ourselves!"

April, 1993

The Chlorophyll Manifesto

by Steve Kogan

Flowers are born free, yet everywhere they are in gardens and flowerpots. How did this come to be? And how were wildflowers constructed by logocentric ideology into religious icons and botanical metaphors? Bravely seeking to break through the iron cage of phallic flower symbolism and at the same time subvert the sexist doctrine of the Trinity, Gertrude Stein attempts to liberate both religion and plants in her famous three-in-one flower proclamation, "A rose is a rose is a rose." But alas, this noble cry is undermined by its very emphasis, for roseness remains embedded in language, trapped in human speech. Her line is, in fact, a bourgeois recapitulation of a monkish belief in flower-power, according to which flowers gave off emanations that could be imprisoned in glass boxes and used to break through conventional constructions of the physical and linguistic world. The idea was a noble gesture on behalf of plants that nevertheless led to the oppressive custom of keeping flowers pressed in books or framed in glass, aesthetically inscribed by romantic ideology in the ballet, *"Le Spectre de la Rose."*

And so, to paraphrase Marx's opening of his pedestrian manifesto on the economic roots of history, I say that, yes, a specter *is* haunting the West, but it is a spirit not yet imagined in the most radical critiques of capitalism, racism, sexism, homophobia, ageism, lookism, and omnicide, in which the prime tool of skepsis has not even *guessed* at the true nature of ideological gaps, the fundamental meaning of *what has not been said*.

Hitherto, and including the latest perceptions of prejudice, every oppressed minority was assumed to have a voice, a voice that was muted, suppressed, enslaved, subverted, and ignored, but a voice nevertheless. Thanks to recent studies by Ague and Weltgeist, for example, we are now aware of the fact that among the many paintings of Mont St. Victoire by Cezanne, *not one oppressed proletarian* appears in any of the works, despite the fact that three generations of impoverished shoemakers were known to have had their shop in the village just behind the hill to the south-east of the mountain. Cezanne deliberately privileged the hill in order to hide all traces of poverty, when he could have easily included the shop by going 6 miles to the northeast. His pictures of Mont. St. Victoire thus create the false impression that he viewed it from every angle, in order to totalize his own prejudice and ensure that his father's considerable fortune from his bank in Aix-en-Provence would not be tainted by any subversion of this bourgeois-pastoral image. (Cezanne's inability to rebel against his father, like Herman Melville's, is thus hidden by the pseudo-innocence of his nature imagery, on the one hand, and his false portrayal of himself as a radical artist breaking with tradition, on the other — seen in this light, of course, his inability is also affirmed.)

Untergang and Cogito have similarly investigated the history of the blacksmith family living under the Rialto bridge in Venice, which was never included by Guardi or Canaletto in their dozens of so-called "Scenes of Venice." And Principia Femina, in her ovular study *Prolegomena to a History of What Has Not Been Said*, similarly redefines 1) Shakespearean tragedy (King Lear's homosexual lover *never* appears outright in the play), 2) Courbet's painting of "The Flayed Rabbit" (the abuse of a deaf mute on June 14, 1855, one mile away, does not even have iconographic mention in the work), and 3) Poe's "The Fall of the House of Usher," in which, to quote Femina, "Poe did not see the connection between the condition of white women in the 19th century and slavery."

All these buried voices, as I remarked earlier, once had real speech, speech that was denied by the anti-historical prejudices of white male hegemonic thought but nevertheless could be heard expressing suppressed rage in the shared communal experience of bars, bedrooms, and brothels. This much is clear and by now has been incorporated in the most progressive schools and critiques.

And now I introduce the true revolution in the revolution, for radical critique is itself subverted by the principle it seeks to undermine. *Radical critique is bourgeois prejudice disguised as radical critique.* In every instance (I cannot stress this too strongly), the suppressed voices now emerging once were real (children of repressed lesbians can thank radical feminists if they so desire; children of oppressed proletarians can thank revolutionaries, and so on); whereas there has not yet been a revaluation of that which has not been said on behalf of *that which cannot speak.*

The most subtle and yet most powerful prejudice facing the world today is *Plantism*, the deliberate suppression and subversion of the Otherness of plants. Indeed, the very word plant betrays the hegemonic desire to bury, to put underground, *to hide from consciousness.* Plantistic chauvinism, operating in the deep structure of language, thus oppresses the Other by projecting onto it the very act of suppression which it employs and falsely ascribes to plants. It is we humans who speak of "planting seeds," thus associating the word with burial through plantistic ideology, deliberately ignoring neutral, floral-free terms such as "seed embedment" and "reproductive earth-immersion." Worse yet, plantistic language controls our very notion of causality. We speak of ideas and events "having roots," "branching out," "stemming from," "blossoming," etc. Such language represents an expropriation of the legitimate and independent rights of plant processes. It lurks not only in logo and phallocentrism, Eurocentrism, racism, and sexism, *but also in their opposites in radical theory.* Quantitatively speaking, there is just as much plantistic chauvinism on the left as the right. Plantistic language is so pernicious, so demonic that not even the most careful attention, the most heightened awareness can escape this insidious and all-pervasive prejudice, as I myself unconsciously betrayed in my description of "the economic *roots* of history" in Marxist analysis. We speak of the "bloom" of youth, the "flower" of a generation, the "rooting out" of criminals, the "thorny" questions of marriage, etc., and in every case, a false and oppressive imagery is at work, a demeaning of an organism that cannot speak on its own behalf or refuse to be a plaything of metaphor, an object of semantic tyranny *even if it should be liberated.*

And here I present the central thesis of all anti-plantistic thought, of which this writing itself can only be, at best, a poor approximation of what finally must be said, for just as Africans can be the only true scholars of Africa, and only lesbians can honestly speak for lesbians, so too, every living thing is its own authority and the only organism capable of knowing who or what it is. Without any linguistic connection between humans and the floral world and standing in the existential void before the irrevocable Otherness of plants, we nevertheless proclaim the only valid theoretical principle on which scientific plant-consciousness can stand: ONLY PLANTS CAN SPEAK FOR PLANTS. Any dilution of this fundamental truth inevitably brings us back to the sources of plantistic hegemony, exemplified even in a construction as plant-friendly, as floraphiliac as the mystic study of plant auras, in which phallologocentrism was nevertheless at work in the attempt to penetrate the essentially *unconscious* and *inaccessible* world-spirit of plants.

The fact that botanical symbolism has been used among all the higher cultures to represent powerful life processes demonstrates the lengths to which human consciousness will go in linguistically colonizing nature for purposes of control. Expressing joy and independence beyond the most grasping, domineering ideology of human happiness, plants are the thing itself, the *ding an sich* of pure bliss, the oneness that humans, even the most wretched and oppressed, have attempted to expropriate in order to further their own selfish aims of projecting a lost natural innocence. Of all victimized life forms, plants have suffered the most, because they are their own paradise, their own Garden of Eden, not just once, but every day, and have the right to be left *absolutely alone.* EVERY GIFT OF FLOWERS, EVERY FLOWER POT, EVERY VEGETARIAN MEAL IS AN ACT OF DEMONIC INSANITY.

Given the fact that the language of plants is alien to all forms of speech, including the Otherness of oppressed peoples, we call for the immediate *abolition of all human connection with plants.* The liberation of women alone would receive new strength, for one of the most pernicious symbols of sexism is the 2,000 year old association of the subjugation, the tearing out of the ground, and the killing of flowers for the purpose of seducing women, as symbolized to this very day in the cult of the Valentine card and the sending of flowers by wire, not to mention the barbaric practise of giving them to sick people in hospitals, thus turning them into passive objects to be gazed upon, into *slaves of plantistic fantasy.*

We hear legitimate outcries today against pornography, against the exploitation of women's bodies in pornographic magazines, films, and advertisements, but there is as yet no concerted outcry, indeed, not even the dimmest awareness that plants are ruthlessly enlisted in sexist imagery. I cite but one instance, anecdotal but decisive: the New York City subway ad that shows a man kissing a seduced woman (enslaved by the false consciousness of love), in which a *bouquet of flowers* appears on the side, deliberately sealing the oppression that is projected in this construction of romantic ideology. The caption is too self-revealing to need further deconstruction: "1-800 FLOWERS. The Mating Call." When bourgeois advertising inscribes on our consciousness "Say It With Flowers," radical skepsis can lead to only one conclusion: *A bouquet of flowers is rape sublimated through plant symbolism.* The medieval depiction of women as flowers, through which a feudal tyranny colonized the consciousness of its time, is one of the most degrading moments in western history, embodied in that so-called popular medieval work, *The Romance of the Rose.* Jean Genet's attempt to undermine this abuse by turning the equation woman = flower into an image of homosexuals in his pseudo-radical work *Our Lady of the Flowers* is but the latest in a long line of what must be seen as double false consciousness. "Prisoners are flowers" he states at the beginning, thus setting the ideology of plantism in the context of homosexuality, a prejudice that subverts the radical content of this so-called avant-garde work of art.

The example of Genet opens out into a world of demonic plant oppression, for the apparent modern break with tradition is itself one of the great sources of domination today. It is a little known yet glaring truth (little known because of plantistic blindness) that anti-floralism is at the heart of modern literature. From Poe and Baudelaire through Kafka, Genet, and science-fiction (seed-pods taking over the earth), anti-floralism has been the unspoken principle at work, just as in the past, an elitist pro-floralism was the ideology of botanical tyranny. Kafka's entire neurosis is summed up in a statement to Felice Bauer that the sight of one rose was oppressive and that two together was almost unbearable. In Poe, the prejudice is blatantly expressed in his characterization of Roderick Usher (the words are telling), in which Poe writes that "the odor of certain flowers *oppressed* him." I need not dwell on Baudelaire's shameless, decadent exploitation of plantism to perpetuate this so-called anti-traditional outlook, supposedly on behalf of destroying the false idealism surrounding traditional plant imagery; and yet, his key work, *The Flowers of Evil*, is nothing but plantism in new form. American literature has its most virulent plantistic poetry in Whitman's *Leaves of Grass*. And contrary to recent neo-Marxist and deconstructionist studies, it is not capitalist oppression or the subversion of authorial textuality that is the key to Melville, but *Plantism*, articulated in what amounts to the culminating tract of 19th-century plantistic viciousness, *Billy Budd*.

I will not belabor the point, already made by radical critiques, about the fraudulent masterpieces in the canon of western tradition. Nevertheless, the idea must be driven home: from Homer's simile of the generations of man as the autumn leaves blowing in the wind and the Gospel's subjugation of plants in Luke's passage on the lilies of the field, to Dante's appropriation of flowers in the Catholic symbol of the mystic rose, *plantism is at the heart of the Western colonization of spiritual life, as vegetarianism is the opium of Oriental thought*.

There can be only one conclusion to this record of brutality disguised through plant symbolism: *Revolutionary consciousness is empty without scientific plant-consciousness*. A guide to plantistic art and language by Weltgeist and Untergang is in progress, extracts of which appear below:

Prejudiced	**Neutral**
uprooted	removed
plant (n.)	chlorophyll producer
plant (v.)	seed embed
fruitful	productive
roots	nourishment network
bud	potential floral form
flower	vegetational scent system
garden	floral installation

It follows that if Melville had been truly radical, he would have named his work *Billy Potential Floral Form*. Similarly, had Genet been the avant-garde writer he appears to be, he would have called his first novel *Our Lady of the Vegetational Scent Systems*.

Against a background of oppression, cloaked in the canon of Western aestheticism, the watchword is vigilance, eternal vigilance for the liberation of plants! The freedom of Flora is nourished by vegetable consciousness!

Art To Be Avoided

Baudelaire, *Les Fleurs du Mal*; Hieronymous Bosch, "The Garden of Earthly Delights"; Dante, *Paradiso*, Cantos 30-32; Genet, *Notre Dames des Fleurs*; Goethe, "The Metamorphosis of Plants"; Joyce Kilmer, "Trees"; Andrew Marvell, "The Garden"; Herman Melville, *Billy Budd*; Renoir, all still lifes; Allessandro Scarlatti, "The Garden of Love"; Shakespeare, most sonnets and all garden scenes (*vide Richard II* and *Romeo and Juliet*); Robert Louis Stevenson, *A Child's Garden of Verses*; Van Gogh, "Cypresses"; Wagner, "Forest Murmurs"; Whitman, *Leaves of Grass*; etc.

Critical Inquiry into Plantism

As yet a nascent field because of widespread, institutionalized Plantism, but gaining attention. See particularly recent studies by Stephen Greenblatt, *Shakespeare's Gardens: The Diffusion of Social Energies in Elizabethan Imperialistic Fairy Tales;* Gary Taylor, *Reeinventing Flora: A Subversive Reading of Pastoral Poetry;* Michael Rogin: *Herman Melville: Plantistic Literature in 19th Century American Culture;* Michel Foucault, *The Pollen of History: Plantistic Historiography from Herder to Spengler;* Stanley Fish, *The So-Called Garden Poem from Marvell to Keats: A Study in Plantistic Interpretive Communities;* Mikhail Bakhtin, *Subversive Shepherds: A New Look at Dresden Porcelain;* The Death Valley Collective, *Our Plants, Our Selves;* Martin Bernal, *Green Athena: How Ancient Greece Stole Botanical Symbolism from Nubia;* and soon to be released by the Institute for Advanced Studies at Princeton in cooperation with Weltgeist and Untergang, *A Guide to Non-plantistic Language*.

January, 1993

Reductio Ad Absurdum

Reductio Ad Absurdum

POLITICALLY INCORRECT NEWS STORY: Alice Springs, Australia (AP) "Aborigines attacked three policeman with frozen kangaroo tails in a remote Northern Territory town — then ate the evidence, a court was told today. Senior Constable Mark Coffey told Alice Springs Court that the three officers were attacked Thursday by 15 aborigines carrying frozen kangaroo tails bought at a local store. The officers, who were also pelted with rocks, suffered cuts and bruises but were not seriously injured. Six men were arrested and charged with assault. But a police spokesman said the kangaroo tails won't be introduced as evidence because it is believed they were eaten by the aborigines." — Submitted by reader John Knowlton.

ANOTHER POLITICALLY INCORRECT STORY: Houston (AP) University of Houston officials have said they will appeal a ruling that a Russian immigrant was expelled from the school's graduate history program because of his ideas, not his performance. State District Judge Don Wittig on Monday ruled in favor of Fabian Vaksman, 37. Vaksman has waged a three-year state and federal court battle seeking to complete his doctorate in history. Vaksman said he fell into disfavor with the department because he vigorously asserted anti-Marxist views. This conflicted with the orthodox Marxist philosophy he said had been prevalent among many history professors.

ANOTHER SUCCESS OF THE DUMB SHIT LIBERATION MOVEMENT: The following document is provided by the State of New York to people taking its real estate license test: "Your examination application slip will be marked either PASSED or FAILED and returned to you by mail. Numerical scores are not given to prevent possible discriminatory employment practices based on achievement levels."

HARASSMENT HIGH: The School Board of the Nicolet High School District, governing the most prestigious high school in the state of Wisconsin has adopted a harassment policy which identifies not only the usual "protected categories" — race, sex, sexual orientation — but adds criminals. "The Nicolet High School District is committed to fair and equal employment opportunity for every person regardless of age, race, color,...handicap,..marital status, sex, sexual orientation....arrest record, conviction record...

"Intimidation and harassment can arise from a broad range of physical or verbal behavior (by employees, non-employees or students) which can include, but is not limited to, the following:

- Physical or mental abuse
- Racial, ethnic or religious insults or slurs
- Unwelcome sexual advances or touching
- Displays of sexually explicit or otherwise offensive posters, calendars, or materials referring to another person as a girl, hunk, doll, babe, or honey
- Making sexual gestures with hands or body movements
- Intentionally standing close or brushing up against another person
- Inappropriately staring at another person or touching his or her clothing, hair or body
- Asking personal questions about another person's sexual life
- Repeatedly asking out a person who has stated that he or she is not interested...

"An employee or supervisor may be held individually liable as a harasser and subject to the same penalties which may be imposed upon employers under state or federal law. A student harasser may be subject to individual liability and discipline."

These kids may never graduate.

PEDOPHILIA UPDATE: The University of Massachusetts at Amherst has revised its non-discrimination code to include pedophiles as a protected minority. In 1990-1991, the school's Affirmative Action and Nondiscrimination Policy contained a clause specifying that its protections "shall not include persons whose sexual orientation includes minor children as the sex object." There are two things that are disturbing about all this. First, why protect pedophiles? (Is it now okay for a man to sexually harass a 7 year old boy, say, but not a 27 year old woman?) And secondly, why the term *sexual orientation?* Does this mean that we are in for brain dwarfing debates about whether pedophilia is chemical or choice? Will there be—in the compulsory Gay, Lesbian and Bisexual Studies courses of the future—seminars on Humbert Humbert as the Ahab of pedophiles, trying to lampoon a sweet young thing? Is there no behavior which U Mass and other enlightened campuses will agree deserves simply to be called *deviant?*

BITING THE HAND THAT FEEDS: Mary Johnson, editor of *The Disability Rag*, a civil rights journal, attacks **Jerry Lewis** for raising hundreds of millions of dollars to help disabled people. "Helping 'those people' by making them be like us — normal, not disabled — is one thing," she sneers. "Helping them to be equal and remain disabled is something entirely different." Once again the old saw is proven: no good deed goes unpunished.

AIDS ON $5 A DAY: While Gay activists flood the nation's high schools with condoms, condemning anyone who doesn't sign on to their agenda as sentencing gays to death, **Bob Damron's** *Address Book*, a kind of *FODOR*'s for homosexual travelers, enters its 28th publishing year. Available at large bookstore chains such as Barnes & Noble's Bookstar outlets, the guide lists gay accommodations and sights of erotic interest in all 50 states, Canada, the Virgin Islands, Costa Rica and Mexico. It includes not only sex establishments and businesses, but such free-lance possibilities for sex with strangers as "Cruisy Areas." Thus, for example, if you are thinking of a vacation in Decatur, Alabama, "Cruisy areas include: *Amtrak & Greyhound Depots (AYOR) *Beltline Mall *Delano Park nr. Picnic Tables *Point Mallard Park - Swimmin' Hole (Summers) and *'The Pumps' (AYOR). (AYOR = At Your Own Risk.)" Ads in this indispensable guide include one in living color for the Leland Hotel in San Francisco featuring a prone naked male *derriere* with the headline: "In San Francisco, the Perfect Spot to Lodge..." In introducing the section on Mexico, editor **Dan Delbex** shares this tip: "Much of Mexico is very poor. Consequently, many boys may be available for the price of a cocktail..." The 1992 edition of Damron's *Address Book* is dedicated to the memory Delbex, who died of AIDS on October 5, 1991, at the age of 35.

GAG ME WITH SOME SELF-ESTEEM: One of the most nauseating moments of **Tom Hayden**'s autobiography, *Reunion*, came when he revealed just how political the personal could be for Sixties leftovers: *"Jane was starting to cry. I kept flipping slides of grotesque young Saigon women, talking about the breast and eye operations performed to turn them into round-eyed, round-bodied Westernized women...Suddenly I understood why she was weeping: I was talking about the image of superficial sexiness she once promoted and was now trying to shake. I looked at her in a new way. Maybe I could love someone like this."* Now comes **Gloria Steinem** with a similar revelation in her new autobiography, *Revolution From Within*. In a passage that qualifies as the Feminist Whine of the Year, she explains (and explains away) her once tender feelings for boyfriend and *U.S. News & World Report* owner **Mortimer Zuckerman:** *"And perhaps most of all, if I had fallen in love with a powerful man, I had to realize that I was in mourning for the power women need and rarely have, myself included..."* Steinem may not have had a baby of her own, but it cannot be said that she doesn't know what motherhood is, given the time she spends in this book feeding pablum to the child within.

ACADEMIC QUOTE OF THE MONTH: *"Prostitution may very well have confirmed colonial fantasies about white men's privileged access to the bodies of black women, but it also confused racial segregation and the racial and gendered distribution of money: in the bodies of the prostitutes the liquid assets and body fluids of white and black men mixed promiscuously."* Anne McClintock, "The Scandal of the Whorearchy: Prostitution in Colonial Nairobi," Transition #52, Oxford 1991.

THE PROTOCOLS OF THE ELDERS OF BLACKNESS: Recently, the Langsam Library of the University of Cincinnati requested members of the university community to name their favorite book. **Eric Abercrumbie**, the Director of Minority Programs and Services, submitted the following response: "My favorite book is The Holy Bible because it provides the blackprint for salvation. Also, it represents the true truth regarding Afrocentric human creation and existence. In spite of white racist efforts to enslave black people and fallacious symbols and information, the true historical and sociological documentation clearly represents that black people were the original people and that all of humanity came from the womb of black women. Furthermore, according to society's classification of race, it is evident that Jesus is a black man. Therefore, even though white racists have presented the idea that black people have contributed nothing to humanity, The Holy Bible clearly indicates that we have made the most important contribution."

GLOSSOLLI: Jentz Martin, specialist assistant/Americans With Disabilities Act Coordinator at the University of Wisconsin (Milwaukee) offers these no-no's in referring to people with disabilities: "Afflicted With — connotes pain and suffering. Most people with disabilities are not in pain, nor do they suffer. Confined To A Wheelchair — a wheelchair doesn't confine; it frees someone. Deaf And Dumb — People who are deaf have healthy vocal cords. If they do not speak, it is because they have never heard the pronunciation of words. Invalid — This word means literally 'not valid.' Everybody is valid."

ALCOHOLICS SYNONYMOUS: In October, the residence advisers at Columbia University's John Jay dorm organized a series of group sessions for Alcohol Awareness Week. The PC advisers arranged separate groups for blacks, women, gays and lesbians. White heterosexual alcoholics need not apply.

BLOODSUCKERS: At Duke University, this year's Halloween tribute was sponsored by the Gay and Lesbian Association and Screen/Society. It was a Lesbian Vampire Film Festival— an evening of lipstick porn featuring titles such as *Mark of Lilith*, *Because of the Dawn*, *Love Me True*, and, of course, that old classic, *Sucker.*

BACKLASH: Pauline Bart, sociologist at the University of Illinois, has not been able to teach her courses this semester and may be severed from the school. Bart claims she is the victim of a "backlash" on the part of men who are against her "therapeutic" attempts to make her classes safe for the "large numbers" of women in them she believes have been raped. But last spring Bart stepped over the line as far as Donald Dixon, a black social work major, was concerned. Dixon alleged that Bart had said in class that he "fit the profile of a male black rapist." Bart denied the accusation but admitted that she felt Dixon and two other men had "threatened" the women in her class by "disruptive" comments. Abandoned by the administration, Bart left behind this percu as her intellectual legacy: "There are not as many female rapists as male rapists."

HALF MAST: During the L.A. riots, militant students tore down the American flag at Ohio State's Bricker Hall. The group responsible was a student-faculty organization called ACTION or Afrikans (sic) Committed to Improving our Nation. One of the students with whom this action did not sit well was **Jordana Shakor**, a black psychology major. Her father, a career military man, had recently died. "There was a flag shrouding his casket," she said. "[It] has been precious to me after that." Soon after Shakor organized a peaceful rally to replace the flag burned by ACTION, she was attacked in the student newspaper by **Kareem Rashaad**: "The flag is the greatest symbol of hypocrisy the world has ever known. Everywhere this flag has gone it has meant nothing but rape, death and destruction for all non-white people who had the unfortunate experience of coming in contact with it....That's why we torch the flag and say 'burn hypocrisy, burn.' Do you finally get it my sister?" The nearby Amvets post decided to recognize her at their next meeting, where they presented Shakor with a flag and a certificate of appreciation. Ohio State vice president Linda Tom was supposed to be present at the ceremony but failed to show.

JOCK CORRECTNESS: **Rick Burns** is the women's soccer coach at Mount Holyoke, a college that has been swept under the feminist tide. In an article in the *NCAA News*, he described the pressure exerted on him by politically correct players to watch his p's and q's. In particular he's been told not to use the term "girls" or "guys" in reference to players. He tried "ladies" but was quickly put right. "Women" was the acceptable term. But, as Burns observed, "Hustle over, women" just doesn't seem to fit. And in fact, when Burns referred to an opponent as a "tall woman" he was reprimanded and told to use the term "vertically endowed." He was also asked not to use the term "subs" by a player who felt it was hierarchical and therefore demeaning. She suggested "others" as a substitute. At one point during the schedule the team captain came to him and said that there was "some concern" that he was mentioning one particular player's name too often in half-time discussions. The player in question had scored 60% of the team's goals during the last two seasons. When his article appeared, even though Burns pledged himself to sensitivity, it ignited a firestorm at Holyoke. Burns was denounced by some team members for being "sexist" and one team member in the *Mount Holyoke News* came close to calling for his resignation.

BROOMSTICK LIB: At Cornell University the new Culture Studies Department describes its mission as the critique of the domination exercised by "ruling classes, and especially men" over subject minorities through "the control of writing and its technologies." Incoming Freshpeople are required to take one seminar from the Culture Studies program, and among the new offerings is *Writing About Witches*. According to its catalogue description *Writing About Witches* "will focus on the politics of witchcraft; we will consider why it is that writing about witches almost always springs from the fear, hatred, or persecution of a type of individual or group, and why writing about witchcraft is also writing about power: supernatural power, divine power, the power of the Church, the power of the mind."

GOSH ALMIGHTY: **Robert Price** has issued a Really Revised Standard Version of some Gospel texts made acceptable for the higher educated. Matthew 12:10-13 goes like this: "And behold, there was a person who was manually challenged. And they asked **Jesus**, 'Is it lawful to heal on the Sabbath?' Not that there was anything particularly wrong with him in the first place, mind you! so that they might accuse him of bias against the differently abled. He said to them, 'What person of you, if he or she has one sheep and it falls into a pit on the Sabbath, will not lay hold of it and lift it out? Of how much more value is a sheep than a man! But people have rights, too. So it is lawful to do good on the Sabbath.' Then he said to the person, 'Stretch out your hand.' And the person stretched it out, and it was temporarily abled like the other."

SEXUAL PERSONAE NON GRATA: Somehow **Camille Paglia**'s *Sexual Personae* made its way onto the 1992 Summer Reading List at Connecticut College. This sent the Women's Studies Committee and other faculty into a feminist tizzy. A parade of faculty members warned the committee of the "dangers" of including the Paglia text. According to Professor **Frederick Paxton**, Chairperson of the Summer Reading Committee, the complaints ranged from "Too long, too dense, and too difficult, to it's bad scholarship, illogical, anti-women, hate-literature, as bad as *Mein Kampf* or **David Duke**." **Robert Baldwin**, Assistant Professor of Art History said Paglia's book was "offensive to human beings, especially women." Afraid to be seen as censors, the academics settled for reducing the status of Paglia's book—it would not be part of "the orientation focus" of the list—and by countering with a new addition, **Susan Faludi**'s politically correct best-seller *Backlash*.

LOOT SUITERS: "A fashionable beggar approached a downtown worker during Los Angeles's three days of rioting and asked for money to buy food.

"He was wearing a new suit with tags still on," **Herb Sanders** of suburban Van Nuys said in a letter published in the *Los Angeles Times*.

"The sleeves on the jacket were rolled up along with the legs on the pants. A piece of rope held up the pants. He had on a new pair of Reebok shoes that didn't match."

Sanders said the man asked for change to buy food.

"I asked him, 'Did you spend all your money on your new suit and shoes?' With a smile he said, 'No, I'm a looter, and I got this new suit and shoes looting.'"

At that point, Sanders asked, "What do you think of the Rodney King situation?"

"I don't follow sports anymore," the man replied.

WITH MALICE BEHIND-THOUGHT: The following statement was provided by the Office of Affirmative Action of the University of Massachusetts at Amherst in response to a query from reader **Louise Dewey** of Littleton, Mass., about dropping its exclusion of pedophilia from the protected category "sexual orientation" in its discrimination code: "The fact is that an earlier version of our Affirmative Action Statement, in discussing our desire to not discriminate on the basis of what is customarily called 'Sexual Orientation' went out of its way to be clear that pedophilia was not acceptable. When that version was revised it became clear that it would be impossible to spell out the various unacceptable practices (for instance, those that were illegal) and so we dropped back to using the customary brief statement which is almost universal nowadays. One or two alert and malicious characters picked up this change, and elected to interpret it as an endorsement of pedophilia. It was no such thing." Well, since they brought it up, why is pedophilia regarded as a "sexual orientation," or, if it is, how does it differ from other "sexual orientations?" Why, unlike all those other illegal and/or unacceptable practices, was pedophilia singled out in the first place? Could it have to do, possibly, with some internal struggle among the politically correct?

SEX HACKERS: The following message was spotted on "Athena," an expensive MIT Communications Network, generally reserved for technical exchanges and subsidized by federal funds:

Slave,

Signs of the brewing interest in the upcoming s/m study break have reached me by phone, computer, and direct communication....We will play a game of show and tell—EVERYONE IS STRONGLY ENCOURAGED TO BRING IN HER OR HIS SEX TOYS AND ANY OTHER EROTICIZED OBJECTS. We will get a chance to ask the questions we've never dared to ask. We will get a chance to reveal all. We are hoping to have a LIVE S/M SCANDALOUS DEMONSTRATION. As I write, rumors that a very cute blond boy with a slight southern drawl will be fisted before your eyes, as well as rumors that a Morrissey-type poet with art-fag hair will be suspended by ropes and whipped, have not been verified....

Your master,

Joe

P.S. The AIDS Quilt will be shown at Tufts this Saturday and Sunday from 10-9 in Cousen's Gym on the Medford Campus....

It would perhaps be a superfluous *explication de texte* on our part to note that it is the postscript that makes this item work.

BOVINE EMISSIONS: For sheer environmental flatulence we thought it would be hard to top **Paul Ehrlich**, who in 1969 predicted that the Earth had only a few years to live and who has continued to make equally inaccurate prophecies of doom since then without ever bothering to do a balance sheet on his handicapping. But Ehrlich now has to take a back seat to **Jeremy Rifkin**, author of the recently published *Beyond Beef.* Here is the spiritual core of the book:

"Moving beyond the beef culture is a revolutionary act, a sign of our willingness to reconstitute ourselves, to make ourselves whole... By doing battle with 'the world steer,' a new generation expresses its sensitivity to the biosphere and its regard for the plight of the poor. By eliminating beef from the human diet, our species takes a significant step toward a new species consciousness, reaching out in a spirit of shared partnership with the bovine..."

The world steer? Is this a Hegelian concept? Make ours medium rare.

FEMALE PROBLEMS AT BROWN: This is an actual document circulated by the English Department:

Memorandum to: Members of the English Department

Subject: Camille Paglia's Talk

When rumors began circulating that Camille Paglia was being brought to Brown, many of us who call ourselves feminists, do feminist-informed work, and oppose Paglia (both politically and intellectually) found ourselves in an untenable situation. To publicly oppose Paglia's appearance would have been to play into the hands of those who sponsor and support her, by ostensibly closing off 'free speech.' Given the current political climate (both within and outside the English Department), opposing Paglia's appearance was not a viable option."

ENVIRONMENTALIST OF THE DECADE: We have a mystery candidate.... **Ronald Reagan**! Why? Because he brought the USSR to its knees by knitting together the tattered strands of the Truman Doctrine and fighting the Cold War to a conclusion. In so doing he stopped the environmental devastation which was part and parcel of the communist enterprise. Growth is the ideology of the cancer cell, and in the Soviet Union growth, forced with draconian methods from the 1920s onward, was particularly carcinomic. In their new book *Ecocide in the Soviet Union*, **Murray Feshbach** and **Alfred Friendly Jr.** describe the toll of 75 years of Bolshevism. More than half the Russian population breathe air with five times the limit of dangerous chemicals. The former Soviet Union has only 10% the number of cars as does the United States, but 67% of automobile pollution. Nuclear accidents, other than Chernobyl, have made parts of European Russia glow in the dark. The equivalent of one Exxon Valdez oil spill occurs every six hours in Siberia. (To speed up construction of oil pipelines, cutoff valves were installed every 30 miles instead of every 3 miles, so a break dumps 30 miles of oil onto the ground.) The Siberian forests are disappearing at a rate of 5 million acres a year, a faster rate than the rain forests of Brazil. According to *U.S. News and World Report's* April 13 issue, the socialist planners used nuclear bombs as a sort of super TNT. During Communist rule more than 130 nuclear explosions were used for geophysical explorations, to create underground pressure in oil and gas fields or simply to move earth for building dams. The growth at any price mentality led to 20% of all metal production being dumped into landfills. There were 270 malfunctions at nuclear power facilities last year, but despite warnings from government officials that all Soviet nuclear power stations are in hazardous condition it is impossible to shut them down, since they provide as much as 60% of the power in certain regions. According to **Vladislav Petrov**, a law professor at Moscow State University, if the current environmental regulations were enforced, 80% of the country's factories would be shut down.

Now, thanks to Reagan's willingness to face down the Evil Empire, these depredations will no longer be necessary to feed communist growth and Russians can perhaps begin to soothe their scorched earth. There is a lesson here for vaporish leftists, who, unable to give the U.S. credit for anything, have tried to convince us that the USSR came to an end simply because of internal contradictions. Yet, this was no immaculate miscarriage, but the result of pressure from R. Reagan, environmentalist of the decade and ecologist *malgre lui.*

DOUBLE VISION: Ferrum College is a small Methodist liberal arts college, located in Franklin County, Virginia, the moonshine capital of the world. Last fall, black students at Ferrum responding to **Spike Lee**'s fashion statements began wearing X hats around campus. They also began sporting T-shirts with pictures of AK-47s and the slogan "By Any Means Necessary" on them. Then this spring, some white students decided to answer with a fashion statement of their own. They designed hats with the X circled and crossed out. Immediately they were hauled before a panel of three deans, who told them this was unacceptable hate speech. Whereupon, the Black Student Union held a demonstration in front of the deans' houses because "they hadn't acted fast enough."

SQUISH: A new movement is spreading on college campuses. Strong Queers United In Stopping Heterosexism originated at Cal State, Northridge a couple of years ago. Now a second chapter has been started at San Diego State. In addition to giving speeches to classes SQUISH has put up billboards with catchy slogans like "I thought all sorority girls were sluts" and (on the other side) "SQUISH knows this shit's got to stop." SQUISH also holds die-ins and kiss-ins. "Our die-in," explained spokesman John Sanders, "is where a bunch of queers lay down on the ground as if dead and get chalked in by the police to show how we're treated by society."

HARVARD LAW LECTURE: The distinguished academic **Ice-T** has been touring college campuses this spring delivering lectures on law enforcement in a free society. Speaking before portraits of robed jurists at Harvard Law School he told a capacity crowd he never thought his lyrics "Die, die, die, pig, die" would offend people. "I thought everybody hated the police," the visiting lecturer said. Ice-T went on to boast "I've got my thumb on the pulse of 50,000 killers" and that he has founded a group of gang members in Los Angeles called *Hands Across Watts*— "basic killers," he called them, "getting ready to move on the police."

RACIAL JUSTICE: Five days before the start of Black History Month, three racial slurs against blacks written on pieces of notebook paper were found posted on the door of the Black Student Union's building on the Williams College campus. Williams had not had a racial incident in two years. The messages were duly denounced by a chorus of campus activists. Three days later, **Gilbert Moore Jr.**, a black student, told administrators that he had posted the messages as part of a project for a course on anarchism he was taking. His intention he said was to promote more campus discourse on race relations. Moore was suspended for a semester. The Black Student Union supported the suspension. "We denounce all racist activity," their statement said.

BAD TASTE: At Stanford University, in celebration of their annual Condom Week, the school's *Ye Olde Condom Shoppe* held a condom drive. With a display table set up in the middle of White Plaza, the school-funded organization handed out bags of condoms accompanied with a questionnaire. Students were asked to compare each condom in a number of different categories, including taste.

STAYING ABREAST AT VANDY: The avant garde at **Vanderbilt** University has painted itself into a corner. Art professor **Donald Evans**, while giving a slide show on the controversial **Robert Mapplethorpe**, slipped in a few nude photos of himself and his wife. A female student in Evans' class promptly filed a sexual harassment complaint. In his defense, Evans said that his work with women's breasts was one of the main reasons that Vanderbilt hired him in the first place.

THE BEARDED LADY: The following letter by California Polytechnic professor of Philosophy and Women's Studies **Mary Crane** appeared in the American Philosophical Association Newsletter, publication of the most prestigious professional association of academic philosophers: "I am a white lesbian, forty-eight years old and I have a beard. Sort of a double goatee affair that grows on either side of my chin. I have it for about 16 years...But hardly anyone else seems to like my beard. Most women will, if forced to discuss it, affirm (in the spirit of the times) my right to it, while affirming their equal right not to have a beard. Then, they go on to make enough unsubtle remarks to let me know that they think I would look much nicer without a beard. I have suffered several serious and painful rejections because of the beard. Still, as far as I can see, I do not have much choice about exposing this beard. To shave is to refuse to do something about the institution of sexism...When women are denied our beards...it is because of sexists' fears of the consequences of any erosion in a system based on strict sex role conformity...I want all the bearded ladies in the world to come out, celebrate ourselves and one another. If you have a beard and you are female and you do not let it grow, I want to challenge you to think about why you keep it shaved. Shy is that 'your choice?' If it's fear of the loss of a job, let's get an ACLU lawyer to defend us. After all, we do have a right! But again, it is more than right...It is a need to celebrate the beauty that is naturally ours in our beards."

MOVE OVER, MAYA ANGELOU: The following poem was required reading for "Gender In Writing," a Freshman English section taught by **Linda Garber:**

The enemies of She Who call her various names

a whore, a whore,/a fishwife a cunt a harlot a harlot a pussy/a doxie a tail a fishwife a whore a hole a slit/a cunt a bit a slut a slit a hole a whore a hole/a vixen/a piece of ass/a dame-filly-mare/dove-cow-pig-chick-cat-kitten-bird/dog-dish/a dumb blonde/you black bitch-you white bitch-you brown-bitch-you stupid bitch-you stinking bitch you little bitch-you old bitch-a cheap bitch-a high class bitch-a 2 bit whore-a 2 dollar whore-a ten dollar whore-a million dollar mistress a hole a slut a cunt a slit a cut a slash a hole a slit a piece of shit, a piece of shit, a piece of shit.

SENSITIVITY UBER ALLES: Administrators at Georgetown University are planning to expand the definition of sexual harassment to include actions directed at groups. The new policy was inspired in part by an incident with the Georgetown rugby team. The team had sung an old standard based on the Knock Knock Who's there? routine, the answer being Tijuana. "Tijuana who? Tijuana bring your mother to the gang bang." The team was not punished, according to Dean of Students, **Renee DeVigne**, because its song, though offensive was not directed at a specific individual. English Professor **Leona Fisher**, one of the supporters of the new policy, acknowledged that "[Sexual harassment issues] do come up against free speech," but said "I would rather that the sexual harassment be punished than the free speech be let go." Yes, Leona, there was a Stalin.

PHOBIC QUEER: A poster plastered at sites in Washington D.C.'s gay community and reprinted in the Washington *BLADE* reads as follows:

<u>QUEERS READ THIS</u>

I HATE GAY MEN!!! They stand around looking at the world through the rose-colored lens of a JR's Cape Cod while QUEERS DIE EVERY DAY!! They talk of television and discos while QUEERS FIGHT FOR OUR LIVES, and then GAY MEN CALL QUEERS RADICALS. BUT WITHOUT THOSE RADICALS, you FAGGOTS WOULDN'T HAVE A TRACKS TO POSE IN!!! THERE'S A WAR AGAINST QUEERS AND NO PRETTY NEW SWEATER IS GOING TO SAVE ANYONE'S ASS!!!

I HATE GAY MEN because they think conformity is survival, because they think invisibility is a good substitute for happiness. BECAUSE THEY THINK SECOND CLASS IS CLASSY!!! I HATE GAY MEN because they care more about the gym and the party and brunch at Annie's then they do about THEIR OWN RIGHTS AS HUMAN FUCKING BEINGS!!! Because they drink their 75-cent drinks and go home and fuck unsafely in the dark and pretend it was safe in the morning on their way to their closeted lives at work where wearing a tie makes them think they have equality. I HATE GAY MEN because they WOULD RATHER PUT THEIR ASSES ON A BARSTOOL THAN PUT THEM ON THE LINE!!!

I HATE GAY MEN BECAUSE THEY THINK OUR LIVES AREN'T WORTH FIGHTING FOR!!!

Pentagon officials take note.

GLORY HOLES DOWN ON THE FARM: **David Sacks**, editor of the *Stanford Review,* reports in the January 25 issue: "The Stanford Administration demands that its students be 'welcoming and accepting' of homosexual behavior. In bathrooms throughout campus, but particularly in the libraries and history corner, holes have been drilled between the walls of toilet stalls to facilitate anonymous bathroom sex. One restroom in the South Stacks of Green Library is a 'horror story' according to a library employee, who described the bathroom's unusual stench and the homosexual graffiti covering the walls. Messages, such as 'horny young male' and 'inexperienced male seeks same' as well as others too obscene to be printed in these pages, proliferate, listing times when like-minded desperadoes can connect. A student told me of his experience in the South Stacks. Unaware of its reputation, he entered for legitimate purposes. While he used a urinal, another student leered at him disturbingly and then walked towards him menacingly — while masturbating. Shocked and offended, he fled before this obviously unbalanced homosexual could physically accost him. Unfortunately, such stories abound: a friend of mine was solicited in Meyer Hall the night before an exam, and, to his gastroenteric dismay, had to flee the toilet mid-use. Of course Stanford, held in the sway of moral relativism and the thrall of gay lobbying and pressure tactics, is powerless to prevent this public imposition." Pentagon officials take note.

MICHAEL JACKSON'S PENIS: In the second week of February, this year, the College of Humanities and Social Science at UC Riverside held a conference on "Unnatural Acts." The program included "Taking on the Phallus," "Beyond the Bathroom Door," "Boys Will Be Girls," "Dreaming Arnold Schwarzenegger," "Fucking (with Theory) For Money," "Michael Jackson's Penis," "Lesbians Who Kill," and "Amelia Earhart in Drag." Conference papers will be published in book form by the University of Indiana Press.

FOOD FIGHTS: Columbia University's *Coalition to Free the Haitian Refugees* recently held a hunger strike on the campus quad. A few days into the protest, members of Columbia's College Republicans decided to have a picnic adjacent to the protesters with their "Abolish Guantanamo" signs. Though the Republican youth were run off, they returned two days later with a grill and held a barbecue amid chants of "Racists Eat While Haitians Die!" from the hunger strikers. Campus administrators and security eventually made the Republicans pack their food and grills and go elsewhere.

POINTS OF DARK: **Charles Ranchal** is a Los Angeles Crip (i.e., one of the area's two most vicious gangs) with a record of at least one manslaughter. He is also one of **Bill Clinton**'s "Faces of Hope" invited to attend the inauguration as a special presidential guest because he was "one of the organizers of last spring's gang truce." A new rap single by social prophet **Ice Cube** and other raptivists called "Get the Fist" explains the street significance of the truce that Clinton's advisers must have missed: *"I said it was just a few good men when we were fightin'. It'll be more good men now that we're united ... Niggas in my hood been gettin' loose and buckin' through. But now we're gettin' wiser ... What happened to the drive by killers? Ain't nothin pumpin' no more, cause brothers now chillin'. From every hood, the block, the corner, the street. Now black on black the other color gets beat."* In other words, black gangsters can now unite to attack white, brown and Asian-Americans all the time instead of only on special occasions like the L.A. riot.

PC XMAS: The following politically correct Xmas gifts were featured in a column by **David Rose** of the *Fresno Bee*. High on his list was this: "Acclaimed by critics and audiences, an important and moving PBS series is now available on video. The *Damn You White Man* series, hosted by Bill Moyers, explores the rich and varied cultures of the New World and details how all of them were virtually wiped off the face of the earth by belligerent white invaders with big guns. Guaranteed to induce intense guilt in anyone of Northern European ancestry. Thirteen hours on seven videotapes. $129.95." Also the challenging new board game *PC State*: "You're an associate professor who must lecture his way across the campus of an ultra-sensitive Northeastern university without offending women, African-Americans, Hispanics, Japanese, Chinese, Taiwaneses, Koreans, Pacific Islanders, Aleuts, Albinos, Jews, Christians, Muslims, Buddhists, Hindus, Druids, atheists, homosexuals, bisexuals, asexuals, the overweight, the underweight, the elderly, the hearing impaired, the visually impaired, mobility impaired, and people with no fashion sense. Players must give a dozen lectures without using any of the 1,745 words or phrases banned as offensive by the university. One slip-up, and you get two weeks' suspension and lose tenure. Two mistakes, and you're stoned to death by an angry mob and your worthless carcass is dragged through the streets of the town behind a natural-gas-powered Volvo. $16.95."

DR. SPOCK IS NOT THE MOTHER OF MY CHILD: In an address to the Bisexual, Gay and Lesbian Student Association at Stanford, **June Jordan,** $70,000+ a year Professor of Afro-American Studies at UC Berkeley, bi-sexual poet, and recipient of numerous awards including a Rockefeller Grant and an NEA Fellowship, had this to say: "I can voice my ideas without hesitation or fear because I am speaking, finally, about myself. I am Black and I am female and I am a mother and I am bisexual and I am a nationalist and I am an antinationalist. And I mean to be fully and freely all that I am! Conversely, I do not accept that any white or black or Chinese man — I do not accept that, for instance, Dr. Spock — should presume to tell me, or any other woman, how to mother a child. He has no right. He is not a mother. My child is not his child." Lucky him!

FAUX RAPE: The San Diego *Union-Tribune* recently printed a story about a 49 year old woman (she is nameless because she was promised anonymity by the police) who emerged naked above the waist from a dressing room at a Nordstrom department store, and began screaming that she had just been sexually assaulted by a man who put a hunting knife to her throat and threatened to kill her if she didn't cooperate. The woman said that the man removed her gold wedding band, Seiko watch and gold chain, and took $133 from her purse. Then, using pieces of duct tape, he bound her hands, sexually molested her with a tire iron and forced her to perform oral copulation. Police spent the next 12 days investigating the highly publicized rape after putting together a composite portrait of the alleged rapist that *Union-Tribune* writer Sharon Jones says "resembled President Bill Clinton." Then, as Southern California feminists were charging that no institution in society was free of rape, the supposed victim failed a lie detector test. DNA tests of stains on the sweater she was wearing—she claimed that she had spit out the rapist's ejaculate—showed the semen to be her husband's. Confronted by San Diego police investigators with this fact, the woman said that she always carried her husband's semen in her purse because it was useful as a facial cream to prevent wrinkles and was indeed carrying a vial of it on the night of the attack and that the rapist found it and spilled it onto her sweater. By this time the police realized that they had something bizarre on their hands. After further interrogation, the "victim" admitted that she had staged the entire event, including molesting herself with the tire iron and using some of her husband's semen to substantiate the hoax. A pathetic addendum to this pathetic case was supplied by Sherry Arndt, identified by the *Union Tribune* as "coordinator of California's foremost sexual assault response program." Told about the hoax, Arndt said: "That woman is a victim of something. She's crying out. She probably was molested as a child."

LOYALTY OATHS: The following was distributed to students at The University of Minnesota Law School in response to "offensive racist graffiti" found on lavatory walls. The pledge was to be signed in front of a witness and returned to school administrators:

"As a member of the University of Minnesota Law School community, I, by my signature, state my commitment to tolerance of those with a viewpoint, life-style, or heritage different from my own. In an intellectually vibrant community, the exchange of differing ideas is challenging and important. However, I do not condone acts and expressions of bigotry and hatred. I fully realize that if I do not take leadership in promulgating these

values on campus, I will diminish the benefits of my education and severely restrict my personal, professional, civic and social growth and achievement. I take responsibility for educating myself about others different from me and enhancing my awareness and understanding of disability and of the impact of racism, sexism, homophobia, and other forms of intolerance, on society and on me."

THE ACRONYM WHICH DARE NOT SPEAK ITS NAME: The Creative Underground Network of Truthful Sisters (C.U.N.T.S.) is a covert feminist organization at U.C. Santa Barbara. In a recent showing, the C.U.N.T.S. plastered the university with fliers that read "The Best Way To A Man's Heart Is Through His Chest" and — the time honored favorite — "Dead Men Don't Rape". Earlier this year, these feminist guerrillas launched a crusade against fraternities and sororities. They dressed themselves in black robes and hoods, stood along fraternity and sorority row during rush week and sung songs that made fun of the Greek system and its "rape culture." The only people who know these women are the Santa Barbara Police. Apparently, a number of the C.U.N.T.S. were arrested while placing "Keep Biting Back, Sisters" bumper-stickers on the backs of police cruisers.

SMACT-UP, PART DEUX: During last month's homosexual march on Washington, D.C., the Andrew Mellon Auditorium was the headquarters of the National S&M Leather/Fetish Conference. Some 1,600 people gathered for six hours of exhibits which included leather-clad men whipping each other's butts and slide projections of men "fisting." For those interested in souvenirs, the *Washington Times* reports that an assortment of "leather whips, full-length body racks, stockades, hoods made of chain, cattle prods and other 'electro-torture' devices" were for sale.

Letters

Letters

Dear Sirs, Ladies & all you turning worms:
Yes! YES! YES!! YES!!!
It's about goddamned time.

Gene Austin
Hanford, California

A new publication slamming political correctness and liberalism? Wow, what a novel idea. What ever will they think of next, a televised talk show for small-minded bigots that suffer from fears of impotence? Oh pardon me, they've given Rush a show, now haven't they.

This "decency" that conservatives talk about incessantly shouldn't have a thing to do with sexuality or political ideology. Decency is treating people with respect regardless of how intimidating you find their uniqueness. I don't understand why being rude and condescending to those you don't agree with has become an attribute. Down in the South we call such behavior as "being ugly," which is a rather apt expression of these culprits' character.

Since you find politically correct speech so abhorrent, I'll close with an appropriate salvo. Fuck off, you small-minded, pseudo-intellectual, conformist, neo-fascist, xenophobic bastards.

Love and kisses,
Carol Ann Causey
Savannah, Georgia

I once sold *Ramparts* an article on catching undercover agents. My wife's and my conversion to conservatism began in the early 70s while "returning to the land" in Northwest Arkansas. Appealing for food stamps to a paraplegic Vietnam veteran who was working as a screener in that office shamed me enough that I buckled down and got serious about making a living. From there it was all uphill, but I am much the better for it.

I now manage the largest "Choose and Cut" Christmas tree farm in Southern California, near Magic Mountain in Valencia, and suffer karmic kick-backs from the likes of Tom Hayden and his league of anti-pesticide screwballs. Oh well. I look at them like weeds and aphids — just another pest to deal with, hoping the EPA will soon register a product for their control.

Mike Milligan

Remove my name immediately from your mailing list. It's quite obvious that all of you are pathetic, scared, mostly male, whites afraid to let go of the silver spoon you were born with in your mouth — it belongs in your ass.

Peter A. Kouides, M.D.

Last week I found an unsolicited copy of your "trashy" paper in my mailbox. I do not know how I got on your perverted mailing list, but if you ever send me any more of your garbage I will not only file a complaint with the Postmaster but also with the FBI and the City of Alendora Police.

Richard M. Bertholf

You fellows have one driving motivation — you want to free yourself from your mothers' all-encompassing vaginas. Fear and hatred of females oozes from this publication. It's surprising to know that my anatomy scares you so. You folks are attempting to turn back the tide of an inevitable social transformation. You won't win. You've already had 4,000 years at the helm and the order you attempted to create is rotting. It's time for change.

Susan Nunn

Thanks for the inspiration to work harder against you. What in the name of reason does your misogynist gang of frightened little boys expressing their neurotic castration fears in *Heterodoxy* have to do with the study of popular culture? I oppose male violence and male privilege, so please take me off your mailing list.

L. Jenscson
Eugene, OR.

You criticize Catharine MacKinnon extensively. Why? Because she is strong? Capable? Articulate? And she is infinitely more published than you? Then you praise profusely Camille Paglia, who sold out women to get tenure, who secretly wants to dry hump Madonna. The world is changing. You simply have to put your tiny penises back in your pants and accept it.

Another tenured female
Harvard Graduate

I thought you might be interested to know that you have a lesbian, vegan, PC-bashing libertarian among your new subscribers (and no, I'm not ugly). Good work!

Love,
Karen McNeil
Oakland, CA

Thank you for your naming of U. Wisconsin's Donna Shalala on your list of Ten Worst College Administrators.

My favorite Shalala story is that she was "surprised and distressed" at the rise of anti-Semitism on campus in the weeks following the campus visit of Louis Farrakhan (which she had sponsored and paid for).

Carol Noll

PS: Heterodoxy? As opposed to what? Homodoxy?

Your readers might more clearly understand the phenomenology of the "P.C." movement if they were more familiar with the recent history of totalist religious cults (and similar political and self-actualization groups). What happened to Alan Gribben at the University of Texas (shunning) is a common cultic phenomenon. After all, Gribben didn't have a mere intellectual difference with his tormentors — he was actually trafficking with Satan's legions.

Similarly, when University of Minnesota coeds are "ordered" by their professors to tell their classmates that they are lesbians, they are being directed toward the hallowed footsteps of the People's Temple flock of the Rev. Jim Jones, whose inner circle (the Planning Commission—shortened, ironically, to "P.C.") was regularly required to confess to being gay or lesbian (see Jeannie Mills' *Six Years With God*, if you have a strong stomach). Mr. Collier's phrase in the Gribben article about "occult folk rituals" is far from coincidental.

Robert H. Chesky, M.D.
Brighton, Michigan

Since I am a politically active, progressive, female, bi-sexual, socialist, pro-choice intellectual, I am sure my views will be of little interest to such knee-jerk reactionaries as yourselves, but I feel compelled to remind you that the entire "PC" issue (reminiscent of cointelpro operations) is clearly an invention of right-wing fascists.

Why don't you guys get real jobs?!?!?!?

"Correctly" Yours,
Louise D. Brown-Marsh

I was happy to receive your May issue of *Heterodoxy*. The reader response from the left-wing pinheads is especially amusing. You know you are on the right track when you provoke such a response. Perhaps a program of gift subscriptions to the politically correct would send them completely over the edge. I would be happy to participate in sponsoring such a subscription.

Michael Grant
Oklahoma City

Please cancel. We will bury you!

Unsigned

Of COURSE I am in favor of spreading Political Correctness worldwide. The main problem with my aim is that the present so-called exponents of Political Correctness have it all wrong. They are blasphemers. They are spreading bovine flatulence. They don't know their masses from scrolls in the ground.

Beef is good for you and good for the planet. Lean beef has the same percentage of cholesterol as lean turkey. Cattle eat stuff that you and I and most animals cannot digest; stuff that grows on land that will not grow the veggies that you and I can eat. Without the protection of mankind, beef cattle would not exist on this planet. The gasses that cattle release are good for the environment. They react with the overabundance of ozone to produce more carbon dioxide and water vapor that collect in the upper atmosphere. These in turn capture the sun's warming rays and are important in protecting the earth from the ice age that would otherwise be rapidly approaching. Meanwhile, the small percentage of sulfides in these gases make the earth appear from outer space as inhospitable. This protects us from alien invaders. Have you never wondered why the flying saucers have not come in force and subdued us? To them we appear to be a stink ball.

Millard Perstein
Sedona, Arizona

Your front page picture of a PC rioter was inaccurate.

This picture is representative of the kind of spurious disinformation campaign you and people like you spread. Superficially, what you say appears to make sense, but then there are these huge leaps of logic that just don't make sense if you examine the facts.

1. The looters in the civil unrest (precipitated by police brutality, captured on film and then supported, against all facts, by a not guilty verdict in a court of law, compounded by the frustration of people who cannot get jobs or other services because of the color of their skin) were not in the age range of the guy in the picture's parents.

2. Most of the looters were not African-American.

Both of these facts are well documented; as you well know. But when you are in the business of creating and spreading propaganda—what do you care about facts? You and your ilk are terrified that if African-Americans are ever in substantial positions of authority, reason would tell you, based on the treatment we have received in this country by your forefathers, and now by you (their sons) in a different guise —we should be thinking about revenge in whatever form it takes. All this other stuff is just a smoke screen.

Ainita Truth

Inglewood, CA

I recently received a copy of *Heterodoxy* in the mail. When I got to the "Reader Response" column imagine my surprise to find the adolescent diatribe of a "tenured female Harvard graduate" suggesting that you should "put your tiny penises back in your pants" and that Camille Paglia's greatest wish was to "dry hump Madonna." I don't understand what penis size has to do with the feminist agenda. This must be something that is taught only at Harvard.

Donald Otto
Bothell, Washington

As loathe [sic] as I am to squander a postage stamp, much less twenty minutes of time in composing this letter, I must [insist] you remove at once my name from your mailing list. Your rampant hate-mongering and lowbrow trumpeting of such reactionary non-scholars as Camille Paglia align you with the neo-Nazis of last summer's Republican Convention.

Sincerely,
Karin Coddon
Department of English
Brown University

I had reservations about subscribing — until I walked through my school's main entrance and saw Professor Leonard Jeffries, in full African regalia, on videotape, blathering his racist wet-dreams. This reminded me why PC needs to be opposed.

No name

I am so angered and enraged by your magazine that it has only *deeply* inspired me to continue to fight for equality, feminism, and true "political correctness." At age sixteen I have already become very involved and aware in my community and world. Not only did your publication upset and disgust me, but it also made me very sad because in 1992 people still think like you all do. It really made me want to cry to think that the male role models I am supposed to grow up with are people like you all.

Sincerely,
Misha Snyder
Baltimore, Maryland

I am 11 years old and I cannot thank you enough for publishing this wonderful paper. I go to public school in D.C., and to a lifelong conservative, that is hell. My schoolmates are a bunch of feminist, liberal, PC, vegetarian multiculturalists. *Heterodoxy* is just the thing for recovering from a six and a half hour school day surrounded by them.

Conservatively yours,
Sam Munson

(Sent to the Editor of *The New Republic*):

Are you aware that the mailing list of your subscribers is being sold to *Heterodoxy*, a publication of unrelenting hatred and bile? Please stop it.

Daniel Yanow
San Francisco, California

Thanks for *Heterodoxy* and the copy of *Deconstructing the Left* by Collier and Horowitz. I come from a family whose cat was named Malcolm X (in 1967), so I'm desperately in need of finding my moorings. Your books and magazine are helping.

Robert W. Sale
San Diego, California

Surely your mysteriously well-funded adolescent endeavor would be more aptly named "Hetero-Dixie," or even better, "Hetero-Dicks."

Yours in mutual hostility
Barbara Schulman

Dear Doxies,

Raised in Cincinnati, Ohio, I was a lesbian feminist in the late seventies. Imagine my shock when I moved to radical, liberal, collegial Madison, Wisconsin, and discovered who I had been following. We're talking narrow-minded, puritanical. The arrival of S-M, leather and butch/femme dykes was a herstorical dialectic inevitability. Hope they made it to Madison. I didn't stay around to find out. So, I appreciate the motive behind your rag.

Yours truly,
Devorah Krause
Willits, California

Being a "red diaper baby" and a renegade/refugee from the Left, I've appreciated the efforts you have made to get the Left to experience what should be its "crise de conscience." Unfortunately, but not unpredictably, the Left seems to have just paused for a moment, excused itself by its good intentions ("it wasn't what we wanted") and proceeded on its arrogant, self-righteous way. It never learns from its experience because it never pays the price — others do, usually in the millions.

Don Tabor
New York City

After scanning your garbarge [sic], one can only think "who says Hitler was wrong?" Don't send anymore. I don't want it.

(Illegible signature)

I must confess that your publication confused me at first. Then I got it. I'm on to you guys now. You are all radical feminists. Why else would you create a publication so senselessly vicious as to be totally discreditable?

Jill Derby, Ph.D.
Lecturer, Consultant
Anthropology
Gardnerville, Nevada

Your bigoted little rag makes me sick. I just sent a check for $25 to the ACLU. Thanks for the motivation!

No signature

Stop sending me your trash; I'm not the slightest bit interested in anything you have to say. Go to hell.

Joan Ehrenberg
Political Science
Long Island University

Too bad you wasted your money sending your racist, fascist, homophobic drivel to another radical feminist pagan like me.

No name

May I suggest a possible contributing factor to the growth of PC on campus? Take a group of intelligent people, confine them to an environment that requires that they work only 10% of the time, with no risk attached to job performance, and there will be trouble. PC would disappear overnight if the bastards had to work hard 8 hours a day and be held accountable for their performance.

John Brinson
Allentown, Pennsylvania

I still can't understand how such a wonderful publication could emanate from the epicenter of craziness there in California!

Thank you for putting things into another (and in my mind, correct) perspective.

Thank you again for presenting another point of view.

Foster W. Cline, M.D.
Evergreen, Colorado

Sigh! I'm afraid I have to admit to being one of the humorless, gullible souls who believed Judith Schumann Weizner's satire in the March *Heterodoxy.* I *did* do a double take on "Sacrevache" but then succumbed to the suspension of disbelief with which all avid newspaper readers must currently arm themselves.

I am curious, though. Is Michael Brandow's review of the Whitney Biennial also a put on? It's so hard to tell these days. Life in America seems to have become a diorama of the absurd.

Wilma J. Moore

Eat shit and die mother-fucker. I don't ever want to see this garbage again. You queer loving sons of bitches. I vote we line you fuckers up and give you the firing squad treatment. Shove this up your ass.

Unsigned

I'm quite shocked that sadomasochists formed a group and wanted to march in a parade. Disgusted.

To be proud of being so "sick" is disgusting. People who want to torture other people are "animals." You don't deserve to be tax deductible. Go tie each other up and torture yourselves. Disgusting.

Unsigned

Enclosed is my order form for more *Heterodoxy* / Horowitz-Collier books. I've just finished reading *Surviving the PC University* and was so impressed I am ordering a second copy for a friend — someone who works in the academy and must put up with such nonsense (spurious sexual harassment charges, etc., etc.) on a regular basis.

I have yet to receive my first issue of *Heterodoxy* (I just entered my subscription) but, on the basis of this book, find it hard to contain my enthusiasm — something of the order of "Where have you been all my life?" In point of fact, I wouldn't have been searching until roughly five years ago — the approximate moment when I found myself incapable of reading the "Village Voice" without revulsion or disgust. Since then: a slow drift to, if not out - and - out conservatism, then something damned close. My real aim is independent thinking but, of course, this smacks of the Left's much-hated "individualism". There being no place for me on the Left, I'll simply move to the Right, thank you very much.

Daryl Haney

A group of feminists marched across our campus with a sign saying: "DEAD MEN DON'T RAPE!" At a government sponsored play reading, I heard the guest playwright recollect how he seduced a 14 year old boy while hired as his swim instructor. The university respected the feminists' right to protest. The audience applauded the playwright's sensitive reading from his play, written for his early "lover," who had since died of AIDS.

Thank you for *Heterodoxy*. It has calmed me knowing that there are others out there who will not be shouted down by the politically correct.

Jonathan Campbell
Nova Scotia, Canada

Gentlemen,

Kudos to your excellent publication. You've confirmed what I've suspected for quite some time: the true home of bigotry, sexism, and intolerance in America is on the politically-correct left. I'm continually amazed at how supposedly "educated" professors and teachers continue to give voice to this pseudo-intellectual, fascist garbage. From the racist ethnic militant groups and their fantasy land history to the blatant hatred of lesbian-feminist dogma, these bitter people are the very things they accuse the extreme right of being. Perhaps someday soon the so-called leaders of these morons will have their people goose-stepping across every campus in Amerika.

Sincerely,
M. Booth
Elk Grove, PA

You Pigs! Take my name off of your mailing list. I do not wish this type of bullshit that you print in my mist (sic). And in reference to "Black Murder Inc." and the slander against the Black Panther Party, I having been a info specialist for the party and having for greater knowledge of all of its chapters around the country wish there was a "squad" to stop your oink.

Power to the people,
Dee DeVille

I thoroughly enjoy your efforts in support of societal fairness and in opposition to P.C. These hypocrites came out of the "closet" in the 60s and 70s and demanded to be heard under their 1st Amendment rights. Now, in the 90s, they are attempting to abrogate those same rights for anyone who challenges or disagrees with their extreme views!

Warm Regards,
Devereaux Leahy
Ventura, CA

I have recently received a disgusting publishing entitled *Heterodoxy.* I did not subscribe to this publication nor do I care to ever see it again in my mailbox.

It is papers like this, and people like you, that keep our country in total turmoil. Your attitudes, as seen through your paper, are the reasons our country has the problems it does. Hence, if you're not part of the solution, you are part of the problem.

I found the language to be particularly vile, which, as an adult I can deal with, but, obviously your circulation manager and the rest of you society drop-outs did not consider for one moment, the hands this paper might fall into once it arrived at my home, i.e. MY CHILDREN. Okay, I have no children, but, you didn't know that!

Advise me who the person is responsible for initiating this subscription to enter my home.

I want to hear from you soon.

Marvin L. Mann
Loveland, Ohio

To the misinformed, misguided, mindless Bigots who publish this crap please remove my name from your mailing list. As an Afro-American physician and former member of the Black Panther Party, I find the blatantly racist, sexist, homophobic leanings of your rag to be most amusing, almost funny except for the fact that I consider you and your ilk to be dangerous. Please perform an act with your genitals and rectum that is probably physically impossible, but for an asshole of your nature quite plausible.

C. Hinson M.D.
Scottsdale, AZ

However I got a sample copy of your March issue I am grateful. As a clergyman in the Evangelical Lutheran Church in America I find myself gagging almost daily now on inclusivity, multiculturalism, political correctness, affirmative action/quota systems, etc. Once I considered myself orthodox with an ever so slight tilt to the left, I am now in the heterodox camp, a deviant who was once mainstream.

Keep up the good fight. It is worth it even if, in the end like Zorba the result is "a splendiferous crash."

Cordially,
Rev. Ronald H. Weineit
Rincon, Georgia

With the stench of putrefied Fish still emanating from Duke and the same old Shalala now ready to bludgeon the country into submission to the PC/quota agenda, I am delighted to sign up for a subscription.

As a professor at the University of Maryland, I fought the likes of what you were some twenty-five years ago — and lost. Now Professor Emeritus, I have fewer teeth but still lots of bite.

Welcome to the side of the good guys!

J. Silverman
Silver Spring, MD

It was an absolute waste of my time to look at your stuff—with your militant views, you go on colonizing the globe like your masters, the Brits, and you call this a Christian attitude. God is watching you.

Unsigned

Whoever you are,

You insult my intelligence, and you insult my sensitivity by sending me an unsolicited copy of *Heterodoxy*. Remove my name from your mailing list forever! I do not want garbage in my mailbox and your revolting paper is indeed garbage, I am so angry that you may publish such a piece and mail it as a "non-profit organization." May you never prosper.

Vivian House
(Mrs. Harold House)
Graniteville, South Carolina

I am a non-tenure-track white male who, upon receiving his doctorate in 1987, ran headlong into reverse discrimination ("affirmative action"). I've lost count of the number of women—most of them without doctorates—who have leapfrogged over me into tenurable teaching appointments during the past six years. My sense of real justice—as opposed to "social justice"—prompted me to raise the issue in print, in a letter to the *Chronicle of Higher Education* dated May 24, 1989, in response to an article openly advocating re-education and thought control ("moral education") for white males who have the temerity to question runaway preferential programs for blacks. That led to my first confrontation with Political Correctness: I learned that it is not Politically Correct for a white male job-seeker in today's market to do anything except admit the villainous nature of the entire breed, and play the role of sacrificial animal. I still have the angry, hate-filled letter from a black literature professor—with tenure no doubt—accusing me of being a racist. My willingness to fight back against this horse manure may yet get me excommunicated altogether after this year. I cannot help but laugh at the morons in your letters column who chant the PC mantra of *racism, sexism, homophobia,* and worse. (Didn't some idiot even threaten to call the police??!)

Keep up the good work,
Steven Yates, Ph.D.
Temporary Assistant Prof.
Department of Philosophy
Auburn University

Please remove my name from your mailing list, I do not wish to receive any further copies of your publication "*Heterodoxy*."

Thank you,
Mary Kay Ash
Mary Kay Cosmetics, Inc.
Dallas, Texas

Dear Boys,

This letter is soaked in my own menstrual blood. Does that disgust you? Does it make your wienes (sic) shrink? You pathetic hypocrites.

You want to silence us so you can write all over us with your pens/ penises/ But you forgot one thing: all womyn make their own supply of idelable (sic) ink! You cannot erase our writings.

And if you try, we'll just have to have an old-fashioned wiene roast.

An Angry Womon

Contributing Authors

DAVID JOHN AYERS is currently working on his doctoral thesis in sociology.

K.L. BILLINGSLEY is a staff writer for *Heterodoxy.*

BILL CERVENY is the Managing Editor of *Heterodoxy.*

PETER COLLIER is the Co-Editor of *Heterodoxy* magazine.

ANNE DEBORAH is a registered nurse in Oakland.

JOHN ELLIS is the author of *Against Deconstruction.*

BARBARA RHOADES ELLIS is a faculty wife at U.C. Santa Cruz.

MICHAEL FUMENTO is the author of *The Myth of Heterosexual AIDS* and *Science Under Siege: Balancing Technology and the Environment.*

ANITA SUE GROSSMAN is editor of *The California Scholar.*

DAVID HOROWITZ is the Co-Editor of *Heterodoxy* magazine.

SARAH HOROWITZ is a journalist for Pacific News Service..

SCOTT KERR is a columnist for the *Shepherd Express* in Milwaukee, Wisconsin.

MICHAEL KITCHEN is a former Navy ensign, and editor of *The Gauntlet.*

STEVE KOGAN teaches English Literature at Hebrew University.

JAY OVEROCKER is a journalist in Los Angeles.

NEIL PATEL is a free-lance journalist in Washington, D.C.

STEVEN PLAUT is an economics professor at Hebrew University.

TURK RICHARDS is a playwright in Boston, Massachusetts.

ALYSON TODD is a campus coordinator for the Madison Center.

JUDITH SCHUMANN WEIZNER is a humorist and a musicologist who lives in New York.

Index